The ignorant bystander?

Manchester University Press

The ignorant bystander?

Britain and the Rwandan genocide of 1994

Dean J. White

Manchester University Press

Published by Manchester University Press
Altrincham Street, Manchester M1 7JA
www.manchesteruniversitypress.co.uk

British Library Cataloguing-in-Publication Data
A catalogue record for this book is available from the British Library

Library of Congress Cataloging-in-Publication Data applied for

ISBN 978 0 7190 9523 8 hardback

First published 2015

Typeset
by JCS Publishing Services Ltd, www.jcs-publishing.co.uk
Printed in Great Britain
by CPI Group (UK) Ltd, Croydon, CR0 4YY

To Mum, Dad and Jenn

Contents

Preface

This project would not have been possible without the help and support of a number of people. First I must thank the various interviewees who agreed to speak to me, many of whom spoke about their role in the response to the genocide for the first time. Some of the interviewees are named throughout the book, others preferred to remain anonymous. Secondly, thank you to the various government officials who responded to my very many Freedom of Information requests; their assistance was definitely beyond what I expected. Thirdly, I must thank Professor Sylvia Ellis and Professor Matt Baillie Smith for their guidance and support. Finally and most importantly, thank you to my family who have supported me throughout.

Preface

[illegible]

Abbreviations

DEC	Disasters Emergency Committee
DPKO	UN Department for Peacekeeping Operations
EU	European Union
FAR	Forces Armées Rwandaises (the Rwandan army)
FCO	Foreign and Commonwealth Office (UK Foreign Office)
JEEAR	Joint Evaluation of Emergency Assistance to Rwanda
MOD	Ministry of Defence
NGO	Non-governmental organisation
OAU	Organisation for African Unity
ODA	Overseas Development Administration
PMQ	Prime Minister's questions
R2P	responsibility to protect
RAF	Royal Air Force
REME	Royal Electrical and Mechanical Engineers
RoE	rules of engagement
RPF	Rwandan Patriotic Front (largely Tutu rebel group based in Uganda that invaded Rwanda in 1990)
RTLMC	Radio Télévision Libre Mille Collines (Rwandan radio station)
UN	United Nations
UNAMIR	United Nations Assistance Mission in Rwanda
UNHCR	United Nations High Commission for Refugees
UNOMUR	United Nations Observer Mission to Uganda-Rwanda

Introduction

'Lord, save us; take us to your Paradise; Lord, forgive us our sins; welcome us into your Kingdom.' These were Reverien Rurangwa's mother's last words: 'Lord, save us', over and over again. As the rest of the world watched the football World Cup, commemorated the fiftieth anniversary of D-Day or witnessed the end of Apartheid as South Africa held its first free elections, Reverien, his mother and close family huddled in a wooden hut, hiding from a gang of armed men. Reverien had been sitting silently for three days without food or water when suddenly the hut's door was kicked open. He recognised the man who casually walked in; it was Simon the quiet bartender from the bar in the shopping centre in the village. But now the man who used to sell banana beer and cigarettes carried a machete. Reverien's family - his younger brothers and cousins, his uncle, his grandmother, his mother - all cowered. Seeing the machete they knew their fate. Uncle Jean was the first to receive a blow. Quick as a flash Simon slashed at Jean's throat; blood shot across the hut, covering the children, causing them to scream in terror. More men crowded in behind Simon; all were armed with machetes, garden hoes or homemade clubs and all were known to Reverien. This was Rwanda in 1994.[1]

In the one hundred days from 7 April to 18 July scenes like this were tragically common in the small central African country of Rwanda. Unlike the Nazi Holocaust, the genocide in Rwanda did not require ghetto clearances, meticulous scheduling of train timetables or the building of industrial death camps. Instead, like Reverien's family, Tutsi were killed, often by friends, neighbours or even family, where they were found: at home, at school, at impromptu road blocks or gathered in churches where they wrongly hoped for some sort of sanctuary. In truth no one really knows how many people died in Rwanda that year; none of the contradictory numbers that have been offered concerning victims of massacres or of refugees fleeing from or returning to Rwanda is substantiated. Alan Kuperman uses extrapolations from the 1991 census and survivor data to claim very precisely that the figure was 494,008; Alison Des Forges in what is considered by many as the definitive account of the events of 1994 quotes 'at least half a million'; General Romeo Dallaire, the commander of United Nations (UN) peacekeeping troops in the country, typically refers to over 800,000 having been killed; and Shaharyar Khan, who during the second half of 1994 was the UN Special Representative to Rwanda, places the figure at between 800,000 and

850,000.[2] Linda Melvern, quoting figures from the Red Cross, is at the higher end of estimates, claiming one million were killed.[3] The sad reality is that we will never know the final number of dead. The fact that whole families and communities were murdered means that there were often no survivors left to report the missing, and the lack of accurate census information means that it is impossible to know even how many Tutsi were living in Rwanda before the genocide. However, based on these various estimates, it seems that a figure of around 800,000 killed in approximately one hundred days is not unrealistic. This makes Rwanda the quickest genocide ever experienced, with a killing rate five times that of the Nazi Holocaust.[4]

Yet whilst hundreds of thousands of people were being slaughtered, as US President Bill Clinton was later to suggest (rather disingenuously of himself at least), 'all over the world there were people like me sitting in offices, day after day after day, who did not fully appreciate the depth and speed with which [Rwanda was] being engulfed by unimaginable terror'.[5] Ironically, though, in the months before the killing began in Rwanda, genocide had again been brought to the fore of international consciousness. Steven Spielberg's film about a German industrialist who saved over 1,200 Jews during the Holocaust first appeared in cinemas in late 1993, and in March 1994 it won the Academy Award for Best Picture. But few in the West drew lessons from what they saw on the screen or linked the events in Nazi Germany to what was unfolding in Rwanda.

In his autobiography, written sixteen years later, former UK Prime Minister Tony Blair recorded the profound effect seeing *Schindler's List* for the first time had on him. Watching the film, in spring 1994, made him think of the responsibility individuals and states have to come to the assistance of others; accepting that the responsibility to help those geographically near was beyond question, he continued:

> But what of situations we know about, but we are not proximate to? What of the murder distant from us, the injustice we cannot see, the pain we cannot witness but which we nonetheless know is out there? ... If we know and we fail to act, we are responsible. A few months [after I saw *Schindler's List*], Rwanda erupted in genocide. We knew. We failed to act. We were responsible.[6]

Testing this assertion is one of the two main aims of this book. First it considers the response to the events in Rwanda from a perspective that to date has been largely ignored by academia – the response of the United Kingdom (the UK). It sets out to address Tony Blair's claims about this specific crisis: did the UK know, did it fail to act, was it responsible? Secondly, more than being just about Rwanda, this book aims to explore British humanitarian intervention more generally. Using Rwanda as a case study, the book explores the various influences and actors that impact on foreign policy making, particularly related to the decision to intervene in overseas crises; these other actors include Parliament, the media, the public, non-governmental organisations (NGOs) and the civil service bureaucracy. The focus is the Rwandan case study, but in the final chapter, by looking at the more recent crises in Libya and Syria, the book explores whether the response to the genocide demonstrates more universal rules of what leads the British Government to intervene in humanitarian crises in far away countries or alternatively, and more commonly, to do nothing. This is then intended to be less a book about the actual course of genocide as it played out in Rwanda and more a consideration of British intervention in the late twentieth and early twenty-first centuries.[7]

Why the UK?

Given that so little has been written about the UK and Rwanda, and indeed Britain and intervention, it is maybe appropriate first to explain why the British response to this one crisis is a valuable case study subject. The UK has been chosen because of the belief that the UK has a military and diplomatic footprint that makes it a powerful and influential member of the international community. Despite its obvious decline since the end of the Second World War, 'it is notable that Britain has always been treated as a world power, and its influence recognized, sometimes unwillingly, by friend and foe alike'.[8] As the Government claimed in 1994, 'The UK plays a unique role in the world's affairs. A member of NATO, the European Union, the Western European Union, the Commonwealth, the Group of Seven leading industrial nations and a Permanent Member of the UN Security Council: no other country holds all these positions of international prominence and responsibility;'[9] the same can still be said some twenty years later. The UK also has a recent history as an active participant in international interventions: since 1990 British troops have been deployed in the former Yugoslavia, northern Iraq, Afghanistan, Angola, Libya, Sierra Leone, Mali, and twice made significant contributions to the Gulf War coalitions. And thirdly, the UK's position in the international community is affected by its close relationship with the US. As a partner, or as some would suggest an agent,[10] of the US, the so-called 'Special Relationship' arguably means that on the international scene the UK punches above its weight. The UK then is one of the few countries potentially capable of significantly influencing world events.

The final reason for a study of the British response comes from General Dallaire, who has written, 'the level and type of involvement of these three Western countries [the US, France and UK] in the genocide in Rwanda was unique and therefore worthy of special attention';[11] to date the UK has not received the special attention Dallaire suggests is needed. The response to the Rwandan crisis, as Mark Curtis indicates, has until now been an event that has been written out of British foreign policy history.[12]

What is meant by humanitarian intervention?

In the years preceding Rwanda's genocide, following the end of the Cold War and the US-led coalition's success in the first Gulf War (1991), humanitarian intervention looked to be on the way to becoming an international norm. The peaceful collapse of communism and the end of East–West proxy wars appeared to herald a new period of foreign policy and a refocusing of foreign policy and military might, in Western countries at least, away from the superpower standoff and towards the achievement of moral good. The change in the diplomatic sphere even led US President George Bush (Senior) to speak of the coming of 'a new world order'. There was now, Bush and others believed, an opportunity to use a combination of military force and humanitarian aid to bring peace to the world. Consequently, in the first half of the 1990s alone, there was intervention in Somalia, Angola, Western Sahara, Bosnia, Haiti, Cambodia, Croatia, northern Iraq and, of course, Rwanda. In fact, more UN missions were launched in the first five years of the 1990s than in the UN's previous four decades of operation.

Despite the sudden increase in intervention, in many cases the international community's response to crises was seen by many as not going far enough. Certainly in the case of Rwanda, the criticism of governments for not having responded sooner or more rigorously is strong. Ingvar Carlsson, for example, condemns the UN Security Council for its inaction, noting:

> The parties to the 1948 Genocide Convention took upon themselves a responsibility to prevent and punish the crime of genocide. The Convention explicitly provides for the opportunity to bring such a situation before the Security Council. The members of the Security Council have a particular responsibility, morally if not explicitly under the Convention, to react when faced with a situation of genocide.[13]

Dallaire *et al.* accuse the UK, US and France of 'shirking their legal and moral responsibilities' in Rwanda by failing to act sooner, and Linda Melvern makes the claim that, having established a peacekeeping mission to Rwanda, the UN became 'responsible' for the country's future and had an obligation to do more.[14] This argument continues that the international community should have launched a more robust humanitarian mission to Rwanda and sooner than it did – the international community had a responsibility to do something. That 'something' is generally meant as putting troops on the ground; Dallaire, Melvern and Carlsson all argue that 'humanitarian intervention' was the only appropriate response.

One succinct definition of what they mean by humanitarian intervention is provided by Adam Roberts: 'humanitarian intervention is coercive action by one or more states involving the use of armed force in another state without the consent of its authorities, and with the purpose of preventing widespread suffering or death among the inhabitants'.[15] This definition captures the essential features of humanitarian intervention: it is a military response; it is by an actor outside of the state; consent is absent; it involves the use, or the threat of use, of force; and there are humanitarian motives. Humanitarian intervention can also be seen as sitting somewhere on a continuum of military action, which has war at one extreme and peacekeeping at the other. Whereas war is combat against a designated opponent, for gains in territory, resources or power, humanitarian intervention is motivated, not by a thirst for more power, but by a humanitarian concern for the welfare of others. Humanitarian intervention also is not necessarily against a known opponent; in humanitarian missions the military will often be deployed to stand between civilians and potential attackers, which could include armies, militias or gangs, where, as in Rwanda, the line between the person to be protected and the potential threat is not necessarily obvious. But nor is humanitarian intervention traditional peacekeeping, which is based on consent, neutrality and a limit on the use of force to self-defence only. In a traditional peacekeeping mission, troops will typically be deployed between two parties who have reached a mutual peace agreement. Marrack Goulding, the head of UN peacekeeping missions in 1988, summed up traditional peacekeeping as 'Peacekeeping soldiers carry arms only to avoid using them; they are military forces, but their orders are to avoid, at almost any cost, the use of force; they are asked in the last resort to risk their own lives rather than open fire on those between whom they have been sent to keep the peace'.[16]

When we talk of humanitarian intervention, then, we are implying more than passive observation of a peace agreement. Troops on a humanitarian intervention mission will typically undertake a wider range of tasks, including protecting aid convoys, enforcing safe zones or confiscating and destroying weapons, and importantly troops would be permitted to use lethal force to protect non-combatants. This, then, is the sort of mission that the above commentators suggest should have been deployed to Rwanda. In reality it is far from the mission that did deploy. Why did the international community and the UK in particular not respond to the crisis in Rwanda in the way that many suggest they should have? To answer that question we need to begin by looking at the various factors that influence the decision to intervene.

Responding to a foreign crisis

Despite the increase in number of humanitarian missions, the typical response of any government to a humanitarian crisis overseas is to do nothing, however overwhelming the evidence of suffering, and this lack of response applies to some of the most serious crises. Weiss for instance notes the absence of a meaningful international response to the ethnic violence in the Darfur region of Sudan, despite the fact that US Secretary of State Colin Powell described the events as genocide in September 2004, and despite the fact that 422 US senators unanimously voted in July 2004 that the Sudanese Government was pursuing a strategy of genocide, and despite the fact that in September 2004 the EU Parliament described the events as 'tantamount to genocide'.[17]

There are many and varied reasons why non-intervention has proved to be the norm. Arguments against include the belief that intervention is justified on the grounds of protecting human rights, and yet this is a concept that is not universally accepted:[18] intervention is simply a post-colonial method for the West to interfere in the affairs of developing states;[19] or humanitarian crises falling out of violent conflict are an inevitable part of state building and therefore cannot be resolved.[20] However, in 1990s Britain, perhaps the most persuasive argument against intervention was the belief that it simply did not work. Amongst Conservative MPs, ministers and Foreign and Commonwealth Office (FCO) and Ministry of Defence (MOD) civil servants there was a widely held view that intervention in someone else's war would 'do more harm than good' and this refrain was therefore fairly common amongst MPs debating intervention in Bosnia.[21]

The general argument was expressed in various different ways, but all combined to mean, as the Foreign Secretary at the time, Douglas Hurd, recalls, the majority of Tory MPs were 'sceptical of the need for even … limited intervention'.[22] Roger Howard, for example, describes one strand of the argument as: 'A "humanitarian war", or any conflict justified on the grounds that it is in another's best interest, is clearly oxymoronic because of the death and devastation that military intervention will inflict.'[23] Tim Murithi distils another as: providing humanitarian aid to civilians in a war zone inevitably results in the conflict being prolonged, as the distribution of humanitarian aid confers power on the recipient, and – if diverted to support the war effort – actually sustains war.[24] In the UK, the British army's involvement in the Northern Ireland Troubles was also cited as an argument against intervention.[25] Both the MOD and FCO, for example, warned against intervention in Bosnia on the basis that Northern Ireland demonstrated how easily troops could become 'bogged down' in peacekeeping operations.[26] Douglas Hurd, who for a time had been Secretary of State for Northern Ireland, similarly held this view and freely warned counterparts of the lessons Britain had already learned about peacekeeping. At the Hague Peace Conference in 1991, Hurd argued against deeper engagement in Bosnia by referring to Northern Ireland where the British had been 'fighting from village to village and street to street … for 22 years'.[27]

The natural position of the British political elite in the early 1990s was, then, to be suspicious and wary of intervention. There was a fear of being dragged into someone else's war or of actually worsening the situation on the ground. So if non-intervention was, and remains today, the norm, and there was such suspicion of the concept of intervention amongst the British Government in the 1990s, what then motivates the interventions that have happened, including the intervention in Rwanda in 1994?

National interest

The answer to this question falls into one of two general schools. Firstly, states participate in humanitarian missions out of an obligation to protect the international peace and to promote human welfare and rights regardless of national borders. This liberal hypothesis promotes the idea of morality in foreign policy making. A second and more widely accepted school of thought contends that rather than morality it is national interest that triggers intervention. As Laura Neack suggests, 'the pattern of state participation, the geographical distribution of operations, the various accounts of the failures and successes of individual operations, and the accounts of the perceptions and intentions of the peacekeeping states suggest that states become involved in UN peacekeeping mainly to serve their own interests'.[28] Drawing on empirical data, she points out that in the period 1945 to 1990 the top ten countries involved in UN missions were made up of what she describes as the middle powers (Canada, Australia, Italy, Ireland), the Scandinavian countries, (Norway, Finland, Denmark) and emerging powers (Brazil and India): all countries that had an interest in promoting their own standing in the international community. She therefore claims that involvement in peacekeeping missions in this period was grounded entirely on serving national interest rather than out of moral obligation or concern.[29]

Like Neack, Michael Smith argues that to suggest states participate in humanitarian actions for anything other than self-interest is delusional; governments 'only act when it is in their interests to do so and therefore when they engage in humanitarian intervention they are really pursuing some other agenda'.[30] Aidan Hehir agrees, 'In the absence of a sense of community, states are compelled to act strategically, not morally, and aim at all times to maximise the national interest and protect their security. Therefore, a concern for those suffering abroad does not motivate states to act unless there are national interests involved.'[31] Smith continues, 'states are necessarily self-interested creatures and are by definition unable to act in any other than self-interested ways. To expect them to do so – to support a genuinely humanitarian action – is to engage in self-delusion, error and hypocrisy'.[32]

One weakness with this argument that national interest motivates intervention is the fact that 'national interest' is such a nebulous term that it has become almost meaningless. Despite the ubiquity of the term, commentators, politicians or journalists, more focused on sound bite than clarity, only rarely attempt to define what they mean by national interest. Neack, for example, includes in her definition of national interest, promoting a state's place in the international community.[33] Paul Diehl suggests that access to resources, the national interest of oil-hungry Western states, has led to the high number of peacekeeping missions in the oil-rich Middle East.[34] And Fabrice Weissman suggests that Tony Blair invoked national interest to justify British intervention in Sierra Leone when in fact what was more significant was the Labour Government's desire to demonstrate its ethical foreign policy to the domestic electorate.[35] In all of these examples 'national interest' justifies intervention, but what is meant by national interest is quite different. As Ian Budge notes, 'it is a mistake to assume that there is a readily identifiable general British "national interest" to be served by its foreign policy. Usually there are competing interests, one of which successfully asserts a claim to be the "national interest" while the others lose out.'[36] As one Cabinet-level minister told this author, pretty much any action can be described as being either in or against the national interest.[37] Britain's role in the recent interventions in Afghanistan and Iraq, for example, can and have been described as either in or against national interests, depending on one's political persuasion and view of Britain's place in the world.

This indefinability surely means any argument based on national interest alone does not adequately explain intervention. Of course it goes a long way in explaining non-intervention – after all, why would a country do something that was not in its own interests? But it fails to explain why countries move from a position of non-intervention to actually intervening. And this is what happened in Rwanda: initially the UK did not intervene, but then slowly there was an increase in the level of financial aid donated in response to the crisis and eventually British troops were sent to the country. Yet at no stage did Britain's traditionally defined interest in Rwanda change. There must then be more to humanitarian intervention than national interest alone.

International law, sovereignty and international responsibility

An alternative explanation is that rather than national interest it is international law that compels countries to respond to humanitarian crises overseas. Since 1945 the international community has codified numerous treaties covering human rights and humanitarian law, including, most pertinently in the case of Rwanda, the United Nations' Convention on the Prevention and Punishment of the Crime of Genocide (the Genocide Convention). Article VIII of the Convention calls on the United Nations to take action 'appropriate for the prevention and suppression of acts of genocide'. There is then an argument that humanitarian intervention in cases of extreme human rights abuses is an obligation under international law and this has led some to claim that 'global elite bystanders [the UK included] ... are liable to charges of complicity in genocide if they fail to undertake their positive obligations, such as prevention and suppression of acts of genocide'.[38]

International law certainly governs intervention but to suggest that the obligations on a state are clear is an over-simplification. For example, signatories to The Genocide Convention pledge to 'prevent', 'suppress' and 'punish' genocide, they do not pledge to intervene to 'stop' it. Nor do individual states pledge to intervene themselves; rather the Convention says, 'Any Contracting Party may call upon the competent organs of the United Nations to take such action'. This clearly places the onus to prevent and suppress genocide on the UN rather than any individual government. Nor is the Convention particularly clear on what constitutes genocide. Article II of the text states that 'genocide means any of the following acts committed with intent to destroy, in whole or in part, a national, ethnical, racial or religious group'. This definition leaves open debate about intent, what constitutes a 'part' of a group and whether the group being subjected to violence is indeed a national, ethnical, racial or religious group. The slightly less than clear wording of the Convention has therefore led some, including in the UK senior Conservative Party ministers, to argue that the Convention provides a right to intervene, rather than an obligation.[39]

The legal 'requirement' to intervene is also complicated by the concept of state sovereignty which has traditionally been a more powerful idea in foreign policy thought than the protection of human rights. On the one hand, for example, the Genocide Convention calls for an international response in certain circumstances, on the other the founding UN Charter states in Chapter I, Article 2 'Nothing contained in the present Charter shall authorize the United Nations to intervene in matters which are essentially within the domestic jurisdiction of any state'; and it is this prioritisation of the sanctity of state sovereignty that was the more powerful concept amongst British Conservatives in the post-war period. In 1983, for example, Prime Minister Margaret Thatcher condemned the US invasion of Grenada '[we in the West should not interfere] in the affairs of a small, independent nation, however unattractive its regime'.[40] She went on to tell the BBC World Service, 'We in western countries use our force to defend our way of life. We do not use it to walk into other people's countries, independent sovereign territories.'[41] The 1991 Gulf War, on the other hand, was justified as war to defend sovereignty; Douglas Hurd recalls, 'No-one doubted Saddam Hussein was a wicked man who had done terrible things to his own people and to others. It would be better if he went ... But we were not going to war to rid the world of an evil rule. We were acting very specifically to reverse an act of aggression.'[42]

Conservative foreign policy in the 1980s and 1990s was clearly more focused on realist and state-centred promotion of economic prosperity, rather than on liberal ideals of protecting human rights. During the 1980s, for example, Thatcher deployed three Royal Navy vessels to the Arabian Gulf, not in any way to influence the war between Iran and Iraq or to come to the aid of civilians caught up in the fighting, but instead to keep the commercial shipping lanes open. The approach to the developing world was also largely driven by trade; Thatcher recorded in her autobiography how she tried to build trade relations with Indonesia despite being aware of 'serious human rights abuses' in the country.[43] As John Coles notes, under Thatcher, it was clear that the top two priorities of foreign policy were firstly safeguarding the country's security and secondly promoting its prosperity.[44] For Thatcher and the Conservative Party more widely, 'what the developing world needed more than aid was trade'[45] and consequently a belief in the inviolability of state sovereignty generally trumped calls to intervene in foreign countries to protect and promote human rights.

The foreign policy focus on security and promotion of economic prosperity, combined with obvious suspicion or cynicism of intervention meant that in the years prior to 1994 Britain was far from one of the leading contributors to humanitarian missions in terms of troops deployed; of the thirty-two UN peacekeeping missions that came before the 1994 deployment to Rwanda, British troops were deployed in only seven.[46] In the early 1990s there was, though, an evident, but small, shift in the Government's rhetoric. Perhaps triggered by growing calls for reform of the UN Security Council, the Government began to talk of Britain's responsibility to be an active participant in peacekeeping missions. As Lawrence Freedman suggests, throughout the early 1990s the FCO 'remained keen to see Britain justifying its place as a permanent member of the Security Council through conspicuous support for Council sponsored operations', to do otherwise was 'missing an opportunity for exercising international influence'.[47] In the 1994 survey of policy, the Conservative Research Office therefore wrote, 'As some threats recede, new ones arise ... Our contribution [to the UN] is the second largest: and we will continue to play a full part in the expansion of UN peacekeeping operations'.[48] Similarly, in 1996, Michael Portillo (then secretary of state for defence) in an address to Parliament on possible deployment of troops to Zaire said, 'We recognise our humanitarian obligation. We take pride in our membership of the UN Security Council, but it carries with it clear duties.'[49]

During John Major's time as prime minister there was a shift, partly driven by changing international circumstances following the end of the Cold War and partly by a slightly more liberal ideology than that held by Thatcher. Major certainly seemed more ready to approve British involvement in humanitarian intervention; for example, in 1991 he demonstrated his willingness to ignore state sovereignty and championed the international response to the Kurdish refugee crisis in northern Iraq. Percy Cradock, by now one of Major's foreign policy advisers, suggests, 'as Major saw it, a middle way had to be found between the prohibitions of Article 2 of the UN Charter, forbidding all interference in a country's internal affairs, and humanitarian affairs'.[50] But the fact that Major led calls for this one intervention in Iraq and also led a Conservative Party that spoke of being more willing to take part in UN operations does not mean that suddenly the Conservative Government had shifted to the more liberal, ethical, human rights-based foreign policy that Tony Blair would announce when Labour came to power in 1997. Non-intervention remained the norm under Major, and when he did authorise intervention – for example, in Bosnia and northern Iraq – the decision was made slowly and cautiously. There was certainly no sudden headlong rush to become more involved in peacekeeping. As Malcolm Rifkind told the Tory Reform Group, 'we must make sensible decisions about which operations we support and which we leave to others'.[51] Or as Hurd wrote in his memoirs, 'the doctrine of humanitarian intervention will never be universal; it will always depend on time place and circumstance'.[52]

So whilst international law, and specifically the Genocide Convention, had little influence in compelling the British Government to intervene in cases of extreme human rights abuses, there was something of a tenet that Britain had a responsibility to be an active participant in peacekeeping missions. There was a belief that permanent membership of the Security Council not only conferred certain rights on Britain but also brought certain obligations. However, throughout the 1980s and 1990s this was tempered by a strong belief in state sovereignty; the understanding that the international community should not interfere in the internal affairs of a sovereign state dominated British foreign policy thinking. So, like the national interest argument, international law and a belief in international responsibilities fails to fully explain why and when a government decides to intervene.

Bureaucracy

Despite this concentration of foreign policy-making power in relatively few hands, there is a school of thought that argues foreign policy is not actually made but rather develops out of bureaucratic interactions; intervention countries drift, or get dragged, into intervention slowly and incrementally. In analysing any government policy-making process, consideration therefore needs to be given to the question of where and how decisions are actually made.

In the case of foreign affairs, it is typical for policy to be controlled by a small group within the political executive. In the UK, for example, the triumvirate of foreign policy is generally held to be the prime minister, the foreign secretary and the defence secretary.[53] It is this inner circle that potentially has the power to direct and shape foreign policy. Political leaders may think they determine policy; however, it is bureaucrats who determine on what issues they focus their time, what intelligence on what crises reaches them and then most importantly enact the policy, whether it be through representing the country at the UN or commanding troops on the ground. But this bureaucratic involvement in shaping policy has inherent weaknesses which lead, potentially, to sub-optimal decision making. For example, conscious of the sheer volume of material created within a bureaucracy (for instance, as early as 1951, long before the advent of e-mail and mobile phones, Foreign Secretary Herbert Morrison recorded that 'under present day conditions the burden on the Foreign Secretary is excessively heavy', continuing that he only ever got five hours' sleep a night),[54] bureaucrats must filter what information actually reaches decision makers. In any bureaucracy there is therefore a need for a great deal of time-consuming knowledge sharing amongst experts, each with only a limited role within the system. This creates the problem that, as information is passed from individual to individual, the content of the message becomes increasingly distorted, key information is disregarded as seemingly unimportant and information simply takes too long to reach decision makers on the bottom-up route through the organisation. The assumption that the political elite in a bureaucratic system firstly make all the decisions and secondly make those decisions in possession of the full facts is clearly inaccurate – as Tullock notes, 'in practice, high level officials frequently demonstrate publicly the most egregious ignorance concerning the area that they allegedly supervise'.[55]

Another weakness of bureaucracies is that they tend to become insular. Takeda and Helms, for example, note the inability of bureaucracies to consider outside information.[56] Christopher Coyne believes this can also be seen in government departments, he calls this 'organisational patriotism' whereby bureaucracies believe their organisation is superior to others.[57] This organisational patriotism, or inter-departmental tension, can lead to fairly serious failings. Coyne, for example, notes how ineffective the US State Department and the Pentagon were in working together in the post-war reconstruction of Iraq[58] and Sherard Cowper-Coles (former British ambassador to Kabul) records similar British failings in Afghanistan due to friction between the FCO, the Treasury, the MOD and the Department for International Development.[59] Such parochialism can obviously be problematic when looking at humanitarian intervention, which requires the involvement of various bodies.

Finally, there is evidence that bureaucracy makes it difficult to alter policies or shift the direction of foreign policy; as Takeda and Helms argue, bureaucracies do not deviate from a failing courses of action.[60] Allison identifies a second manifestation of this phenomenon in his study of the Cuban missile crisis, suggesting that bureaucracies also operate with a bounded 'repertoire' of processes. Rather than rationally and systematically considering all responses to a crisis, a bureaucracy will adopt the first satisfactory response that it comes across within the standard operating procedures that it works from. The effect of this is that bureaucracies tend to respond to a crisis in the same way that they responded to previous similar crises. As Allison suggests, 'the best explanation of an organisation's behaviour at t is t - 1; the best prediction of what will happen at $t + 1$ is t'.[61]

A bureaucratically driven response to an unprecedented humanitarian crisis such as Rwanda is therefore unlikely. Bureaucracies are clearly constrained by their established way of thinking, by the speed with which information flows through the organisation and by unwillingness to consider information coming from outside sources, such as NGOs with more knowledge of the situation. In such circumstances, bureaucratic inertia is likely to prevent intervention rather than drive it. The only way for such inertia to be overcome is by top-down direction from the political elite to act and this is precisely what happened in the case of Britain's intervention in Iraq. Anthony Seldon notes the decision to champion the relief effort came from John Major himself and not the FCO; in fact, whilst working up the speech he would use to launch the idea, Major joked to his private secretary, 'Of course the Foreign Office won't like it ... but sometimes one has to prepared to take a flier at things'.[62]

Public opinion and the media

The generally held view historically was that public opinion had limited influence on foreign policy; more recent studies, however, seem to suggest this may no longer be the case.[63] Writing before the 2003 Iraq War and the 2011 Syria crises, Geoffrey Robertson argues that greater exposure to the world, through television, the internet and travel, has kindled a 'potent mix of anger and compassion' which produces a democratic demand for something to be done every time a humanitarian emergency appears on Western television screens.[64] Andy Storey suggests that Western governments have been forced to respond to this change in the public: 'with the end of the Cold War, Western governments are, for the most part, less interested in developing countries *per se*; the main impulse behind any action is more likely to be public relations rather than strategic interest'.[65] In this school of thought, foreign policy, like domestic politics, is driven by politicians seeking to gain advantage at the polls by enacting policies popular with the electorate – a demographic which obviously does not include those suffering in far away crises. The public, the argument goes, set a region of acceptability in foreign affairs and, by taking this into account, political elites are either constrained or pushed towards action in response to international events.[66] If the public demand action the government must do something and if the public show no interest, neither will politicians; governments are forced to respond to the public's demands or risk unpopularity – the ultimate sanction for an elected politician.

So if public mood influences government, what leads the public to support a response to certain foreign crises and not others? Looking at the question of public acceptance of military intervention (including humanitarian intervention), Bruce Jentleson and Rebecca Britton reached a two-part conclusion.[67] Firstly, they showed there is no direct relationship between a state's vital interests and public support for military intervention; secondly, it is overly simple to argue that the public oppose intervention with high stakes. As evidence of the first conclusion they point out that the majority of the American public initially supported intervention in Somalia in 1993 despite no obvious national security interest. In support of their second claim they demonstrate that the vast majority of Americans supported intervention to prevent North Korea acquiring nuclear weapons in the late 1990s despite the high likelihood of massive US casualties in any such intervention. The interesting point that Jentleson and Britton do not make is that these two examples illustrate a further point. In the case of Somalia there was no obvious national interest, however described, and US causalities were expected to be very low; whereas in Korea the opposite was true, there was a clear threat to national security but casualties were expected to be very high. There is a correlation between public acceptance of likely casualties and the perceived level of national interest; the American public would not have supported intervention in far away Somalia if high casualty rates had been forecast. Of course this is exactly what happened after the Battle of Mogadishu, when eighteen US soldiers were killed and the American public immediately turned against the US involvement.

This theory that governments are forced to act, out of neither a liberal impulse nor strict national interest, but rather because they are responding to public pressure stimulated by media coverage, has become known as the 'CNN effect'. Jakobsen describes the mechanics of the effect as, 'Television images of atrocities à journalists and opinion leaders criticise government policy in the media à the pressure on the government "to do something" becomes unbearable à the government "does something"'.[68] Various authors have pointed to the CNN effect to explain intervention in a number of cases. Mark Nelson, writing in the *Wall Street Journal* in April 1991, for example, suggested that John Major and George Bush launched Operation Provide Comfort on the back of a public 'tidal wave of outrage' against Saddam Hussein's treatment of the Kurds in northern Iraq.[69] It is, however, the US intervention in Somalia that is held up most frequently as evidence of the power of the media. Bernard Cohen, for example, is quoted as suggesting that the media led President Bush to send troops to Somalia: 'By focusing daily on the starving children in Somalia ... TV mobilised the conscience of the nation's public institutions, compelling the government into a policy of intervention for humanitarian reasons'.[70] And Nik Gowing has suggested it was television that then led President Clinton to withdraw troops: 'the gruesome images ... of one dead US Special Forces crewman being dragged through the streets of Mogadishu forced ... President Clinton's announcement of a phased US withdrawal from the Somalia UN operation'.[71] The supposed power of television, and twenty-four-hour television news in particular, to influence the response to foreign crises eventually led former UN Secretary General Boutros-Ghali to suggest, 'CNN is the sixteenth member of the Security Council'.[72]

However, Jakobsen's study of the role played by the media in five separate interventions in the early 1990s concludes that the CNN effect alone is not sufficient to explain intervention. Instead Jakobsen states that in cases of 'traditional national interest' the government is not at all influenced by the media, rather it will intervene regardless of the level of media coverage and public support; in such cases the government will typically use the media to mobilise international and domestic support. In cases where there is no traditional or obvious national interest, Jakobsen argues, 'the CNN effect [will] put the issue of intervention on the agenda but the decision whether or not to intervene [will be] ultimately determined by the perceived chance of success'.[73] For Jakobsen, the media at most puts a crisis on the agenda, but more typically government action precedes media coverage rather than the opposite being true. Agreeing with this,

Jonathan Mermin suggests that in the specific case of Somalia, journalists focused on the possibility of US intervention only after it had first been advocated in Washington.[74] Robert DiPrizio's examination of intervention supports this view; he claims that the role of public opinion in George Bush's decision to intervene in northern Iraq in 1991 has been overstated.[75] In this case, he argues, the evidence is that public opinion possibly speeded up the decision-making process, but Bush would have followed the same course of intervention regardless. This, then, is evidence of the accelerant influence of the media, meaning that media coverage can shorten decision-making response time, but not necessarily change the eventual decision. DiPrizio, Mermin and Jakobsen all therefore agree that the media place an issue on the international agenda, but coverage does not of itself lead to intervention.

Chance of success

For Jakobsen, neither traditionally defined national interest (threats to security or economics) nor the CNN effect are sufficient to explain why Western governments have intervened in the post-Cold War period. A high chance of success, he argues, must be present if intervention is to be seriously considered by governments. He notes, 'Intervention is highly unlikely unless the chances of success are perceived as good', continuing, 'once [a conflict] has [been] placed on the agenda, the perceived chances of success become the principal factor determining whether an enforcement operation will take place'.[76] It is at this point that we must make a distinction between cases where there is a traditional national interest (for example, economic or security interests) and those where there is none. Jakobsen suggests that where there is a clear national interest the calculation of whether the costs of intervention outweigh the benefits (which can be defined as success) becomes more flexible. He demonstrates this by suggesting, like Jentleson and Britton, that countries are more willing to bear casualties when security or economic interests are threatened than when they are not. A finding of national interest therefore sets the bar lower in the calculation of whether success is likely, making an enforcement action more likely.

Certainly, many authors point to this phenomenon in practice. As we saw above, Jentleson and Britton noted this in the cases of Somalia and North Korea. Mary Kaldor suggests this is also what was seen in Bosnia in the early 1990s.[77] As European countries and the US initially judged the violence in Bosnia to have little impact on their national interest a high hurdle was set before intervention would be authorised. This, Kaldor argues, meant European countries, initially seeing no threat to their own security or trade relationships and fearful of being dragged into the war, provided only limited and ineffective peacekeeping, rather than more assertive humanitarian intervention. Having acknowledged to themselves that they were not going to intervene in a meaningful way, Western governments, particularly France and the UK, looked to redefine the situation to justify their limited response to their domestic media and electorate; 'the Serbs were too strong to attack', the 'Bosnians could not be helped', 'there was nothing we could do'.[78] Yet as the crisis in the former Yugoslavia expanded it became apparent that it did threaten European interests – there was a risk of escalation and conflict widening geographically or of a refugee crisis spreading across Europe - consequently the chance-of-success threshold was lowered. This reassessment meant troop-contributing nations were willing to incur higher costs, both monetary and in terms of casualties, and the peacekeeping operation was expanded.[79] As the perceived threat to the national interest increased, the readiness to intervene similarly grew and the old excuses and risks were somewhat downgraded – despite nothing changing on the ground, suddenly the chance of success was considered acceptable and peacekeeping expanded.

David Rieff's work on Bosnia also illustrates that, as with all decision making, the debates on likelihood of success and therefore whether to intervene in a humanitarian emergency are influenced by past experience. In this particular case experts drafted in by the British Government argued that airpower alone had never won a war and could not stop the Serbian aggressors; that the Serbs had held up twenty-seven Wehrmacht divisions in the Second World War; and that Bosnia was an ideal country for guerrilla warfare and conventional armies had no history of defeating such tactics.[80] These factors, Rieff argues, all combined to convince policy makers that the chances of success were low. This is not an isolated incident; examples of decision makers drawing on historical analogies are rife. Bennett reminds us that 'Anthony Eden, taking decisions on Suez as Prime Minister in 1956, looked back on his experiences as Foreign Secretary in the 1930s ... [and] Ministers faced with the Argentine invasion of the Falklands thought about what happened in Suez'.[81] Of course, as all events are unique, when a decision maker latches onto an historical analogy there is a real risk that the ultimate decision is made more in response to that past crisis rather than the current one. As we will see, this was certainly the case for the US over Rwanda.

A refinement of Jakobsen's theory would therefore be that when, based on past experience, states anticipate high costs of intervention set against the perceived national interest (in terms of monetary cost, lives lost or the impact on other priorities), they naturally and instinctively become less inclined to launch any humanitarian intervention mission. Conversely, if a government assumes a humanitarian mission can be achieved with relatively low costs and high benefits, intervention becomes much more likely.

Race

The final issue to consider here is the argument that race influences, or potentially impedes, humanitarian intervention. Certainly, with specific reference to the

Rwandan genocide there have been suggestions, including from Boutros-Ghali, that the West was willing to watch thousands of Africans be killed, yet was quick to respond to the rich (read 'white') man's crisis in Bosnia.[82]

Throughout history the public and governments have adopted clichéd stereotypes of foreigners: throughout the Second World War, for example, American policy towards Japan was driven by a public view that all Japanese were fanatical, savage and inhumane; in the UK, debates on granting independence to India were shaped by the commonly held belief that carnage and confusion would follow because of the 'feeble' mindedness of those who would govern the country after the British left;[83] and, more recently, there has been an evident shift in the treatment of Muslims in the US and UK following the 11 September attacks.[84] This framing of thought based on race has influenced thinking on Africa more profoundly than that on any other continent.

It was Henry Morton Stanley who first opened up Africa for the Western general public in the late nineteenth century, and Stanley's descriptions of a continent 'still fixed deeply in barbarism' have stuck indelibly in the Western psyche.[85] The image continued into the twentieth century with Hollywood portrayals, such as the Tarzan films, *Zulu* and *The African Queen*, exaggerating to absurd levels the negative perceptions that most Americans and Europeans had of Africa. In Hollywood and literature, Africa, and its people, was dark, dangerous and violent. This image of Africa remained the dominant one in the UK at the time of the genocide. Richard Dowden, for example, suggests that despite the fact that millions of Africans have never experienced war or famine, that is the overwhelming image of Africa; 'Say "Africa" to people who have never been there and they will describe a sick and starving child and men with guns'.[86] The dominant image of Africa is that it remains a violent continent and significantly this violence is understood not as rational but as simply ancient and savage. As Peter Dahlgren has argued, this has led to Africa being portrayed as the polar opposite of the predominantly white West: '"They", the people of [Africa] appear as unstable and prone to violence. Incessant glimpses of disorder and violence serve as a reminder that these societies continue to act out their essential character; they are virtually driven by violence. "We" on the other hand the industrialised West, are typified by order and stability, a higher form of civilisation.'[87] The consequence of this 'violent savage' framing is ultimately that the West stops seeing victims. Under this analysis Africans become responsible for their own fate, making it difficult for the Western public to sympathise with innocent civilians caught up in violence or even to recognise that their suffering is a humanitarian crisis.

There is a second and alternative view of Africa. That is, although the West shows little sympathy for suffering caused by war, the Western public does respond very strongly to suffering that is perceived to be of natural causes (whether it is or not). In this interpretation the dominant news images of Africa are of refugees, famine and starving children with flies in their eyes; a 2002 VSO report, for example, noted that '80 per cent of the British public strongly associate the developing world with doom-laden images of famine, disaster and Western aid'.[88] It is this image that is reinforced so frequently in the media and on an annual basis on British television during Comic Relief or Children in Need. The West has consistently demonstrated a willingness to respond to this sort of crisis. However, as Ibrahim Seaga Shaw argues, this 'emotive framing' of Africa leads not to a fuller understanding of the continent or genuine calls to redress human rights abuses, but instead to superficial calls for aid.[89] In this analysis, African suffering is understood to need emergency food and water rather than political engagement.

Summary

Having explored the various potential influences on the decision to intervene, we are left with a rather unsatisfactory explanation. All too often each of the various influences is looked at in isolation, but of course this is not at all how decision making works in the real world. No foreign secretary or prime minister ever works through a checklist of public opinion, media coverage, international law and race before making a decision to deploy troops. Instead their understanding of a crisis is framed by what they read in the press, see on the television, learn from civil servants, know from history and hear from members of the public, and their response is influenced by their interpretation of national interest, the perceived chances of success, the response of other nations and the crisis's relative importance to other events and domestic priorities. An explanation of foreign policy making that fails to address this myriad of different influences is an incomplete one.

What we can say categorically is that no one factor seems to explain fully the decision to intervene. National interest alone appears to be unsatisfactory; media coverage seems important but not sufficient and international law is not something that motivates intervention. There is no formula that predicts when a state will or will not intervene: governments intervene in countries that appear to have little or no impact on national security and economic interests; they respond to crises that demand front-page headlines and to crises that appear as no more than a footnote; and they intervene in Africa one year and not the next; they intervene in response to comparatively minor events and ignore other crises that by rights should be called genocide.

But we can see some trends. The factor that appears consistently is the suggestion that intervention only happens when it is believed something can be done at an acceptable cost (in terms of money, lives and standing in the international community). The US, for example, was willing to intervene in Somalia despite no obvious national interest because the anticipated cost was small. Or, as we have seen, the British and French Governments' response to ethnically motivated violence in Bosnia shifted over time as the perceived threat to national interests increased. In these cases, governments believed they could achieve something positive at an acceptable cost. It is also apparent that it was political elites that took the lead in forming policy. The media did not push governments to intervene; indeed in the cases of Libya in 2011 and Bosnia in the 1990s the press were fairly cautious and British involvement in Mali in 2012 was announced by Prime Minister David Cameron with hardly any prior press coverage of the crisis. The working hypothesis of this book is therefore that intervention only occurs when three factors align. First there must be a recognition that a humanitarian crisis exists; secondly, there must be political will at the very top of government to intervene; thirdly, governments intervene only when they feel they have a chance of success, when they perceive, based on the evidence available to them (through sources that include a less-than-perfect bureaucracy, the media and history) that the benefits of intervention outweigh the likely costs. Different factors may combine to put an issue on the agenda – media coverage, parliamentary pressure, debate at the UN, intelligence sources, or an obvious threat to national security – but once on the government's agenda the decision of whether or not to intervene becomes largely a judgement of whether the likely benefits outweigh the likely costs. In the vast majority of cases the answer is 'no' and governments do nothing, but just occasionally governments decide the answer is 'yes' and intervention is launched.

The remainder of this book explores this hypothesis by focusing on the events in Rwanda in 1993 and 1994. It begins with a brief exploration of the history of Rwanda from pre-colonial times to the outbreak of genocide; I make no claims to say anything original in this particular chapter and readers already familiar with the history of Rwanda may wish to move straight to Chapter 2. Chapters 2, 3 and 4 then explore the British response to the crisis in three stages. Chapter 2 addresses the first stage, a period in which Britain can be seen firstly as having only a remote connection with Rwanda and secondly as failing to understand the crisis in Rwanda; Britain was at this stage the 'ignorant bystander'. The chapter looks at the period prior to the outbreak of genocide as well as exploring Britain's involvement with the Tutsi rebel army and the decision to send a UN peacekeeping mission to Rwanda. In the second stage Britain became aware of what was happening in Rwanda but chose not to intervene; Chapter 3 therefore examines why the UK seemed to have moved from being the ignorant bystander to the 'indifferent bystander'. It explores the period of May and June 1994 and looks at discussions at the UN, the response to the refugee crisis in Tanzania and the British response to the French decision to deploy to Rwanda. In the third stage Britain actively became involved in the crisis; aid to the region was massively increased, there was public and media pressure for the Government to intervene and British troops were finally deployed. However, it has been suggested that even in this period Britain was the 'bystander who did too little too late'. Chapter 4 therefore examines the response to the refugee crisis which developed in Zaire and then the decision to send British troops to Rwanda. Finally, in the Conclusion the various influences on policy making are assessed and consideration is given to Tony Blair's suggestion that the UK bore responsibility for the events in Rwanda.

Notes

1 R. Rurangwa, *Genocide: My Stolen Rwanda* (London: Reportage Press, 2009), p. 40.

2 A. Kuperman, *The Limits of Humanitarian Intervention: Genocide in Rwanda* (Washington DC: Brookings Institution Press, 2001), p. 122; A. Des Forges, *Leave None to Tell the Story: Genocide in Rwanda* (New York: Human Rights Watch, 1999), p. 1; R. Dallaire, *Shake Hands with the Devil: The Failure of Humanity in Rwanda* (London: Arrow Books, 2004), p. 5; S. Khan, *The Shallow Graves of Rwanda* (London: I.B. Tauris, 2000), p. 1.

3 L. Melvern, *Conspiracy to Murder: The Rwandan Genocide*, revised edn (London: Verso, 2006), p. 4.

4 A. Jones, *Genocide, War Crimes and the West* (London: Zed Books, 2004), p. 232.

5 P. Auerswald *et al.*, *Clinton's Foreign Policy: A Documentary Record* (The Hague: Kluer Law International, 2003), p. 220.

6 T. Blair, *A Journey* (London: Hutchinson, 2010), p. 61.

7 Readers wanting a more general history of the Rwandan genocide are directed to: Des Forges, *Leave None to Tell the Story*; Melvern, *Conspiracy to Murder*; or G. Prunier, *The Rwandan Crisis: History of a Genocide* (London: Hurst & Co., 2005).

8 G. Bennett, *Six Moments of Crisis: Inside British Foreign Policy* (Oxford: Oxford University Press, 2013), p. 173.

9 A. Cooke, *The Campaign Guide 1994: A Comprehensive Survey of Conservative Policy* (London: Conservative & Unionist Central Office, 1994), p. v.

10 M. Curtis, *The Ambiguities of Power: British Foreign Policy since 1945* (London: Zed Books, 1995), p. 183.

11 R. Dallaire *et al.*, 'The Major Powers on Trial', *Journal of International Criminal Justice* 3 (2005), p. 862.

12 M. Curtis, 'Britain's Real Foreign Policy and the Failure of British Academia', *International Relations* 18:13 (2004), p. 281.

13 I. Carlsson, 'The UN Inadequacies', *Journal of International Criminal Justice* 3 (2005), p. 844.

14 Dallaire *et al.*, 'Major Powers', p. 887; L. Melvern, 'The Security Council: Behind the Scenes', *International Affairs* 77 (2001), p. 108.

15 A. Roberts, 'The So Called "Right" of Humanitarian Intervention', in *Yearbook of International Humanitarian Law 2000* (The Hague: TMC Asser, 2001), p. 4.

16 A. Lebor, *Complicity with Evil: The United Nations in the Age of Modern Genocide* (New Haven: Yale University Press, 2006), p. 15.

17 T. Weiss, *Humanitarian Intervention* (Cambridge: Polity Press, 2007), p. 54.
18 R. Howard, *What's Wrong with Liberal Interventionism: The Dangers and Delusions of the Interventionist Doctrine* (London: Social Affairs Unit, 2006), p. 24.
19 A. Bellamy, 'Whither the Responsibility to Protect? Humanitarian Intervention and the 2005 World Summit', *Ethics & International Affairs* 20:2 (2006), pp. 143–5.
20 Massad Ayoob, *The Third World Security Predicament: State Making, Regional Conflict and the International System* (Boulder: Lynne Rienner, 1995).
21 For example: Hansard, HC Deb, 26 July 1993, vol. 229, cols 848–9; Hansard, HC Deb, 7 February 1994, vol. 237, col. 25.
22 D. Hurd, *Memoirs* (London: Abacus, 2004), p. 492.
23 Howard, *What's Wrong with Liberal Interventionism,* p. 66.
24 T. Murithi, 'NGOs and Conflict Resolution in Africa: Facilitators or Aggravators of Peacekeeping?', in O. Furley and R. May (eds), *Peacekeeping in Africa* (Aldershot: Ashgate, 1998), p. 278.
25 J. Gow, 'British Perspectives', in A. Danche and T. Halverson (eds), *International Perspectives on the Yugoslav Conflict* (London: Macmillan, 1996), p. 89.
26 P. Dixon, 'Britain's "Vietnam Syndrome"? Public Opinion and British Military Intervention from Palestine to Yugoslavia', *Review of International Studies* 26 (2000), p. 114.
27 B. Simms, *Unfinest Hour: Britain and the Destruction of* Bosnia, (London: Penguin Books, 2001), p. 10.
28 L. Neack, 'UN Peace-Keeping: In the Interest of Community of Self?', *Journal of Peace Research* 32:2 (1995), p. 184.
29 *Ibid.*, p. 194.
30 M. Smith, 'Humanitarian Intervention: An Overview of the Ethical Issues', *Ethics & International Affairs* 12:1 (2006), p. 70.
31 A. Hehir, *Humanitarian Intervention* (Basingstoke: Palgrave Macmillan, 2010), p. 62.
32 Smith, 'Humanitarian Intervention', p. 70.
33 Neack, 'UN Peace-Keeping', p. 182.
34 P. Diehl, *Peace Operations* (Cambridge: Polity Press, 2008), p. 59.
35 F. Weissman, *In the Shadow of 'Just Wars': Violence, Politics and Humanitarian Action* (London: Hurst & Co., 2004), p. 63.
36 I. Budge, *The New British Politics* (Harlow: Pearson Longman, 2007), p. 536.
37 Anonymous interview with author.
38 H. Cameron, *Britain's Hidden Role in the Rwandan Genocide: The Cat's Paw* (Abingdon: Routledge, 2013), p. 24.
39 Anonymous interview with author.
40 M. Thatcher, *The Downing Street Years* (London: HarperCollins, 1993), p. 331.
41 Quoted in M. Rikfind, 'Britain Restored in the World', in R. Subroto and J. Clark (eds), *Margaret Thatcher's Revolution: How it Happened and What it Meant* (London: Continuum, 2005), p. 34.
42 Hurd, *Memoirs,* p. 454.

43 Thatcher, *The Downing Street Years*, pp. 500–3.
44 J. Coles, *Making Foreign Policy: A Certain Idea of Britain* (London: John Murray, 2000), p. 77.
45 Thatcher, *The Downing Street Years*, p. 169.
46 www.un.org/en/peacekeeping.
47 L. Freedman, 'Defence Policy', in D. Kavanagh and A. Seldon (eds), *The Major Effect* (London: Macmillan, 1994), p. 279.
48 Cooke, *The Campaign Guide 1994*, p. 580
49 N. White, *Democracy Goes to War: British Military Deployments under International Law* (Oxford: Oxford University Press, 2009), p. 69.
50 P. Cradock, *In Pursuit of British Interests: Reflections on Foreign Policy under Margaret Thatcher and John Major* (London: John Murray, 1997), p. 181.
51 Cooke, *The Campaign Guide 1994*, p. 580.
52 Hurd, *Memoirs*, p. 542.
53 Coles, *Making Foreign Policy*, p. 92
54 J. Dickie, *The New Mandarins: How British Foreign Policy Works* (London: I.B. Tauris, 2004), p. 88.
55 G. Tullock, *The Politics of Bureaucracy* (Lanham: University Press of America, 1965), p. 167.
56 M. Takeda and M. Helms, '"Bureaucracy Meet Catastrophe": Analysis of the Tsunami Disaster Relief Efforts and Their Implications for Global Emergency Governance', *International Journal of Public Sector Management* 19:2 (2006), p. 210.
57 C. Coyne, 'The Politics of Bureaucracy and the Failure of Post-War Reconstruction', *Public Choice* 135 (2008), p. 15.
58 *Ibid.*
59 S. Cowper-Coles, *Cables from Kabul* (London: Harper Press, 2012), pp. 7, 38, 166.
60 Takeda and Helms, 'Bureaucracy Meet Catastrophe', p. 211.
61 G. Allison, *Essence of Decision: Explaining the Cuban Missile Crisis* (Boston: Little, Brown and Co., 1971), p. 88.
62 A. Seldon, *Major: A Political Life* (London: Phoenix, 1998), p. 162.
63 S. Soroka, 'Media, Public Opinion and Foreign Policy', *Harvard International Journal of Press Politics* 8:1 (2003), p. 27.
64 G. Robertson, *Crimes against Humanity* (London: Penguin, 1999), p. 373.
65 A. Storey, 'Non-Neutral Humanitarianism: NGOs and the Rwanda Crisis', *Development in Practice* 7:4 (1997), p. 385.
66 C. Frizzell, 'Public Opinion and Foreign Policy: The Effects of Celebrity Endorsements', *Social Science Journal* 48 (2011), p. 315.
67 B. Jentleson and R. Britton, 'Still Pretty Prudent: Post Cold-War American Public Opinion on the Use of Military Force', *Journal of Conflict Resolution* 42:4 (1998), pp. 406–7.
68 P. Jakobsen, 'National Interest, Humanitarianism or CNN: What Triggers UN Peace Enforcement after the Cold War?', *Journal of Peace Research* 33:2 (1996), p. 206.

69 *Ibid.*, p. 208.
70 J. Mermin, 'Televison News and American Intervention in Somalia: The Myth of a Media-Driven Foreign Policy', *Political Science Quarterly* 112:3 (1997), p. 385.
71 N. Gowing, 'Instant Pictures, Instant Policy: Is Television Driving Foreign Policy?', *Independent* (3 July 1994).
72 L. Minear *et al.*, *The News Media, Civil War, and Humanitarian Action* (Boulder: Lynne Rienner, 1996), p. 4.
73 Jakobsen, 'National Interest', p. 212.
74 Mermin, 'Television News', p. 389.
75 R. DiPrizio, *Armed Humanitarians: US Interventions from Northern Iraq to Kosovo* (Baltimore: Johns Hopkins University Press, 2002), p. 39.
76 Jakobsen, 'National Interest', p. 212.
77 M. Kaldor, *New and Old Wars: Organised Violence in a Global Era* (Cambridge: Polity Press, 2006), p. 61.
78 D. Rieff, *Slaughterhouse: Bosnia and the Failure of the West* (New York: Simon & Schuster, 1996), pp. 154–9.
79 Kaldor, *New and Old Wars*, p. 61.
80 Rieff, *Slaughterhouse*, pp. 154–9.
81 Bennett, *Six Moments of Crisis*, p. 174.
82 R. Holbrooke, *To End a War* (New York: Modern Library, 1999), p. 174.
83 Winston Churchill, in Hansard, HC Deb, 1 August 1946, vol. 426, col. 1256.
84 M. Krenn, *The Color of Empire: Race and American Foreign Policy* (Washington DC: Potomac Books, 2006), p. 102.
85 *Ibid.*, p. 77.
86 R. Dowden, *Africa: Altered States, Ordinary Miracles* (London: Portobello Books, 2009), p. 4.
87 P. Dahlgren, 'The Third World on TV News: Western Ways of Seeing the Other', in W. Adams (ed.), *Television Coverage of International Affairs* (Norwood: Ablex, 1982), p. 53.
88 VSO, *The Live Aid Legacy: The Developing World through British Eyes* (London: VSO, 2001), p. 3.
89 I.S. Shaw, 'Historical Frames and the Politics of Humanitarian Intervention: From Ethiopia, Somalia to Rwanda', *Globalisation, Societies and Education* 5:3 (2007), p. 359.

1

History of the crisis

European colonisation came late to Rwanda. Its remote location and limited resources meant that it was not until 1885 that Germany gained colonial rights to what was then known as Ruanda-Urundi at the Berlin Conference (this territory included modern-day Rwanda, Burundi and parts of Uganda). It was nearly ten years later, in 1894, that Count Gustav von Götzen became the first German, and probably only the second European, to visit the new colony. Unfortunately, von Götzen left no accurate records of what he observed in Ruanda-Urundi; we therefore cannot accurately know how Rwanda changed over the one hundred years from first contact with the West to 1994 when genocide tore the country apart.

By 1894, as in 1994, Rwanda certainly had three separate groupings, though whether these should be described as racial, ethnic, tribal or social remains a matter of debate. As Richard Dowden explains, 'the relationship between Hutus and Tutsis is unique, complex and very difficult for outsiders to comprehend. There are no words in English to describe it. Caste, class, race or tribe do not match the reality.'[1] The Hutu, then as now, formed the bulk of population at around 82 per cent, the Tutsi accounted for a further 17 per cent and the Twa were a small minority of less than 1 per cent. Although it has never been conclusively demonstrated and still remains a controversial hypothesis, it was popularly held by European colonists that the three groupings arrived in Rwanda at different times in pre-colonial history. The Twa, a pygmy race of hunter-gatherers, were allegedly the first to arrive, followed by the Hutu agriculturalists; the Tutsi, pastoralists from the north, arrived last, from the fifteenth century onwards. Colonists generally believed that typically Tutsi were taller, had lighter skin and had more European-looking features than the Hutu, leading them to hypothesise that the Tutu were descendants of Ham, one of Noah's sons, who had travelled to Rwanda from Ethiopia. This gave rise to what has become known as the 'Hamitic myth'.

Despite the uncertainty over the origin of the groups, what is clear is that when von Götzen arrived in Rwanda he found a society governed by a largely Tutsi aristocracy. This aristocracy controlled most of the wealth and land and enjoyed almost feudal rights over the peasantry; but, unlike their Hutu and Twa cousins, the Tutsi peasantry were exempt from the obligation to provide labour services to the Tutsi overlords. There was certainly a distinct Tutsi elite in the pre-colonial period, but, as Peter Uvin points out, it is important to recognise the similarities between the two groups: all shared the same religion, the same language, the same customs and festivals, and inter-group marriage was not rare. Most significantly, it was possible to change group; a rich Hutu could become a Tutsi.[2] As Tony Vaux suggests, although the relationship between the groups was certainly complex, it did not seem to match the 'Western stereotype of Africa [which] demands ... the monolithic, indivisible tribe, liable to fight other such tribes as a matter of custom'.[3]

German control of Ruanda-Urundi proved to be brief, ending during the First World War, when in 1916 Belgian troops entered the capital, Kigali. After the war Rwanda was technically a trust territory, which dictated that its rule was subject to League of Nations oversight, but in practice Belgium was left to govern the country as it saw fit. The Belgians arriving in Rwanda, like the German before them, noted the more Caucasian features of the Tutsi and similarly interpreted this as an indication of their superiority over the Hutu. The Belgian authorities therefore chose to continue the practice of elite Tutsi domination. In 1926, a series of reforms, known as 'les reformes Voisin', were introduced which effectively codified this preference: Tutsi were given positions of power in local government, gifted land to farm, educated at missionary schools and trained as Catholic priests. In 1933 additional legislation required all Rwandans to carry an identification card showing their ethnic grouping. Although ordinary Tutsi peasants also lost out during this period, with many forfeiting land and fleeing north into Uganda, the impact of the reforms was to intensify Hutu resentment of the whole Tutsi minority, not just the elite, and to further polarise the two groups. Whatever the exact nature of the relationship between Hutu and Tutsi before colonisation, the Belgium reforms meant the two groups now perceived themselves to be different.

Tutsi and Belgian domination of Rwanda continued until the late 1950s when the Belgian Government finally accepted the inevitability of demands for independence, both from within Rwanda and Belgium and also from the wider international community. At the last minute, despite having governed through the Tutsi for four decades, the Belgian authorities, foreseeing the almost certain post-independence dominance of the Hutu majority, unexpectedly switched their favour away from the Tutsi to the Hutu. Emboldened by the newfound Belgian patronage, Hutu were encouraged to form political parties and to begin to exert their position as the country's majority. Suddenly in November 1959, false rumours that a Hutu politician had been killed by a gang of Tutsi youth triggered Rwanda's first major spate of ethnic violence. This one rumour was the spark that ignited the tinder box of resentment between Hutu, who as they saw it had suffered years of discrimination, and the Tutsi; it was the start of a Hutu revolution. In the violence no differentiation was made between the Tutsi elite and ordinary Tutsi, all were considered fair targets. Within two weeks over three hundred people had been killed. In response, large numbers of Tutsi fled to Uganda and Burundi. Once begun, the shift to Hutu domination was unstoppable: in 1960 only nineteen of the 229 newly elected *bourgmestres* were Tutsi and in 1961 Hutu took thirty-five of the forty-two seats in the newly formed Parliament. For many outside Rwanda this was seen as a victory for democracy. However, these events led the UN to conclude: 'The developments of the last eighteen months have brought about the racial dictatorship of one party ... An oppressive system has been replaced by another one ... It is quite possible that some day we will witness violent reactions on the part of the Tutsi.'[4]

Rwanda formally gained independence on 1 July 1962; the former Tutsi *mwami* (king) was removed and Grégoire Kayibanda, a Hutu, became the country's first elected president. Kayibanda was a man not afraid to use ethnic violence and terror to cement his position in power. Under the new president, the principles of the 1959 Hutu revolution were confirmed: previous reforms and laws that favoured Tutsi were not only overturned but were reversed and Hutu domination of government and military began. Throughout the 1960s ethnic violence also formed a central pillar of Kayibanda's rule; in 1964 in particular, a raid by Tutsi refugees was firmly put down by the army and a wave of reprisal killings left tens of thousands of Tutsi dead across Rwanda.

In 1973 Kayibanda, a southern Hutu, was deposed in a bloodless coup led by the army Chief of Staff from the north of the country, Juvénal Habyarimana. Despite retaining the policies that limited the number of Tutsi in government, the military and in education, Habyarimana was much more moderate than Kayibanda and under his presidency Rwanda experienced a period of relative economic prosperity and stability that continued into the late 1980s. The seeds of his downfall were sown early. Habyarimana surrounded himself with family members, friends and people from his village. This personal domination of government bred resentment amongst southern Hutu which would eventually lead to political turmoil.

The years of stability came to an abrupt end in the late 1980s when the international price for coffee and tin, Rwanda's only two exports, plummeted and the country became dependent upon foreign aid. As this dependency increased and the end of the Cold War led to growing demands for democracy across Africa, Habyarimana came under pressure from donor countries to renounce the system of one-party government that had been in place since 1974. With no alternative but to acquiesce, Habyarimana begrudgingly allowed the formation of new parties; immediately a number of Hutu-dominated liberal parties opposed to his dictatorship sprang up and the once-stable political atmosphere in Rwanda was overturned.

Meanwhile, the number of predominantly Tutsi refugees in Uganda and Burundi had swelled to some 700,000. These refugees, who had fled official persecution, always held that some day they would return home to Rwanda and by the early 1980s they had formed an alliance whose stated ambition was their return to Rwanda. By 1987 the alliance had formed into the Rwandan Patriotic Front (RPF), a military organisation led by officers with experience of fighting in the Ugandan civil wars and who, because of their support of Ugandan President Museveni, also held senior positions in the Ugandan army. Having failed to reach agreement with Habyarimana on a negotiated settlement to allow refugees to return home, on 1 October 1990 the RPF launched an invasion of Rwanda from Uganda, with the intention of forcing their way back home.

At this point the RPF had around 2,500 soldiers, many of whom had deserted from the Ugandan army and were armed with equipment they had plundered. The Rwandan army (Forces Armées Rwandaises – FAR), on the other hand, was over 5,000 strong and equipped with modern weaponry supplied by France as part of a one-sided military cooperation pact. Despite their numerical superiority, FAR initially suffered losses at the hands of the well-trained, well-disciplined and war-hardened RPF; but by November the RPF had retreated back into Uganda. However, it was not FAR alone that forced the RPF retreat. On 4 October 150 French paratroopers arrived in Kigali to support the Rwandan Government and they were soon reinforced by 450 more French troops sent on the personal instructions of President François Mitterrand; France was effectively propping up Habyarimana. The relationship between France and Rwanda had developed during the 1970s and mirrored the association between Paris and a number of other Francophone African countries. As Daniela Kroslak describes the relationship, it was part of France's 'activist Africa policy' begun by Charles de Gaulle and continued by all subsequent French presidents; it was a policy which allowed France to dominate Africa economically, culturally and politically and as such confirm its role as a global power. [5] The various military pacts which France had with African countries, though, did mean that in cases of war France was obliged to respond, even if it was only to reassure other African leaders that they could trust their French ally.

The RPF, although beaten back, was not destroyed. Throughout 1991 and 1992 its raids continued. Within Rwanda, Hutu ultra-nationalists responded in what was by then the traditional fashion of reprisal violence against Tutsi civilians; over 2,000 Tutsi were killed in revenge attacks. At the same time Habyarimana significantly increased spending on the military and arms; FAR was expanded to some 10,000 soldiers and by 1993 Rwanda, one of the smallest countries in Africa, had become one of its largest arms importers.[6] Linda Melvern has uncovered details of contracts between the Rwandan Government and South African arms dealers worth a staggering US$56 million between October 1990 and May 1991 alone, as well as over $10 million of deals with Egypt in a similar period.[7]

After eighteen months of intermittent fighting, in March 1992 Habyarimana finally gave in to international pressure and announced the formation of a new coalition cabinet which included Hutu opposition parties. The newly appointed ministers were quick to act, first agreeing a ceasefire with the RPF and then beginning peace talks in Arusha, Tanzania. But despite these peace efforts,

Habyarimana quite publicly continued to expand and arm FAR. After numerous false dawns, breaches of the ceasefire by both sides and the signing of various protocols, a final set of agreements, known as the Arusha Accords, was signed in August 1993. The Accords provided for fairly radical change; a broad-based transitional government would be installed until democratic elections could be held, the Tutsi refugees would be allowed home, the two warring armies would be merged, French troops would withdraw and the position of the president would become largely ceremonial. It was this last provision that made it obvious to Rwanda observers that Hutu extremists close to Habyarimana, keen to retain their firm grip on power and control of the foreign aid money coming into the country, would not support the agreement. Despite the signing of the Accords, peace was far from inevitable.

In November 1993 UN peacekeeping troops arrived in Rwanda after the Security Council agreed to oversee the Accords' implementation[8] and at the same time the French troops left. The force, known as the United Nations Assistance Mission for Rwanda (UNAMIR), was mandated to oversee the transition to the broad-based government and the merging of the two armies. The Accords' plans for power-sharing and elections seemed to be a perfect fit with the ideological belief that rapid liberalism and democracy would create conditions of stable and lasting peace that was permeating much of the international community in the immediate aftermath of the end of the Cold War. For some in the UN, the mission was potentially a textbook example of how liberal peacekeeping could work. In practice, the key step of transferring power to the transitional government was delayed repeatedly, usually due to the procrastination and stubbornness of Habyarimana.

By April 1994 the broad-based government had still not been formed and the international community was losing patience. On 5 April the UN Security Council voted to renew UNAMIR's mandate, but a review after six weeks was stipulated in the hope that this would reinvigorate the peace process.[9] Regional leaders also applied pressure, particularly to Habyarimana, who was widely seen as being responsible for the stalling. On 6 April Habyarimana flew to Dar-es-Salaam for a meeting with the presidents of Tanzania, Kenya, Uganda and Burundi, all of whom demanded an end to his procrastination. Scolded, the President boarded his private jet, a gift from the French Government, to return to Rwanda. As the plane came in to land at Kigali, two surface-to-air missiles illuminated the night sky and the jet was shot down; all on board were killed. No one has ever claimed responsibility for firing the missiles.

Within hours an interim government led by army officers and Habyarimana's former supporters took control of the country. Almost immediately road blocks, manned by government-backed militia (the Interahamwe) and FAR, sprang up across Kigali. The next day opposition leaders and influential Tutsi were rounded up and killed in a systematic manner that was indicative of thorough organisation. The killings quickly spread from Hutu opposition leaders to ordinary Tutsi, first in Kigali and then across the country. Among the first victims were ten Belgian peacekeepers captured and executed as they tried in vain to protect the moderate prime minister elect, Agathe Uwilingiyimana. Two days after the killing started, the RPF resumed the civil war and this time rather than intervene, the French, along with the Belgians, acted quickly to evacuate their ex-patriot citizens (the French, on Mitterrand's personal orders, also evacuated Habyarimana's wife and family, granting them asylum in Paris). Having evacuated its own citizens the Belgian Government announced it would also withdraw its troops from UNAMIR; then on 21 April the UN announced that UNAMIR's position was untenable and it would be withdrawn with the exception of a rump headquarters force.

In the absence of international peacekeepers, the pace of genocide was incredible. Alan Kuperman estimates that within two weeks of the violence breaking out 40 per cent of the Tutsi population had been killed, suggesting an average daily death toll of some 18,000 people.[10] Survivors and witnesses recall how Hutu set up road blocks where they casually checked the identification cards of everyone who passed; Hutu were allowed to pass, Tutsi were slaughtered and, as if to demonstrate how orderly Rwandan society was, piled neatly at the side of the road. The Hutu militia hunted out Tutsi in their homes, in the fields, in the hills and in the swamps and surrounded churches where Tutsi had congregated for safety. The killing was largely carried out by hand; FAR had access to guns and grenades but ordinary Hutu killed with whatever weapon was at hand – machetes especially would be used to kill thousands. All the time the Hutu population were egged on by the militia leaders and Radio Télévision Libre Mille Collines (RTLMC), a radio station that pumped out rabid anti-Tutsi propaganda. When local leaders proved too slow to implement the genocide they were replaced and hardcore militia bussed in to complete what was euphemistically called the 'work'.

In May the UN authorised the return of an increased peacekeeping force to Rwanda, but for weeks no new soldiers were deployed. In late June France, publicly expressing its frustration at the UN's lack of progress, announced that it was going to deploy a unilateral mission to Rwanda with the aim of protecting civilians. The mission, known as Operation Turquoise, deployed to the south-west of Rwanda and established a safe-zone. For many Tutsi in the region it remained anything but safe; despite the French presence the genocide continued and it looked for a while as Turquoise's only impact would be to start a new war between the RPF and France. Only after one hundred days of fighting and violence did the genocide end, and then only because the RPF had occupied the country other than the area under French control. The RPF's military dominance was almost total and everywhere the two armies clashed the FAR was forced back. On 4 July the RPF captured Kigali, on 5 July Butare, the country's second city, and on 14 July Ruhengeri, the temporary home of the Government. On 18 July the RPF announced a unilateral ceasefire and installed a new government the following day.

In the face of this relentless drive, huge numbers of Hutu civilians also fled their homes, taking with them only the possessions they could carry. Ordinary Hutu were encouraged by local leaders and RTLMC to escape before the RPF arrived; in a mirror image of what they were themselves ordering, both Hutu leaders and RTLMC warned that Hutu civilians would be indiscriminately massacred by RPF soldiers, who they portrayed as invading Tutsi. Initially approximately 500,000 crossed the border into Tanzania and set up makeshift refugee camps there and a further 200,000 headed south into Burundi. Once the RPF took control of the eastern half of Rwanda, the displaced Hutu turned westward and crossed into the Zairean border region near the town of Goma. In the week ending 18 July alone, some 1.4 million Hutu, by now including the interim Government and the majority of FAR, crossed the border into eastern Zaire. Large sections of the Hutu population, many of whom had either carried out[11] or stood by and watched the quickest genocide ever seen, was by the end of July suffering one of the worst refugee crises that the world had had to deal with.

The international response

Before turning to the more thorough examination of the UK's response, it is worth the slight diversion of briefly considering how other countries responded; certainly some of these responses affected the British. Here the responses of the three main international protagonists in the crisis are considered: the United States, France and Belgium.

The United States

In August 1994 some 2,100 US troops would eventually deploy to Zaire in response to the humanitarian emergency unfolding in Goma in what was called Operation Support Hope. It is evident that throughout the crisis, although there were a few mid-level officials who sought some form of US response, at senior levels the Clinton administration, despite being aware of the genocidal nature of the crisis, actively took steps to avoid becoming involved in Rwanda.[12] Options were considered, but the response was always the same – there was a reason why direct US involvement should be avoided. For example, at one stage a State Department official suggested jamming RTLMC; the idea was rejected by the Pentagon, which raised legal arguments against the plan and highlighted the cost and presumed inefficiency of the scheme before finally arguing that jamming a civilian radio station infringed freedom of speech. As early as mid-April the State Department's legal advisers were considering whether the atrocities constituted genocide. Although they did eventually acknowledge that 'acts of genocide' were happening, in May their advice to the administration was to avoid the use of the word 'genocide' as this could 'commit the [US Government] to actually do something'.[13]

Why the US was so hostile to any intervention can be explained by four key factors. Firstly, the response was dominated by events in Somalia in 1993. Only six months before the genocide broke out in Rwanda, eighteen US Rangers, in Somalia as part of a UN-mandated peacekeeping force, had been killed during a failed mission to capture a Somali war-lord. The horror of the event was flashed across the globe as CNN filmed a dead American being dragged through the streets of Mogadishu. In response, Clinton promised to withdraw all American troops from the country and sought to blame the UN for the deaths. The tendency to 'fight the last war' meant that, come 1994, events in Rwanda were viewed through a Somali lens – the fear of another Mogadishu terrified American decision makers. Without the shadow of Somalia maybe the response would have been different, but as far as the US was concerned, as National Security Adviser Tony Lake was subsequently to suggest, 'Rwanda was a casualty of chronology'.[14]

Secondly, Congress heavily influenced the response. Clinton had taken office better disposed towards internationalism and peacekeeping than any other president, but by 1994 the Republican-dominated Congress had made it clear that it did not support the rising cost of peacekeeping. Although there were a few who called for greater US involvement in Rwanda, the majority in Congress were keen for the US to keep out. For example, after the evacuation of American nationals from Kigali, Republican Senate Leader Bob Dole appeared on the CBS news programme *Face the Nation* saying, 'I don't think we have any national interest here ... I hope we don't get involved there. The Americans are out, as far as I am concerned in Rwanda. That ought to be the end of it.'[15] Ever-conscious of the need for Congressional support to push through domestic reforms, there was no way that Clinton was going to incur the hostility and wrath of Congress over Rwanda.

The third factor is US Presidential Decision Directive (PDD) 25. Although not published until after the genocide had begun, PDD25 was being drafted in April 1994 and was therefore at the fore of decision makers' minds. In the wake of the events in Somalia, the US's future involvement in peacekeeping was reviewed and PDD25 set out when the US would and would not intervene. From now on, military involvement would be measured against set criteria: US interests were at stake; there was a threat to world peace and a clear mission goal; costs were acceptable; Congress, public and allies supported intervention; a working ceasefire was in place; and there was a clear exit route. Rwanda passed only one of the criteria: there was evidence of a humanitarian emergency. In the absence of clear instructions to the contrary from the President, no senior government official was going to champion intervention when it clearly failed to satisfy the new policy.[16]

The final factor influencing US policy was the fear in the White House and the Pentagon that the US was assumed to be the peacekeeper of last resort.

Having seen what had happened in Somalia, Washington feared that supporting any mission, even by voting in favour at the Security Council, would inevitably lead to US involvement. The belief was therefore that if any troops deployed to Rwanda, eventually the US would either have to reinforce the mission or lead some form of rescue. As Samantha Power suggests, there was a 'fear, articulated mainly at the Pentagon but felt throughout the bureaucracy, that what would start as a small engagement by foreign troops would end as a large and costly one by Americans'.[17] For this reason the administration opposed not only US involvement but also that of others.

Like the UK, the US did eventually deploy troops to the region, but only after the genocide had ended and only then into neighbouring Zaire to provide aid in the refugee camps. Jared Cohen nicely sums up the US response in the title of his book on US involvement - *One Hundred Days of Silence*.

France

The French response to the events of 1994 was also influenced by history, though in this case a history going back further than 1993. Since the wave of African independence in the 1950s and 1960s, France had viewed north and western Africa (a largely Francophone region) as falling within its sphere of influence. French presidents since de Gaulle believed that by dominating Africa they cemented their nation's position as a world power and justified their permanent seat at the UN Security Council. French relations with Rwanda had been especially strong as demonstrated by the very close personal relationship between presidents Mitterrand and Habyarimana. However, by the early 1990s France was losing confidence in its dominant position in Africa. As Asteris Huliaras notes, 'The developments in Rwanda were considered by many French politicians, diplomats and journalists as evidence of an "Anglo-Saxon conspiracy", part of a plot to develop an arc of influence from Ethiopia and Eritrea via, Uganda, Rwanda and Zaire to Congo and Cameroon. For them, the "Anglo-Saxons" had a hidden agenda "to oust them from Africa"'.[18]

Some, including Gerard Prunier, have called this French perception the 'Fashoda Syndrome', referring to the 1898 territorial dispute that nearly led the UK and France to war in the small Sudanese village of Fashoda.[19] The syndrome, he continues, explains the tendency within French foreign policy to assert French influence in areas which may be susceptible to British or, since the wave of African independence in the 1960s, US influence. This underlying belief led the French Government to conclude from 1990 onwards that the RPF incursions into Rwanda were supported by the English-speaking Ugandan Government and therefore by extension by the wider Anglo-Saxon world. If France was to retain its close relations with its various client states across Africa it had to stand up to the aggression of the RPF; President Mitterrand was determined to reassure the

French public and African heads of state that France's position in Africa, and therefore the world, would not be threatened. This meant actively intervening to support the Rwandan Government throughout the civil war, which France did between 1990 and late 1993 by sending troops and supplying weapons (indeed, France continued to supply weapons, in defiance of a UN arms embargo, even after the genocide had broken out).[20]

Once the killings began the French political elite steadfastly refused to accept that what was happening in Rwanda was genocide. Throughout the summer of 1994, the French Government described Rwanda as a civil war and called for a ceasefire between the two parties; it justified its relations with the interim Hutu Government on the grounds that this was the only way to encourage it to negotiate. When the French did eventually acknowledge the genocide, they perpetuated the theory of double-genocide. In May French Foreign Minister Alain Juppé spoke of both sides committing crimes and in September Mitterrand spoke of 'genocides' deliberately using the plural.[21]

The French, more than anyone, must have known what was happening in Rwanda in April 1994; as well as deploying troops as part of the effort to evacuate foreign nationals, there were still reputedly military intelligence agents in the country.[22] The close connections with the Hutu regime also meant that the French Government received first-hand intelligence about what was happening on the ground. Yet the French did not intervene until June, did not encourage the UN to intervene more robustly, did not share their intelligence, did not seek to have the Rwandan ambassador removed from the Security Council[23] and made no effort to influence their friends in the interim Government. As Andrew Wallis concludes, 'Whilst Clinton used every trick in the diplomatic book to avoid getting involved in a country in which the USA clearly had no interest, Mitterrand and his military advisers were determined to get the best outcome for France out of the carnage'.[24] This meant deliberately ignoring the genocide and acting to preserve the Hutu Government that France had supported since the mid-1970s; an RPF victory was seen, by Mitterrand and the wider French political elite, as a threat to France's position in Africa and hence its standing in the international community.

Belgium

It was unusual for ex-colonial powers to contribute peacekeepers to missions in their old colonies, yet the Belgian Government was keen to support UNAMIR and Belgian troops formed the backbone of the mission. Why Belgium was the only NATO country willing to offer troops is not clear, but Romeo Dallaire, the commander of UNAMIR, suggests that 'a deal may have been struck with the French for Belgian troops to protect [France's] interests in Kigali after the French battalion was shipped out'.[25] Once in theatre it quickly became obvious to the Belgians that the peace process was precarious and in danger of collapsing. Belgian intelligence appears to have been more aware than most of the growing tension in the country: in November 1993 it noted the distribution of grenades across the country; in December officers warned that youth militias were being trained; and in January 1994 Belgian intelligence officers worked with Jean-Pierre, the Hutu informant who led Dallaire to send what has infamously become known as the 'Genocide Fax'. This fax, sent to UN headquarters in New York, has since been held up by some as the 'smoking gun' that proves that genocide could have been foreseen. In December 1993 Jean-Pierre approached Belgian officers with intelligence about the planning of genocide; he claimed that he was a senior military instructor involved in training the Hutu militia and had seen lists of intended victims. In return for asylum, he promised to lead UNAMIR to a number of arms caches across Kigali. On 11 January Dallaire faxed New York with this information and requested authority to carry out raids on the caches based on Jean-Pierre's intelligence. The request was refused by the Department for Peacekeeping Operations, which evidently feared a repeat of the Mogadishu fiasco, without ever having been discussed with or officially brought to the attention of Security Council members. Based on this catalogue of evidence, the Belgian ambassador in Kigali informed Brussels in early February that UNAMIR should be given a more forceful mandate or be withdrawn. Following this report, Willy Claes, the Belgian Foreign Minister, visited Kigali to see the situation first hand. On his return to Brussels he contacted UN Secretary General Boutros Boutros-Ghali to warn him that given its mandate and resources UNAMIR was ineffective and it was therefore necessary to reinforce the mission. The Belgian ambassador at the UN similarly pushed for reinforcements, but was reputedly told by officials that UNAMIR was considered a low-cost and low-priority mission and expansion would not be considered.[26]

The initial response of Belgium to the renewal of fighting in April 1994 was to argue for a rapid deployment of extra troops. At the UN, Belgium again asked for UNAMIR's mandate and rules of engagement to be changed so that its troops could intervene to stop the violence, but acknowledged they would only actively intervene if there was UN support.[27] There was none; on 8 April the Belgian ambassador informed Brussels that 'certain permanent members' were opposed to broadening the UNAMIR mandate.[28] At home, the Government also came under fierce criticism following the murder of the Belgian peacekeepers, and public opinion quickly soured towards the involvement in Rwanda. In the face of this opposition, and with no international support, the Government did an about-face and on 10 April Belgian paratroopers landed at Kigali airport to assist in the evacuation of Belgian and Western nationals. At the same time Boutros-Ghali was informed of the Belgian decision to withdraw its forces from UNAMIR. The official reason was that UNAMIR was now ineffective and that nothing could be done to stop the civil war.

Once this decision had been made, the Belgian Foreign Ministry set out to convince Security Council members that UNAMIR should be withdrawn completely. The effort devoted to what was effectively a face-saving exercise far exceeded previous efforts to have UNAMIR reinforced; Willy Claes reputedly contacted many of his counterparts personally.[29] As the former colonial power, the Belgian Government was considered, by many, to be the most qualified to speak on what was right for Rwanda. The murder of the Belgian soldiers and the public backlash was clearly the turning point for Belgium; like the US in Somalia, the Government was forced to withdraw and wanted nothing more to do with the country. Like both France and the US, Belgium placed its own national interest before any belief in humanitarianism and the people of Rwanda were left to their fate.

Summary

The genocide unleashed by the extremist Hutu government in 1994 was the bloodiest 100 days of the late twentieth century, possibly the whole century. In just those 100 days some 800,000 people were killed and approximately two million displaced from their homes. In a macabre symmetry the explanation of those 100 days needs to be traced back 100 years to 1894; the arrival of Europeans definitely changed Rwanda and most significantly it changed the relationship between the three 'ethnic' groupings. Colonisation did not make genocide inevitable in Rwanda, but it was a necessary contributory factor. Despite having a hand in the causes of the ethnic violence that plagued Rwanda from independence onwards, the West was far from keen to respond to the genocide; having invested in the peace process that ended three years of civil war the US, France and Belgium simply walked away once the killing began.

Notes

1 Dowden, *Africa: Altered States*, p. 227.
2 P. Uvin, 'Reading the Rwandan Genocide', *International Studies Review* 3:3 (2001), p. 76.
3 T. Vaux, *The Selfish Altruist: Relief Work in Famine and War* (London: Earthscan, 2001), p. 189.
4 UN General Assembly, *Question of the Future of Ruanda-Urundi: Report of the UN Commission on Ruanda-Urundi* (30 May 1962).
5 D. Kroslak, 'The Responsibility of External Bystanders in Cases of Genocide: The French in Rwanda, 1990–1994' (PhD thesis, University of Wales 2002), p. 132.

6 P. Gourevitch, *We Wish to Inform you that Tomorrow we Will be Killed with our Families* (London: Picador, 2000), p. 88.
7 L. Melvern, *A People Betrayed: The Role of the West in Rwanda's Genocide* (London: Zed Books, 2009), pp. 64–6.
8 United Nations, UN S/Res 872 (1993), New York, 5 October 1993.
9 United Nations, UN S/Res 909 (1994), New York, 5 April 1994.
10 Kuperman, *Limits of Humanitarian Intervention,* p. 122.
11 Scott Straus estimates that between 175,000 and 210,000 Hutu were active participants in the genocide, which means approximately 14 to 17% of the adult Hutu population. (S. Straus, 'How Many Perpetrators Were there in the Rwandan Patriotic Front? An Estimate', *Journal of Genocide Research* 6:1 (2004), p. 93.)
12 J. Dumbrell, *Clinton's Foreign Policy: Between the Bushes, 1992–2000* (London: Routledge, 2009), p. 79.
13 Office of the Deputy Assistant Secretary of Defense for Middle East/Africa Region, Discussion Paper, US Department of Defense, 1 May 1994.
14 J. Cohen, *One Hundred Days of Silence: America and the Rwanda Genocide* (Lanham: Rowman & Littlefield, 2007), p. 60.
15 Melvern, *A People Betrayed,* p. 172.
16 H. Burkhalter, 'The Question of Genocide: The Clinton Administration and Rwanda', *World Policy Journal* 11:4 (1994), p. 49.
17 S. Power, 'Why the United States Let the Rwandan Tragedy Happen', *Atlantic Monthly* (September 2001).
18 A. Huliaras, 'The "Anglo-Saxon Conspiracy": French Perceptions of the Great Lakes Crisis', *Journal of Modern African Studies* 36:4 (1988), p. 594.
19 Prunier, *Rwandan Crisis,* p. 104.
20 M. McNulty, 'French Arms, War and Genocide in Rwanda', *Crime, Law & Social Change* 33 (2000), pp. 115–20.
21 A. Wallis, *Silent Accomplice: The Untold Story of France's Role in the Rwandan Genocide* (London: I.B. Tauris, 2007), p. 187.
22 Kroslak, 'Responsibility of Bystanders', p. 306.
23 Rwanda was elected to the UN Security Council in January 1994 to take up one of the ten rotating seats.
24 Wallis, *Silent Accomplice,* p. 201.
25 Dallaire, *Shake Hands,* p. 84.
26 Melvern, *A People Betrayed,* p. 104.
27 The rules of engagement for UNAMIR, as drafted by General Dallaire, did authorise the use of force, up to and including deadly force, to prevent 'crimes against humanity'. Dallaire states that these rules were cribbed from the UN mission to Cambodia and sent to New York and all troop-contributing nations for approval at the start of the mission. Only the Belgian Government responded to Dallaire, and that was to indicate that it did not want its troops to be used for crowd control. The Belgian Government had therefore tacitly agreed that force could be used to stop crimes against humanity, yet when the

genocide began did not feel able to follow the rules that it had signed up to (Dallaire, *Shake Hands*, pp. 72 and 99).

28 Des Forges, *Leave None to Tell the Story*, p. 619.

29 K. Kovanda, 'The Czech Republic on the UN Security Council: The Rwandan Genocide', *Genocide Studies and Prevention* 5:2 (2010), p. 199.

2

The ignorant bystander?

'Rwanda was the classic small country far away of which we knew and wished to know nothing ... The country was poor, overcrowded, French speaking and offered no obvious attractions to us.'[1] These were the words of Edward Clay, Britain's non-resident ambassador to Rwanda, in 1995, succinctly summing up the UK's relationship with Rwanda before the genocide. Rwanda could not be said to have been at the top of Britain's foreign policy priority list – it did not even make the top 100. In the decades before the genocide Britain's relations with, and interest in, Rwanda had variously been described by the FCO as 'minimal', 'tenuous' and 'insignificant'.[2] As 'insignificant' as Rwanda may have been, the UK's position on the UN Security Council meant that in 1993 and 1994 the UK was forced, at least momentarily, to pay some attention to the small country far away.

This chapter explores the period up to 21 April, when the Security Council took the decision to withdraw the bulk of UNAMIR. Beginning with a review of Britain's relationship with Rwanda in the period before 1990, it moves on to consider how the media, Parliament and Government responded to the outbreak of civil war and looks at allegations that the UK supported the RPF in the civil war. It then discusses Britain's involvement in the decision to deploy UNAMIR and finally looks at the British reaction to the resumption of violence in April 1994. Throughout this period the violence was widely misinterpreted in Britain as the resumption of civil war and the FCO's support for the partial withdrawal of UNAMIR was made in the belief that the UN had limited chance of enforcing peace, but could act as a go-between in ceasefire negotiations between the RPF and the Interim Government. The UK was, in this period, the ignorant bystander.

Before 1990

Although British diplomats had been keen to claim large swathes of East Africa in the carving-up of Africa at the 1885 Berlin Conference, once Ruanda-Urundi had been allocated to Germany, Britain seemed to forget about the tiny country. At the end of the First World War, the UK tried briefly to take control of Ruanda-Urundi away from the Belgians, and part of the territory was indeed hived off to British-controlled Uganda, but overall the region was not considered worth a diplomatic battle. After 1919, other than an isolated question in 1926 relating to the Belgian right to demand native work, Rwanda really did slip from the UK's consciousness. Rwanda was not mentioned in the House of Commons again until Jeremy Thorpe asked the Foreign Secretary 'Whether he will instruct the British delegation at the United Nations to raise immediately, in the Security Council, as a threat to peace, the killing of members of the Tutsi tribe by the Rwanda Republican Government, as a violation of the Convention on the Prevention and Punishment of the Crime of Genocide'.[3] This was February 1964 and Thorpe was referring to President Kayibanda's forceful response to the incursion of the Tutsi from Uganda. In response, Peter Thomas, Minister of State at the Foreign Office, agreed that the events in Rwanda did constitute genocide but the Government did not believe that the UN Security Council was the 'appropriate forum for this matter'. Instead Thomas confirmed that the Foreign Office hoped that Rwanda's neighbours could exert some influence over Kayibanda. After this exceptionally brief show of interest in the affairs of Rwanda, the country slipped from the view of the House of Commons for another thirty years.

Media coverage of Rwanda was no more comprehensive. It has been suggested that Africa is the 'dark continent' only in that the media leaves its readers in the dark;[4] this was certainly the case over Rwanda. Throughout the 1980s, for instance, any media coverage of Rwanda invariably focused on the conservationist Dian Fossey, AIDs, or the impact on East Africa generally of falling coffee prices. Nor did Rwanda – which despite its altitude has never shared Kenya or Ethiopia's athletic success – ever really make it onto the back pages of the newspapers, a sure-fire way of attracting British attention. The only times Rwanda received anything more than passing coverage was when it was suggested as a destination for a trekking holiday to view the native mountain gorillas, and even then articles highlighted Rwanda's remoteness and the difficulties facing British tourists. In 1990, for example, Sheila Hayman wrote in the *Independent*, 'Rwanda used to be Belgian, so you have to fly Sabena, from Brussels; your passport has to make two Brussels trips, as there is no nearer consulate to issue a visa. Arranging all these practicalities and fixing up, via fax, a personalised itinerary with Rwanda Explorations Ltd took so much energy and time.'[5]

In the same way that the media and Parliament ignored Rwanda, the Foreign Office, and from 1968 onwards its successor the FCO, also demonstrated a marked lack of interest in the country. In a memo responding to the non-resident ambassador's annual report of 1968, one FCO official wrote: 'Admirable though it [the annual review] is, both its length and detail are, I submit, greater than Her Majesty's Government's very minor interest in Rwanda warrants'.[6] The report had run to no more than one thousand words. The fact that there was no British resident ambassador meant that intelligence was minimal and FCO documents suggest that diplomatic staff visited the country maybe once, or exceptionally twice, a year. In 1977, the non-resident ambassador (at this time based in Kinshasa, Zaire) highlighted that not being present in Rwanda meant that 'one cannot get the "feel" [for the country] that comes to any reasonably intelligent resident'. He continued that mail between Kinshasa and Rwanda could take as long as a year to be delivered, making communication with the country very difficult.[7] The lack of intelligence on the country was highlighted by a short report produced by the FCO African Section Research Department in 1977: 'We have little knowledge of Rwanda in the Research Department. The country has no newspapers and we have no post there. Therefore one can only guess from the absence of bad news that the country is peaceful and stable at present as it appears to have been for the last 13 years.'[8]

It is, however, no surprise that there was an apparent disinterest in Rwanda in this period. From the time that Prime Minister Harold Macmillan delivered his famous 'winds of change' speech, Britain's interest in the Africa as a whole swiftly declined and the continent, with the exception of South Africa, from a British perspective became 'marginal'.[9] Percy Craddock, who would go on to become John Major's foreign policy adviser, for example, recalled, 'when I was the head of the Foreign Office Planning Staff in the late 1960s we produced a map of the world [with] the countries magnified or reduced in size according to the extent of British interests ... South Africa bulked large against a shrunken African continent.'[10] By the late 1980s, other than protecting business interests, particularly in the south, the Government was content to leave Africa to the multilateral organisations, the UN agencies, the EU and international financial institutions[11] or to cede commitments to NGOs.[12]

And if Africa as a whole was no longer a core priority for Britain, Francophone Africa was given even less attention; the UK had diplomatic representation (i.e. a high commissioner) in all Commonwealth countries in 1990, but diplomatic relations in seventeen of the twenty-six Francophone countries were on a non-resident basis. The bilateral aid figures show a similar situation. In 1988, for example, British bilateral aid, on a per capita basis, averaged £4.79 to Commonwealth countries and only £0.12 to Francophone countries.[13] The figures show similar disparity between 1989 and 1994. As a Francophone country, Rwanda fell into this second tier of countries, in what was in reality for the FCO the forgotten continent.

As an aside, in 1965 the Rwandan Government had enquired about the possibility of joining the Commonwealth, mainly with the aim of improving relations with its Commonwealth neighbours, Uganda, Kenya and Tanzania. The response of the Commonwealth Relations Office was fairly dismissive, noting that there was no British tradition in Rwanda and they 'use[d] a different language'; instead Rwanda was encouraged to 'mend fences' with its Anglophone neighbours.[14]

The civil war period – still no interest

The outbreak of civil war in October 1990 did not fundamentally change the level of interest in Rwanda either in the media, in Parliament or at the FCO. It was not, for example, until January 1993 that the first question on the deteriorating situation in Rwanda was tabled in the House of Commons. In response to a question about what the Overseas Development Administration (ODA) was doing to aid Rwandan refugees, Minister of State Mark Lennox-Boyd matter-of-factly confirmed that the UK was doing nothing.[15] Similarly two months later Lennox-Boyd confirmed that the UK Government had made no direct representation to the Rwandan Government over human rights abuses, though the European Community had made a statement on behalf of its member states.

The civil war in Rwanda received as little attention in the media as it did in Parliament. The initial RPF invasion in October 1990 was fairly extensively covered, with articles appearing in all of the broadsheets (a war in Africa generally fails to interest the tabloid press). But it was not until 8 October that the first report was actually written by a journalist in Rwanda; for the first week all reports were filed from Paris, Brussels or Uganda.[16] Although at this stage no newspapers spoke of a threat of genocide, some reports did recall the horror of previous violence in the country. For example, Catherine Watson, writing in the *Independent*, informed readers that the 1959 revolution was 'a brutal revolt: according to one account the Hutu literally cut their tall and elegant Tutsi masters down to size by chopping off their legs at the knee'.[17] However, it is noticeable that much of the reporting focused not on the actual hostilities, but on the French and Belgian efforts to evacuate European nationals. Television coverage was even less comprehensive; ITN reported the outbreak of war only once and even then the focus was on the arrival of French troops in Kigali.[18]

Within a fortnight of the invasion, though, media interest in Rwanda had again waned – in fact, vanished. Reporting of the civil war, or Rwanda more generally, again became sporadic and cursory; only the *Guardian* and the *Independent* reported the 1990–91 peace negotiations. As Greg Philo argues, as is typical of reporting Africa, the absence of large-scale conflict or a pressing humanitarian disaster meant that the media attention shifted elsewhere.[19]

There was a steady trickle of newspaper coverage of the crisis throughout 1992–93, almost all of which was in the broadsheet press, and then more particularly in what can be described as the more liberally minded press: the *Guardian*, the *Observer* and the *Independent*. The war did not, to borrow Lindsey Hilsum's language, 'cross the threshold of significance' that would have seen it covered in the tabloids.[20] It is also true to suggest that it would be entirely possible to miss the coverage (articles were often short and relegated to deep inside the newspapers) or to underestimate the severity of the crisis – by June 1992, the travel section of the *Guardian* was again suggesting Rwanda as a tourist destination.[21] The press also made it clear that the situation in Rwanda was not particularly unique. Richard Dowden, writing in the *Independent,* for example, noted that the end of the Cold War and Western calls for democracy were opening up 'old divisions and local disputes' across Africa, before cataloguing crises in Nigeria, Mali, Senegal, Somalia, Togo, Ethiopia, Djibouti and Congo.[22] As the *Guardian* recorded on New Year's Eve 1992, 'large parts of the globe remain plagued by conflict'; of the twenty-five conflicts listed in the article, the war in Rwanda was considered the one with most hope of being resolved.[23] The sheer number of potential world crises meant that Rwanda was, as Peter Sharp suggested on the ITN lunchtime news in May 1993, 'virtually unreported' and 'overshadowed by Bosnia and Somalia'.[24]

Like the media, the Government and FCO's relationship with Rwanda seems to have been little changed by the outbreak of civil war in October 1990. Bilateral aid remained minimal, at around £400,000 in 1989–90 and 1990–91, falling to only £200,000 in 1991–92 when two English teachers funded by the Overseas Development Agency left the country after the invasion.[25] As the ambassador's annual report for 1990 made clear, 'there was little in way of bilateral relations'.[26] By this time it was the British High Commission in Kampala (Uganda), rather than the Embassy in Zaire, that nominally covered Rwanda, but visits to the country were still rare (between May 1991 and February 1994, the UK did not have an ambassador who had presented credentials to the Rwandan Government). The High Commission in Uganda did maintain telephone contact with the few British expats who lived in the country (mainly missionaries), but there is no record of what intelligence these calls generated, if any.[27] There was also an honorary consul resident in the country – Tony Wood, the owner of a Rwandan coffee plantation. Despite these small efforts the absence of an accredited ambassador combined with the continuing fighting along the Uganda/Rwanda border meant that there was very little first-hand experience or knowledge of the country. The infrequency of travel between the two countries is illustrated by the fact that when making his first visit to Rwanda in February 1994, Edward Clay depended on a map photocopied from The Lonely Planet Guide to East Africa – apparently Clay did not even have a guide to Rwanda.[28]

But, whilst media, Parliament and Government showed little evidence of interest in the situation in Rwanda, some NGOs certainly were concerned. In 1992 Oxfam commissioned a report on the Rwandan refugees; the report warned that 'the ... region remains potentially extremely unstable, and ... unless serious work is done on all fronts to tackle the ... problems of the region ... the potential for further explosive conflict is considerable'. In a second report a year later, Oxfam's representative in Kigali wrote, 'Rwanda stands on the brink of an uncharted abyss of anarchy and violence, and there are all too many historical, ethnic, economic, and political pressures that are likely to push it over the edge'.[29] Amnesty International also attempted to highlight the increasing ethnic tension in Rwanda in the period from the outbreak of civil war right up to the genocide. For example, on 21 February 1991 an Amnesty International statement noted,

'The media in Rwanda is reported to have been advocating revenge and violence against the Tutsi. Hutu vigilantes have been involved in violent attacks on Tutsi.'[30] A year later it informed members that 'since the guerrilla war started in October 1990 several thousand Tutsi have been killed by Hutu vigilantes and members of the security forces'.[31] Yet despite these warnings, neither organisation predicted genocide; Anne Mackintosh, at the time Oxfam's representative in Rwanda, states that as late as February 1994 she anticipated a resumption of civil war but 'did not imagine ... how monstrous' the violence would be.[32]

Did the British Government support the RPF in the war?

Claims that the UK and US were more closely aligned with the RPF than publicly acknowledged have been present from the time of the crisis itself and have been examined in depth by Wayne Madsen[33] and more recently Hazel Cameron. Cameron argues that in October 1990 the relationship between the RPF and the British Secret Intelligence Service (MI6) was so close that 'it is inconceivable that the order for the ... invasion of Rwanda was given without their approval and active assistance'.[34] This theory appears to be based on two underlying assumptions: firstly the RPF was dependent upon the Government of Uganda for arms, finance and logistical support, and secondly that the UK and US both had a strong presence in Uganda and must therefore have been close to the Anglophone RPF. Throughout the crisis many in the French political elite, including President Mitterrand, also believed that the RPF invasion of Rwanda was an Anglo-Saxon plot to evict France from Africa – a proxy war between client armies, the RPF supported by Britain and America, the FAR by France. It was not just the French who thought this; the Canadian Foreign Minister also visited London in 1992 to confront the FCO over Uganda's support of the RPF. Clearly the Canadians also believed that the UK had some degree of influence over Uganda and therefore the RPF.

In support of the argument, there is certainly some evidence of direct contact between the RPF and the High Commission in Kampala. Despite numerous Freedom of Information requests, there is no publicly available evidence of a formal meeting between the RPF and anyone from the FCO before the October 1990 invasion; there is, though, clear evidence that Whitehall was uncomfortable about the meetings in Kampala. The first meeting recorded in the FCO's London files was on 27 November 1990 when two representatives of the RPF visited the High Commission in Uganda and met with the First Secretary and the embassy's Defence Adviser . The record of the meeting, as sent to the FCO and copied to the MOD and Cabinet Office, does strongly suggest, but not explicitly state, that this was the first meeting between the parties. The discussions covered the RPF's thinking on the historical background to the invasion and its objectives, which were said to be to achieve a peaceful settlement with

President Habyarimana. However, there is a suggestion that the RPF wanted to retain some distance from the British; the confidential memorandum recorded, for example, that 'They [the RPF representatives] assured us that they could find adequate volunteers, funds and logistical support to continue fighting in Rwanda for a considerable time ... [But] they would not be drawn on their sources of support, their military disposition or their negotiating stance.' In the report the First Secretary suggested that there were benefits in maintaining low-level contact with the RPF, given its future 'potential importance in Rwanda', but informed London that no pledges or promises of support or aid were given to the two representatives.[35]

The First Secretary met with the two representatives again just days later on 6 December 1990 (the Defence Adviser is not recorded as having attended this second meeting), this time to discuss the outcome of negotiations between the RPF and Habyarimana's Government. In response to the RPF representative's question about the UK's attitude towards the conflict that was by now two months old, the First Secretary recorded his response as, '[I told them] we had no close historical connections with Rwanda and could not see anything that we could usefully do at the moment. In any case, Rwanda was an African problem which should really be solved by Africans.'[36] This second meeting, so soon after the first, worried the FCO back in London, though; again in a confidential telegram London wrote:

> Given that two meetings took place within 10 days we believe there is a risk that RPF may draw the wrong conclusion about the extent of our interest and willingness to become involved in the conflict (not withstanding Smith's clear statement of our position at the second meeting). We therefore think it wiser if you were to decline any early request for a third meeting and let several weeks elapse before agreeing to see the RPF again.[37]

Proponents of this conspiracy also point to the fact that Paul Kagame, as well as other RPF commanders, received training from the British and American militaries prior to 1990;[38] but before wild conclusions can be drawn, this evidence needs to be placed into context. Prior to 1990 many Rwandan refugees had served in the National Resistance Army which had fought a civil war against President Obote of Uganda from 1981 to 1986. After victory in this war the new President, Yoweri Museveni, retained the Rwandans, including Paul Kagame, in what became the official Ugandan army. Kagame served as the head of Ugandan military intelligence from 1986 to October 1990. As an allied country with historic links to the UK, the Ugandan army had, like most other Commonwealth countries, a close relationship with the MOD. The British army, for example, ran a number of junior command and staff courses in Jinja in south Uganda in the late 1980s – one course was even running at the time of the 1990 invasion. Additionally, seven officers from the Ugandan army attended courses at the

Royal Military Academy Sandhurst, the British army's officer training college, prior to 1990 and one attended army staff college in the UK.[39] Although there are no public records of who attended these various courses, it is feasible, given the senior positions they held in the Ugandan military, that amongst the trainees were a number of Rwandans who would later hold positions in the RPF. As Lt. Colonel Mike Wharmby, the officer who commanded British troops deployed to Rwanda in August 1994, noted, 'RPF soldiers and officers held themselves and behaved in a manner which demonstrated their professionalism and suggested they had received training from Western militaries'.[40]

This may all seem suspicious to an outsider but there is no suggestion that the UK viewed this training as being provided to a rebel army; rather correspondence between Kampala and London shows that the training provided to the Ugandan army was seen as a way of strengthening the relationship between Uganda and the UK. For example, MOD records do not show any ethnic Rwandans as having been at Sandhurst; some of the seven officers trained in the UK may have been exiled Rwandans but they were recorded as being Ugandan and the training was made available in their capacity as members of the Ugandan army, not in their capacity as members of a rebel force. Despite Hazel Cameron and Alaine Destexhe's attempts to portray the relationship between the UK and the RPF as sinister, this was training being provided to an allied government with historical links to the UK and it fitted into a perfectly normal pattern of providing training to Commonwealth armies. It is also apparent that it was not just the British and Americans who were providing training to the Ugandan army; in 1989 there were military training teams from Libya, the Soviet Union, China, North Korea and Tanzania in the country and Ugandan soldiers also travelled to India, Cuba and Zimbabwe for training.[41]

A number of inferences with regard to Britain's role in Uganda can also be drawn from declassified US intelligence documents. The CIA, drawing on information from the Defence Intelligence Agency, which is known to have had agents in Uganda throughout the 1990 to 1994 period, stated as early as 5 October 1990 that FAR had 'foreign support', yet at this early stage there was no mention of foreign support for the RPF.[42] Two months later, by 12 December 1990 the CIA was suggesting that 'Libya may have provided financial and military support to ethnic Tutsi rebels who invaded Rwanda from Uganda in early October'.[43] Given that the British Government was at this time accusing Libya's Colonel Gaddafi of supporting international terrorism, including the IRA in Northern Ireland, and of having planned the bombing of flight Pan Am 103 over Lockerbie in 1988, it seems highly unlikely that it would have supported a rebel group with links to Libya. In none of the CIA documents released to date, many of which were at the time top secret and restricted to US eyes only, does the intelligence agency suggest that the UK had any role in the conflict. This is despite fairly blunt assessments, which the US Government has voluntarily declassified, of the French, Belgian and Ugandan involvement on the two sides of the war.

Nor can the claim that the British supported the RPF be accepted blindly without testing the motivation for any alleged support. As discussed above, Britain really had no interest – economic, historical, cultural or strategic – in Rwanda in 1990. Why, then, would the British support the invasion of a country that had nothing to offer? A possible explanation, given the UK's close relationship with the Ugandan Government, would be to ease the refugee crisis in southern Uganda. However, this explanation cannot be accepted for three reasons. Firstly, the easiest way to solve the refugee crisis would have been through diplomatic efforts; yet there is no evidence of the British supporting this. Secondly, it would have been obvious to anyone that a Tutsi invasion of Rwanda threatened to unsettle the whole region (especially Burundi); certainly a regional war raged for a number of years after the events of 1994. And finally, the British Government was clearly sensitive about its relationship with the Government of Uganda. In this period there was an embargo on selling lethal equipment to Uganda and in 1991 an approach from the Ugandan Government to provide weapons training to game rangers was recorded in a confidential FCO document as having been rejected 'on the grounds that it might be seen as UK connivance in the training of guerrillas'.[44] As well as motive, the conspiracy theory also ignores the actual evidence. As we have seen, the High Commission staff in Uganda had only a very tentative relationship with the RPF. The FCO also claims that no requests for aid, equipment, assistance or arms were ever received from the RPF.[45] In fact all photographs of RPF soldiers from this period show them carrying Kalashnikov rifles and wearing distinctive East German army camouflage clothing – items more likely to have been purchased on the international black market than supplied by the British.[46]

It is of course impossible to completely rule out a claim that a small element of MI6, perhaps a single agent, was more closely aligned to the RPF than we will ever know. Maybe Kissinger's claim about there being no Vietnam policy, just individual agencies, concerned with Vietnam[47] equally applies to the British in Rwanda before 1994. But such a suggestion seems unlikely; the absence of any evidence makes such claims difficult to believe. And even if one does accept the theory of connivance of a small covert element of MI6 this surely must not be taken as official support of the rebels at the highest levels of government. Suggestions that the British military or intelligence agencies in Uganda were deliberately and malevolently aligned with the RPF are not convincing – this was not, as President Mitterrand might have thought, a proxy war between Britain and France fought out between the RPF and the Rwandan Government.

The Arusha Accords and deployment of UNAMIR

On 22 June 1993 the Security Council approved the establishment of the United Nations Observer Mission Uganda-Rwanda (UNOMUR), which was tasked with observing the Uganda/Rwanda border to ensure no military aid intended for the RPF crossed (UNOMUR was later rolled up into UNAMIR). UNAMIR was then established by Resolution 872 on 5 October. The discussions on a possible peacekeeping mission and the subsequent deployment of UNAMIR went largely unnoticed in the UK; not a single question was raised in Parliament relating to the proposed mission and the deployment appeared only very briefly in the press. In fact, in the six month period from October 1993 to April 1994, which was to prove pivotal on the road to genocide, Parliament showed no interest at all in Rwanda, with only two questions being asked in the six months.[48] Neither focused on the nature of the UN mandate or whether Britain should be doing more. In terms of press coverage, in October 1993 the press was more focused on the coup in neighbouring Burundi, which like Rwanda had a volatile ethnic mix of Hutu and Tutsi. The situation in Rwanda looked relatively calm to outsiders and instead the assassination of the President of Burundi and the violence it triggered looked to be the more significant story unfolding in the region. In a headline that could have been recycled just a few months later with only the country changed, Mark Huband wrote, 'Burundi Bloodbath Runs its Course as West Looks On'.[49] Despite the violence in Burundi, no one in the media warned of the risk of Rwanda igniting in similar fashion. George Alagiah, for example, reported from Burundi for the BBC and admits that no journalist can honestly say they foresaw a similar outbreak in Rwanda.[50]

The rest of the UK might have been ignoring events in Rwanda but the FCO had to show some interest in the country, given the debates at the UN. At this stage it would be wrong to suggest the UK took anything like a leading role in the establishment of first UNOMUR and then UNAMIR. David Hannay, the British Permanent Representative to the UN in 1993, for example, records a distinct lack of enthusiasm amongst Security Council members for the proposed peacekeeping mission in September 1993, suggesting that some members believed the mission 'had been landed on the UN's doorstep without adequate preparation or consideration'.[51] The UK was certainly one of those countries. Hannay continues that it was pressure from the French, with some support from African nations, which pushed through the resolution and eventually compelled the Security Council to authorise the mission. In an interview with the author, he stated, 'The French had got themselves trapped [in Rwanda]. They wanted their troops out, but did not want the Habyarimana regime to collapse ... Undoubtedly it was the French who pushed for UNAMIR ... We went along with the original decision with some reluctance but we supported our French allies.'[52] A US State Department report on the draft wording of Resolution 872 similarly makes the point that it was the French who were pushing hardest for a mandate for a UN force.[53]

It is commonly held that the reason for the lack of support for UNAMIR – which commentators suggest resulted in the force being too small with too weak a mandate – was mainly financial. Linda Melvern, for example, suggests that throughout the crisis the UK tried to pass responsibility for Rwanda from the UN to the Organisation for African Unity (OAU), in an attempt to avoid the expense and risk associated with further UN involvement.[54] Then when a few months after the deployment of UNAMIR, in February 1994, the Belgian Government recommended the enlargement of the force, commentators again suggest this was rejected by the UK and US, both of which objected to the increasing cost of UN peacekeeping. Alan Kuperman writes of this decision: 'The United States and Britain blocked this initiative citing the costs of more troops and the danger that expanding the mission could endanger peacekeepers',[55] and Melvern claims that the US and UK 'adamantly opposed' the Belgian plans to reinforce UNAMIR 'for financial reasons'.[56] Despite these suggestions, there is no publicly available evidence to support such a claim; nothing in the public papers, statements of ministers or documents released under Freedom of Information makes reference to budgetary concerns. On the contrary, in March 1994 the UK chaired a meeting at UN headquarters where it called for an increase in the size of the force in Bosnia, and itself promised an additional 900 troops;[57] these seem far from the actions of a country intent on saving money. Rather it appears that the UK, and importantly other Security Council members, supported a small UNAMIR for three practical reasons.

The first reason is explained by Karel Kovanda, the Czech ambassador to the Security Council, who recalls,

> UNAMIR was not very big, and its members were lightly armed; their mandate was rather weak. All this followed from the view of the UN Secretariat (with which the Security Council agreed at the time) that the toughest part was to get the parties to actually reach an agreement; putting it into effect was not expected to be too much of a problem.[58]

The mandate was therefore based on the assumption of consensus between the two warring parties; there was no provision for protecting civilians in the mandate, or deploying a heavily armed UN force, as this was not deemed to be necessary. As one FCO official close to the debates suggests, Rwanda was viewed as a potentially model peacekeeping mission; there was a generally accepted peace settlement and a plan on how to achieve this.[59] The size of the mission was similar to other UN observer missions launched in the early 1990s: the authorised strength of UNAMIR was 2,500, which compares favourably to the UN Mission for the Referendum in Western Sahara (2,500), UN Observer Mission in El Salvador (1,000), UN Observer Group in Central America (1,000) and UN Iraq-Kuwait Observer Mission (1,200). UNAMIR was mandated to do more than observe but even so a force of 2,500 seemed sufficient given the size of the country.

The second reason for UNAMIR's size was the fact that there was genuine concern amongst Security Council members, particularly the UK, New Zealand

and Russia, about the UN becoming overstretched; here we must acknowledge this includes financial overstretch, but the main issue was overstretch of the UN infrastructure, something that could not be simply addressed by increasing funding. There had, in the years 1990 to 1993, been a rapid expansion in the number of UN missions and the number of troops deployed; in mid-1994, the UN was already heavily committed in Bosnia, Cambodia and Somalia and was also under pressure from the US to authorise a mission to Haiti and from Russia to authorise a mission to Georgia. Some Security Council members, the UK included, were therefore sincerely asking whether the UN infrastructure was adequate to cope with this expansion. Simple things, such as the fact that UN Department for Peacekeeping Operations (DPKO) headquarters was not staffed on a twenty-four-hour basis, concerned many of those considering new missions. A CIA briefing paper, prepared on 1 October 1993, reflected this concern, 'The international relief system, already under severe strain, faces burgeoning demands in the future. The resources of the US and other donors will be spread more thinly and donors will have to be more selective about which crises it addresses.'[60] For this reason the automatic approval of any mission, however worthy, was not guaranteed.

The third reason related to fears for the safety of UN personnel. Resolution 872 authorising UNAMIR was issued only days after 'the battle of Mogadishu' in which eighteen US soldiers were killed, and after twenty-four Pakistani soldiers had been killed also in Somalia in June 1993. The UK, US and Russia in particular showed real concern about the potential risk to UN troops being deployed; Russia and the UK therefore insisted on a reference to UN Security Council Resolution 868 being made in the Rwanda resolution. Conscious of a number of attacks on UN peacekeepers, Resolution 868, which had been passed on 29 September 1993, stated that UN troops would be withdrawn from *any* mission where their safety could not be ensured. Despite claims that the two warring parties in Rwanda were supportive of a UN mission, the British contingent at the UN was cautious and demanded wording in the resolution that allowed for the review of the mission's performance. This does not contradict the belief that the mission to Rwanda would be a simple one but it does demonstrate the caution amongst Security Council members. If there was no sign of progress or if there was a threat to the UN peacekeepers the British, from the outset, wanted the right to withdraw the mission.

Despite the spiralling cost of peacekeeping in the early 1990s, which almost certainly had some impact on how most national governments viewed the increasing calls for more peacekeeping missions, it does not seem to have been financial considerations that shaped Britain's support for a small UNAMIR. The documentary evidence implies that Britain had little involvement in discussions surrounding Resolution 872. Hannay suggests instead that Britain gave limited thought to the proposal and went along with the proposed plan mainly because it was being requested by France, Britain's long time ally. The FCO, though, did have reservations about the safety of the troops and the ability of the UN to manage the mission, particularly given the speed with which UNAMIR developed, and in these respects the FCO was right to be cautious. But like other members of the Security Council, it did take comfort from the Secretariat, the French and both sides in the civil war, who all reassured the Council that peace had been agreed and the implementation would be easy – of course this was not to be the case.

Did the British Government foresee the genocide?

Hazel Cameron, in her 2013 book, contends that 'global elite bystanders to genocide ... are liable to charges of complicity in genocide if they fail to undertake their positive obligations, such as the prevention and suppression of acts of genocide ... where reliable intelligence clearly warned of imminent and serious humanitarian risks'.[61] The question must then be asked if the British Government did have reliable intelligence of an imminent threat of genocide in Rwanda before April 1994. As we have seen, the open source intelligence - newspaper and television coverage and correspondence from NGOs - did not foresee genocide. Nor, for most of this period, did the FCO have sufficient presence in Rwanda to gather its own reliable intelligence of the imminent threat. It would also seem unlikely that there was much, if any, MI6 presence in, or focused on, Rwanda. In terms of official information, then, the Government was dependent upon what the FCO could gather from outside Rwanda.

In Africa, this meant intelligence gathered in Uganda and gleaned from the UK's very limited role in observing the Arusha peace negotiations. In Uganda, one would expect a certain level of intelligence and 'gossip' about Rwanda to have filtered back to the High Commission in Kampala via its contact with Ugandan officials and the RPF. However, the infrequency of the memorandums sent back to London suggests that the High Commission showed very limited interest in the on-going war and received little intelligence. There is certainly nothing in the memos from late 1990 through to the autumn of 1993 that suggests the High Commission was receiving intelligence from the RPF or Ugandan counterparts of a risk of a humanitarian crisis in Rwanda. Throughout 1991, 1992 and early 1993 the FCO to a very limited extent also monitored the Arusha negotiations through the High Commission in Dar-es-Salaam (Tanzania), which commented on the discussions once they began. Again the correspondence from Tanzania was patchy, infrequent and not particularly illuminating. The volume of correspondence relating to Rwanda seems to suggest that the FCO still had a 'minimal', 'tenuous' and 'insignificant' interest in Rwanda.

The deployment of UNAMIR from October 1993 did not fundamentally alter the level or nature of intelligence coming out of Uganda. The ceasefire and the presence of UN troops meant that for the first time in a number of years the High Commission felt it was safe to cross the border from Uganda into Rwanda. Fairly soon after UNAMIR deployed, Edward Clay, British High Commissioner in Uganda and non-resident ambassador to Rwanda, made his first visit to Rwanda. He did not go there though with any plan to alter Britain's relationship with the country. Recording his visit of February 1994, Clay wrote to Whitehall, 'The accreditation to Kigali of the first British ambassador for nearly three years may have raised hopes about closer British involvement in and aid to Rwanda. I hope I dispelled these.'[62] The accreditation of an ambassador did mean that London received some eye-witness intelligence on the country, the first for a long time.

Clay visited Rwanda from 22 to 25 February 1994; in that three-day visit he saw for himself what was happening in Kigali and his observations were fed back to London in two reports. He began the first of these: 'Political impasse continues in Rwanda. Most serious danger-point last week now passed, but tension remains high. Habyarimana both the key and a major impediment to implementation of the Arusha Accords. No other options than for the international community to press for the implementation of those agreements.'[63] In the telegrams Clay focused on the political situation, but could not avoid reporting the intermittent violence which was spreading across the country. Clay emphasised the ubiquity of road blocks and soldiers across the country and recorded that during his visit 'individual killings, allegedly mostly Tutsi, numbered between 30 and 50 dead',[64] but he continued, 'it would be dangerous and unwise to try to ascribe responsibility for these killings'. The overriding message coming out of these two reports, presumably the first received in London for a number of years, was that the resumption of *civil war* looked likely; Clay went as far as to suggest that an RPF statement of 23 February attacking Habyarimana amounted to a declaration of war. He recorded that there was limited hope of a peace settlement and that the return of Tutsi refugees to Rwanda was unrealistic. The only option available to the international community, he repeated, was to keep the pressure on both sides to implement the Arusha Accords; in the meantime, he suggested, 'it would be useful to get firm confirmation that the Belgians would be responsible for evacuating our citizens, if it came to that'.[65] Certainly in Clay's reports there is nothing to suggest the possibility of imminent genocide.

It was not just from within Africa that the FCO received intelligence. It has been variously alleged that the UK also had access to supposedly secret communications between the DPKO and General Dallaire in Kigali. Although these cables were not intended to be shared with Security Council members,[66] Linda Melvern claims that the UK mission somehow gained access to them and was therefore well informed about the impending crisis.[67] Unfortunately, there is no evidence that this was the case. David Hannay, Britain's Permanent Representative to the UN, categorically denies that he ever saw the correspondence from Dallaire, but does accept that other officials may have without his knowledge.[68] It would seem odd for someone within the British mission to have had access to the cables but not then share the intelligence with the Permanent Representative. Nor does any of the correspondence between London and New York, released under

Freedom of Information, make reference to anything that appears to have come from Dallaire's cables. One senior FCO official, based in London at the time but with responsibility for UN issues and who was in regular contact with Hannay, certainly makes it clear that they never saw any of Dallaire's correspondence, stating that they were not even aware of the existence of the infamous 'genocide fax' until a number of years later.[69] All that said, it is of course not beyond the realms of imagination that the cables could have been intercepted by MI6 or leaked to a British official – such claims are at the believable end of espionage conspiracy theories. However, if that were the case we must not forget the nature of bureaucratic government as outlined in the Introduction; even if one or two individuals in New York did see Dallaire's daily reports, there is no evidence that this information was widely disseminated and certainly no evidence that it reached decision makers.

The conclusion we must reach, then, is that the British Government in the period up to April 1993 did not recognise the potential risk of genocide in Rwanda; the facts suggest that at the time the FCO simply did not have the resources or the inclination to thoroughly monitor the situation in Rwanda. The best intelligence available to the FCO came from Clay's February trip to Kigali and this warned of the risk of renewed civil war. The FCO quite simply did not see the genocide coming.

The genocide begins: Rwanda becomes headline news

The morning after Habyarimana's plane was shot down, Edward Clay sent a report to London; its contents appear to have influenced the Government's response, certainly for the first few weeks of the genocide: 'The situation in Kigali meantime appears to be calm. We have spoken to our honorary consul. He and Kanyarushoke [the Rwandan ambassador to Uganda] both spoke of there having been some prolonged periods of shooting. But Kanyarushoke believes this was the Presidential Guard reacting hysterically and firing wildly in the air, rather than to kill.'[70] The Clay memo of 7 April focused on the political problems rather than the humanitarian crisis and, like his memorandum from February, highlighted the need for a political solution led by the Rwandans themselves. The memo suggested that rather than responding to an outbreak of violence against civilians, the priority for all parties was to move urgently towards the swearing-in of the transitional government as agreed at Arusha. From this point on, the High Commission in Uganda ceased to be an effective source of information - the renewed violence effectively closed the border between Uganda and Rwanda and the only British representative left in the country, Honorary Consul Tony Wood, was unable to provide any valuable intelligence. Wood was evacuated on 12 April, after having been 'under siege in the capital with just two watchmen and his parrots for company'[71] and despite his best efforts was unable to communicate effectively with the outside world because of the failure of Kigali's telephone system. By 13 April, the High Commission was completely reliant on the unarmed UN observers who patrolled the Uganda/Rwanda border for information; as Clay recognised on 12 April in a memo to London, 'These sitreps are very indirect and necessarily out of date'.[72] The FCO was now reliant on third-party sources for its intelligence on what was happening in Rwanda; this appears to have come from the media, from allied countries (especially Belgium) and from the UN Secretariat.

In terms of media coverage the shooting down of Habyarimana's plane finally made Rwanda headline news. Despite the previous disinterest in Rwanda, the press were quick to report the risk of violence reigniting. On the first day of the violence *The Times*, for example, told its readers that 'UN officials expressed fears of an eruption of tribal violence. Past genocides in the strife-torn central African states [referring here to both Rwanda and Burundi] have resulted in tens of thousands of deaths.'[73] The *Evening Standard*, going to print later in the day, was able to report on 7 April that violence had already broken out in Kigali and quoted the German ambassador to Rwanda, who had reported that the homes of two German families living in Kigali had been damaged by mortar fire.[74] This was the first indication that the story, in the UK press at least, was going to be more about the threat to Westerners than the deaths of thousands of Rwandans.

In the following fortnight four consistent themes characterised the coverage in the media. Firstly, the focus on the threat to Western expatriates in Rwanda dominated early reporting. On 8 April *The Times* reported a 'bloodbath in Kigali' but emphasised that several Belgian citizens had been killed in the fighting;[75] similarly, the *Evening Standard* began its coverage by reporting that ninety British citizens were at risk in the 'war-torn' country.[76] By the following day, *The Times* was reporting that 'expatriates huddled in their homes, too fearful to venture out' and that 'foreigners waited anxiously for news of evacuation'.[77] All of the mainstream newspapers dramatically reported that French and Belgian paratroopers were 'rac[ing] to evacuate Westerners from Rwanda'.[78] Similarly, television news concentrated on the plight of Westerners; on four consecutive nights, beginning 9 April, ITN's coverage of Rwanda focused entirely on the evacuation of expatriates.[79] *Scotland on Sunday*'s report that the evacuation of US zoologists meant Rwanda's mountain gorillas were in danger – which failed even to consider the fate of Rwandan civilians – was the ultimate demonstration of the British media's lack of interest in ordinary Rwandans.[80]

The second theme was the focus on Rwanda's violent past. The press seemed almost resigned to the fact that tribal violence in Rwanda was the norm and should be expected – and accepted. For John Palmer in the *Guardian*, there was a 'traditional enmity' between Hutu and Tutsi which explained the violence.[81] Robert Block, writing in the *Independent*, began an article, 'Since independence from Belgium in 1962, their histories [Rwanda and Burundi's] - inexorably intertwined - have been marked by ethnic hatred and tribal violence. Atrocities are so commonplace that a news magazine once remarked: "Another week, another 300 massacred in Burundi." The observation could have just as easily been made about neighbouring Rwanda.'[82] The *Sunday Times* similarly reported that Rwanda had the African 'continent's most savage history', continuing that 'the cycle of violence is the result of xenophobia, paranoia and geography'.[83] The tone of the article suggested that this cycle simply could not be broken. This theme came out even more strongly on ITN's coverage; John Draper, for example, reported on *News at Ten*: 'The rival Hutu and Tutsi factions have been in conflict for decades'[84] and told viewers, 'There really is little hope of peace'.[85] As early as 10 April, the press seem to have accepted that Rwanda's inevitable fate, a consequence of its tribal makeup, was massive human suffering.

The third factor obvious in the press reports is the misinterpretation of what was happening on the ground. The media's initial response was to describe the violence in Kigali as 'anarchy',[86] 'random',[87] or 'chaos'.[88] Such descriptions ignored the highly orchestrated nature of the killings – in a period of chaos a government does not, as happened in Kigali, deploy garbage trucks to systematically collect dead bodies piled up next to road blocks. And although some reports identified that the Tutsi were the main victims of the violence, there was no underlying recognition that this was an organised attempt to destroy the Tutsi population which was being centrally directed by the Government using pre-prepared lists of targets. The witness accounts coming out of Rwanda were also confused; the press therefore reported variously that the fighting was between FAR and the RPF, the Presidential Guard responding violently to the death of the President, or led by civilian militias. The BBC's Mark Doyle recalls:

> I have to admit that during the first few days I, like others, got the story terribly wrong. Down on the ground, up-close – if you could get close enough safely enough – it did look like chaos. I said so. I used the word chaos. What I could clearly see in the first few days was the shooting war between the RPF and the Government and the dead bodies. It was not clear who had killed whom.[89]

Because of this, the situation was typically interpreted as a resumption of the civil war, rather than as the outbreak of genocide. In this period, for example, words such as 'soldier', 'war', 'troops' or 'fighting' were three times more prevalent in the press coverage than 'child', 'civilian' or 'victim', all of which would have been more suggestive of genocide than war.

The fourth theme is fairly typical of reporting Africa: the press's tendency to illustrate violence as tribal and savage, with all the connotations that that cliché embodies. The Hutu militia, the *Independent* told us, were armed 'with machetes and sharpened bamboo spears',[90] the Glasgow *Herald* wrote of an 'orgy of tribal bloodletting',[91] and the *Evening Standard* said that 'Rwanda with its beautiful, steaming rainforests ... [had] a savage history of inter-tribal warfare'.[92] ITN, having called the situation 'madness', 'tribal slaughter' and 'savagery', even quoted one expatriate as describing Rwandans as like 'animals ... They kill each other worse than animals.'[93] The media representation of the crisis was straight out of *Tarzan* or Joseph Conrad's *Heart of Darkness*, it was stereotypical Africa where savages killed each other for fun, an Africa still fixed deeply in barbarism. The media intensified this tribal framing by failing to make the coverage at all personal. At no point were the Rwandan victims given names and at no point did the press interview Rwandans; rather they fell back on convenient labels of 'a Tutsi' or 'a Hutu' and as is fairly typical of reporting of Africa took their quotes from aid workers, nuns, the UN or fleeing expats;[94] anyone as long as they were not Rwandan.

Although the newspapers might not have accurately reported the crisis or the fact that it was Tutsi and opposition politicians that were being deliberately and systematically killed, they did graphically report the horror of what was happening. Mark Huband, for example, wrote in the *Guardian*, 'In the centre of Kigali, drunken soldiers and gangs of youths brandishing machetes manned roadblocks on streets where piles of mutilated corpses lay'.[95] Catherine Bond, also in Kigali, wrote, 'Rwandan soldiers bayoneted to death two patients at Kigali's central hospital on Monday amid the dying ... At the back of the hospital compound about 40 bodies were piled high, rotting in the drizzle.'[96] The newspapers also were reporting the magnitude of the killings; subsequent evidence would show they were under-reporting the extent of the crisis at this early stage, but the numbers involved were still staggering. Even so, in the context of African tragedies, the numbers being quoted were not of a magnitude that caused outrage and demanded attention. The *Guardian* reported at least 15,000 killed on 12 April,[97] on the same day the *Daily Mail* reported up to 20,000 dead,[98] a figure which was repeated on the front page of the *Independent* the next day.[99] By comparison the famine in Ethiopia, which had been widely reported ten years earlier, had led to some 400,000 deaths.[100] In this respect the media contributed to an under-appreciation of what was happening in Rwanda. It was slowly becoming clear in some of the reports a week or more after the shooting down of Habyarimana's plane that the dead were not victims of war but were deliberately targeted civilians. For example, the *Daily Mail* reported on 16 April, 'A bloodthirsty mob slaughtered 650 children in a massacre in a church in Rwanda, it emerged last night'.[101] Although no papers were yet talking of genocide, it was apparent from the press, but only to those who were following the coverage closely, that there were two crises in Rwanda – a resumption of the conventional civil war and secondly a targeted effort to persecute Tutsi civilians. In fact, on 14 April *Channel Four News* explicitly acknowledged, 'Beside the battle, tribal slaughter goes on with tens of thousands dead'.[102]

Despite the graphic images there was hardly any suggestion in the press that the international community should be doing something; Jakobsen's description of the mechanics of the CNN effect moving from images of atrocities to media condemnation of government inaction to public calls for action does not appear to have been correct in this case.[103] In an editorial of 11 April *The Times*, for example, concluded:

> The anarchy in Rwanda would seem to provide a classic case for armed international intervention. There is a precedent in Somalia. But the analogy is flawed. There is no method in Rwanda's madness. It will not be easy for the United Nations to act as fireman: a number of fires rage and it is not clear who fans the flames. Which parties would be asked to ceasefire against whom? A 'classical' peacekeeping operation could not be mounted at least not without long and careful preparation ... France and Belgium have flown in troops to evacuate foreign nationals. But they cannot cure Rwanda's blood frenzy. It is for Rwandans themselves to do so, before more life is senselessly consumed.[104]

On the same day the *Independent* similarly suggested: 'The slaughter of Belgian members of a United Nations force only highlights the helplessness of the international community'; contrary to what Security Council members had believed only months before, the article continued, 'In any attempt to rank the world's trouble spots according to their potential to benefit from outside help, Rwanda must rank low'.[105] Having emphasised the history of violence in Rwanda, and by framing it as tribal savagery, the media seemed to convince themselves of the hopelessness in this particular conflict; from the outset most of the press were suggesting that it was up to Rwandans, or wider Africa, to solve the crisis. Rather than the images of suffering leading to condemnation of inaction and calls for something to be done, the media used those same images to tell the world that there was little that the West could achieve in Rwanda.

In these first few days only the *Guardian* suggested that it was wrong of the West to accept the inevitability of violence and to avoid becoming involved; in a leading article the paper called for a more 'serious UN peacekeeping effort'.[106] Later it condemned the UN for failing to instruct UNAMIR to intervene, noting 'UNAMIR's weakness and the UN's moral failure as it leaves Rwandan staff to the mercy of marauding soldiers have once more battered its image'.[107] Most of the print media focused on the urgent need to evacuate Westerners and the threat to the UN peacekeepers; the *Guardian* was alone in suggesting, to quote Douglas Hurd, 'that something should be done' and even then not very vigorously, and from deep inside the paper rather than loudly from the front page.

This malaise was similarly reflected in the letters pages. In the period from 7 to 21 April there were only thirteen readers' letters on the subject published in the broadsheet press. Of course newspaper editors have the power to decide which letters they print and therefore this may not be an accurate reflection of the number or tone of letters written; but it must be assumed that if there had been a deluge of readers' letters supportive of intervention, editors would have felt compelled to publish more. Of the thirteen, only three called for more rigorous UN involvement; one of those was from Oxfam and a second from ActionAid.

Two letters argued that, based on the experience of Bosnia, the international community was right to keep out of Rwanda, the rest simply did not address the issue of intervention; instead they focused on the causes of the conflict, the FCO's (mis)management of the evacuation of British citizens or called for Rwandans in the UK to be granted asylum.

If letters to the editor can be taken as a barometer of public interest, however blunt, the public were certainly more interested in, or aware of, the humanitarian crisis in Bosnia than the events in Rwanda, with letters about Bosnia outnumbering those on Rwanda three to one.[108] There were notably more letters in this fortnight mourning the premature death of the American rock-singer Kurt Cobain (of Nirvana fame) or about censorship of violent videos. The evidence of letters sent to newspapers seems to support the claim that the public learn the relative importance of issues through the amount of news coverage those issues receive in the media.[109] Despite the scale and horror of the violence, Rwanda was not the lead foreign story, it did not receive prominent coverage and what coverage there was was unsympathetic. The public generally responded by ignoring the crisis or assuming nothing could be done.

The lack of coverage of Rwanda, relative to Bosnia, and the framing of the crisis as ancient tribal violence and most importantly as a civil war rather than as genocide and a humanitarian crisis seemed to lead the public – and also the politicians who acknowledge that they depended on the media for their intelligence – to conclude Rwanda was a less important issue. There was very limited recognition and understanding of what was happening in the country and therefore it would not be unfair to suggest that a common view was that there was little chance of successfully intervening in Rwanda and it was therefore best or convenient to ignore the problem.

Withdrawing UNAMIR

Again in late April, as was the case when UNAMIR was first deployed, debates at UN headquarters meant FCO bureaucrats were among the few people in the UK giving Rwanda any attention; but now, rather than discussing deployment of troops, the focus was on possible withdrawal. On 21 April UN Security Council Resolution 912 was published; through it the Security Council members declared that they were 'appalled at the large scale violence in Rwanda' and 'deeply concerned by the continuing fighting, looting, banditry and breakdown of law and order, particularly in Kigali'.[110] Yet whilst it 'condemned' the violence against Rwandan civilians, the Security Council '*strongly* condemned' (emphasis added) the violence against UNAMIR, which was a breach of 'international humanitarian law'. The most significant impact of the Resolution was that it effectively ordered the reduction in size of UNAMIR, from some 2,500 troops to only 270. Dallaire, writing ten years later, stated that this one decision was tantamount to the

US, UK and France aiding and abetting genocide in Rwanda.[111] Any criticism of the UK must be set in context and no judgement of the decision to support Resolution 912 must be made based on hindsight knowledge of what we now know happened after 21 April. There are, then, two key questions that we must ask before condemning the FCO for its support of the withdrawal. First, did the FCO recognise that genocide was underway in Rwanda when it voted in favour of the Resolution? Secondly, what did the FCO believe were the alternatives?

Before 21 April no one in the British political elite had publicly described the events in Rwanda as genocide, but in this period could, or should, the Government have been more aware of what was happening? Did the Government, as Tony Blair later suggested, know that thousands of people were being killed in a deliberate and systematic genocide? In answering this question there are, as we have seen, two relevant factors that have to be considered. Firstly, Rwanda as a country was not at all important to the British establishment; it would have therefore been especially hard for events in the 'small country far away' to register with British decision makers. Secondly, the sources of intelligence available to the British were limited.

Although one could argue that being busy, or focused elsewhere, does not absolve an individual or government from its responsibility to intervene in an emergency, it is a factor that must pragmatically be acknowledged, and in this period the crisis in Rwanda was sadly just one of many international crises. As the US ambassador to the UN, Madeleine Albright, records in her memoirs, what she says with the benefit of hindsight can be seen as warnings of impending genocide: '[Rwanda] had to compete for attention against an avalanche of other information from crisis spots around the globe. At the time, there were clashes or extreme tensions in Bosnia, Somalia, Haiti, Georgia, Azerbaijan, Armenia, Angola, Liberia, Mozambique, Sudan, Cambodia, Afghanistan and Tajikistan, as well as on-going defiance of Security Council resolutions by Saddam Hussein's Iraq.'[112] Given the UK's previous disinterest in Rwanda and this catalogue of other crises, many of which had a more direct impact on British interests, it is unlikely that the FCO bureaucracy would have placed intelligence on Rwanda at the top of ministers' briefing papers or red boxes.

In addition to this long list of crises, the British Government faced a number of domestic issues, all considered more significant and more urgent than the growing crisis in Rwanda. As Michael Heseltine, Deputy Prime Minister in 1994, states in his autobiography, in spring and summer 1994 domestic issues, including leadership challenges to John Major and violence in Northern Ireland, were dominating the attention of the Cabinet.[113] In an interview with Anthony Seldon, for example, John Major recalled that he was spending at least 15 per cent of his time on Irish affairs at that time.[114] At the FCO attention was also focused elsewhere; Foreign Secretary Douglas Hurd was dealing not only with the crisis in Bosnia, where an additional 900 British troops were sent in March 1994, and the very negative impact this was having on Anglo-American relations, but also with the highly controversial debates on the voting system to be adopted by the soon to be enlarged European Union. Hurd, and the other FCO ministers, were also, understandably focused on countries and regions that impacted on Britain's more obvious trade and security interests. At the time that Habyarimana's plane was shot down Hurd was on a five-day trade tour of Brazil and the Falklands.[115] For these various reasons, as Hurd's autobiography makes clear, at senior levels of government there was very little interest in and awareness of what was happening in Rwanda, there was simply too much else going on in the world.[116]

Although genocide scholars and regional experts such as Alison Des Forges, looking back at the events of 1990–94, see ample evidence of the impending genocide, in real time and in the FCO's crowded agenda the evidence was less obvious. Baroness Lynda Chalker, FCO minister with responsibility for Africa, openly admits that prior to 1992 she personally knew nothing of Rwanda; only two years after the outbreak of civil war did she really become aware of the issues affecting the country. As she points out, there was very little British aid going into the country, there were very few reports coming out, there were very few British NGOs in the country, and even Ugandan contacts knew little of what was happening in the French-speaking country. She describes FCO contact with Rwandans as 'minimal, occasional and accidental almost'. Chalker recalls that prior to 1994, whenever anyone spoke to her of Rwanda it was invariably about the gorillas.[117] Furthermore, as the academic Michael Barnett – who in 1994 was seconded to the US State Department – points out, it was junior desk officers at the various foreign ministries, who had probably never visited Rwanda and were also responsible for monitoring other Central African countries, that were seeing the intelligence on Rwanda, not anthropologists or historians with an expert knowledge of the country. That these junior officials missed some of the evidence of genocide or failed to bring it to the attention of their overly busy superiors is, Barnett suggests, no surprise.[118] So once the crisis developed this vacuum of intelligence was filled, by necessity, by three sources, the media, Britain's European allies, namely France and Belgium, and the UN Secretariat.

In terms of dependence on the media, Malcolm Rifkind, at the time Secretary of State for Defence, acknowledges that 'essentially what we [Cabinet ministers] knew [of Rwanda] was what we read in the newspapers like everyone else'.[119] It is also alleged that Douglas Hurd was briefed on the crisis by civil servants whose only source of information was CNN. Chalker denies this was the case, but accepts that CNN was one of a few good sources available to the FCO.[120] The reliance on the media meant that the crisis did not receive the government attention that it merited. As shown above, someone dependent upon the media for intelligence would not have foreseen genocide. Media coverage was not sufficiently comprehensive or accurate enough for someone to have reached that conclusion; journalists themselves were not reaching that conclusion. Then, once the genocide did erupt, for the first two weeks at least, as most journalists accept, the press interpreted the killings as simply the resumption of a vicious tribal-based civil war and the scale of civilian deaths was not of a scale that demanded attention. Without further intelligence, or a more thorough understanding of the history of Rwanda, no one could have objectively concluded from the press coverage that what was happening in Rwanda was genocide.

The other key sources for British decision makers were the French and Belgian governments and the Security Council. Drawing on the concept of 'spheres of influence' as the old colonial power and the new great-power sponsor, respectively, Belgium and France were seen certainly by some in the FCO as the Rwanda experts and as having responsibility for the country. One FCO official, for example, told Linda Melvern, 'We tended to believe what the French were telling us'.[121] Rifkind concurs, agreeing that given Rwanda's history the UK Government 'would [have] naturally look[ed] to the French for a lead'.[122] These two countries probably had more intelligence than anyone else on what was happening in Rwanda yet even they failed to anticipate the genocide. The Belgian Senate, in a report on the crisis written in 1997, concluded, for example, that despite the Belgian civilian and military authorities collecting large amounts of intelligence, this was not shared amongst interested parties and consequently any potential warning signs were missed.[123] Within a couple of days of the genocide beginning, both the French and Belgian governments were widely and publicly advocating the need for UNAMIR to withdraw. Once the Belgian Government decided to withdraw its troops from UNAMIR the Belgian Foreign Minister Willy Claes telephoned Hurd directly to explain the decision.[124] Hurd does not record the content of this call, but we can safely assume that, having made the decision to withdraw, Claes would have been keen to paint as dark a picture as possible of the situation in Rwanda, so as to lessen any criticism of Belgium's decision. Karel Kovanda recalls that a similar call was made to the Czech Foreign Ministry in Prague and confirms that Claes did very much argue for the full withdrawal of UNAMIR.[125] In the first days of the genocide both France and Belgium had troops on the ground and both described the situation as anarchy. Both governments spoke of the ferocity of the renewed fighting – the Belgians to justify their withdrawal from UNAMIR and the French to justify their on-going support of the Rwandan Government. Both had a self-interest in presenting the crisis as civil war rather than genocide and the British, with little evidence to contradict that interpretation, appear to have trusted that conclusion.

Finally, in terms of intelligence coming from the UN, those present at Security Council debates highlight that prior to 7 April there was no suggestion by the Secretariat that genocide was on the horizon. Colin Keating, New Zealand's representative in New York, who would later call for a more robust UN response, recalls that in this period the intelligence placed in front of the Security Council did not suggest any possibility of genocide. In a 1999 radio interview he recalled, 'I think really the information suggested that there was banditry, that there was ongoing sporadic fighting, but it was more in the character of skirmishes related to the civil war rather than any suggestion that the civil population as a whole was at risk'.[126] Even after the genocide had broken out, the debate and focus at the UN remained on the war rather than the genocide. Albright recalls,

> As I look back at my records of the meetings that first week, I am struck by the lack of information about the killing that had begun against unarmed Rwandan civilians, as opposed to the fighting between Hutu and Tutsi militias ... oral summaries provided to the Security Council lacked detail and failed to convey the full dimensions of the disaster.[127]

The Security Council, directed by Boutros-Ghali, like the French, the Belgians and the media was concentrating on the war, not genocide.

In the crowded foreign policy environment that the FCO faced, intelligence on the situation in Rwanda was missed and the crisis misinterpreted, for the first two weeks at least, as renewed civil war rather than genocide. Clay's suggestion in March 1994 that the FCO should approach the Belgian Government to discuss the plans for evacuating British civilians from Rwanda was not some Nostradamic prediction of genocide but rather a warning of the likelihood of renewed civil war. Once the violence began in April the British saw what they expected – a civil war; and all their other intelligence sources told them the same. The British Government could not therefore realistically have known of the genocide before 21 April.

Alternative courses of action

The Security Council's initial response to the renewed violence was to issue a Presidential Statement on 7 April, which expressed concern about the loss of life amongst civilians, opposition politicians and particularly the UN peacekeepers. It called on the Secretary General to collect all available information and report to the Council as soon as possible.[128] This report was formally made on 20 April. However, before Boutros-Ghali had chance to report, the Belgian Permanent Representative wrote to the Security Council President, informing him of Belgium's decision to withdraw its troops from UNAMIR. The letter of 13 April argued that because of the 'widespread massacres' and 'chaos' in the country, the implementation of the Accords was seriously jeopardised and therefore Belgium recommended the entire UNAMIR operation be suspended.[129] Partly in response to this letter and following an official complaint from the UK that the Secretariat was not providing the Council with sufficient information, on 14 April DPKO officials briefed the Security Council on what it saw as the two possible options for UNAMIR: either withdraw immediately and fully, or leave UNAMIR in Rwanda for three weeks longer to determine whether there was any prospect of a ceasefire. Finally, the day before Boutros-Ghali reported back to the Council, certain members, possibly but not definitely including the UK, were made aware of a cable from Dallaire. The tone was not overly optimistic:

> The consequences of withdrawal by UNAMIR will definitely have an adverse affect on the morale of the civilian population, especially the refugees, who will feel that we are deserting them. However, in actual fact, there is little that we are doing at the present time except providing security, some food and medicine and a presence. Humanitarian assistance has not really commenced.[130]

Finally, when he did report to the Council on 20 April, the Secretary General presented three options: increase UNAMIR and strengthen the mandate; reduce the force to circa 250 personnel focused on achieving a ceasefire; or withdraw completely.[131] Hannay had suggested the very same options to the Security Council during informal discussions over a week earlier.

Initially there was no consensus on which option was best. A week earlier, on 13 April, Nigeria had presented a draft resolution to the Council on behalf of the Non-Aligned Caucus advocating a strengthening of UNAMIR and following Boutros-Ghali's report Nigeria continued to argue in support of the reinforcement option. On the other hand, the loudest and most powerful voice on the Council, the US, was calling for a full and immediate withdrawal. With violence flaring up across Rwanda and the death of the Belgian peacekeepers, the Clinton administration immediately foresaw another Somalia. American decision makers, viewing the events in Rwanda with fresh memories of Somalia and fearing a repeat of the Mogadishu fiasco, were terrified. Combining this fear with a genuine lack of hope of securing a ceasefire, the US State Department concluded that UNAMIR was achieving nothing other than endangering the lives of the peacekeepers; it must therefore be withdrawn. Even before the Secretary-General reported back to the Security Council, instructions were sent to the US ambassador at the UN, Madeleine Albright, to this effect:

> Department has considered the prospect of additional wide scale conflict and violence in Rwanda, and the threat ... to remaining foreign civilian and military personnel ... Taking these factors into account Department believes that there is insufficient justification to retain a UN peacekeeping presence in Rwanda and that the international community must give highest priority to full, orderly withdrawal of all UNAMIR personnel as soon as possible.[132]

With no peace to keep and violence escalating, the State Department saw the inevitable failure of UNAMIR as a threat to the reputation of UN peacekeeping. Another failed mission, so soon after failure in Somalia, would, they suggested, be fatal to the concept of UN peacekeeping.

The British supported the middle ground option of partial withdrawal. For the FCO there were a number of factors arguing against reinforcing UNAMIR.

Lead amongst these was a concern for the safety of UN troops, which the UK had highlighted at the time of the original resolution authorising UNAMIR. The Belgian soldiers had already been killed and it looked as if the UN was being deliberately targeted. Hannay therefore argued that reinforcement 'was not feasible because of the lessons drawn from Somalia that conditions on the ground' for UN troops and personnel 'could evolve rapidly and dangerously'.[133] Secondly, there was a realistic acknowledgement within the FCO of the fact that it would be almost impossible to find governments willing to contribute troops to the force should reinforcement be approved. The events in Somalia, blatant US opposition to the reinforcement plan, the Belgian campaign to have UNAMIR withdrawn, and an RPF statement that it would attack any force, including the UN, that stood in their way would certainly make most potential troop contributors cautious. Even if troops were found, there was then the difficulty of transporting them to Rwanda when the UN did not control the airport. Regardless of the ability to find reinforcements, the FCO also recognised that the existing UNAMIR force was crumbling. Already Belgium had withdrawn its soldiers - the most proficient and best equipped in UNAMIR – and within days of violence breaking out the largest contingent, the Bangladeshis, were in a state of near mutiny.[134] As one FCO official later admitted in an interview, in many respects Resolution 912 did not force the withdrawal of UNAMIR, it simply reflected what was already happening; troop-contributing nations were withdrawing their soldiers without the Security Council ordering them to.[135] For these reasons the UK rejected reinforcement.

The FCO did not believe reinforcing UNAMIR was a realistic option, but nor did it support full withdrawal. Whereas Washington argued that anything short of full withdrawal risked the reputation of the UN, the British delegation at the UN expressed the opposite view and maintained that a full withdrawal would highlight the impotence of UN peacekeeping; the impression that the UN ran with its tail between its legs at the first sign of trouble would, the UK argued, have consequences for future missions. In direct contradiction to the US view, Hannay also argued that complete withdrawal would worsen the situation on the ground. Here he seems to have been drawing on Dallaire's assessment of the situation: UNAMIR was not achieving much but it was at least providing some security and was able to act as a go-between in ceasefire negotiations. Hannay was therefore willing to stand up to the US; he recalls how he was approached by Madeleine Albright before the vote on Resolution 912:

> In the margins of the first consultation I was approached by Madeleine Albright. She said her instructions were to propose the immediate withdrawal of the peacekeeping force, its whole rationale and mandate having been invalidated. What did I think? I said I thought that would really not do. The peacekeeping force might not be able to carry on with its original mandate, but it might be able to perform some humanitarian tasks and to save lives. The UK would not

> be supporting any requests for a withdrawal. Could she not get her instructions changed?[136]

Despite not fully understanding the situation in Rwanda, the British appreciated that UNAMIR was doing important, if limited, work in protecting civilians at a handful of sites across Kigali and that, more significantly, UNAMIR was uniquely placed to negotiate between the warring parties. Reflecting Edward Clay's earlier messages, the British believed that the only way to stop the violence was by the two sides implementing the Arusha Accords and this was more likely with a UN presence in the country. In New York, the British view won out. Albright, bypassing the State Department, phoned a senior official at the National Security Council: 'I first asked them for more flexible instructions, then yelled into the phone, demanding them'.[137] Albright eventually voted in favour of the partial withdrawal plan.

Dallaire's suggestion that the UK should be held complicit in the genocide for approving Resolution 912 does not hold up to the facts. Given the context, any suggestions that reinforcement of UNAMIR could have been approved are unrealistic. What was more likely at the time was that the US view would win out and UNAMIR withdrawn completely. The British, and Hannay in particular, were instrumental in preventing this from happening – Mark Curtis' suggestion that the British mission to the UN is little more than a puppet of the US seems, in this case at least, to be contradicted by evidence.[138] If anything the UK's intervention prevented a worse outcome for Rwandans – complete withdrawal. And, given the FCO's contemporary understanding of events in Rwanda, the decision to support the partial withdrawal option makes sense. The FCO on 21 April did not appreciate that genocide was underway; instead they saw what they expected – a resumption of civil war. Such an interpretation led to the conclusion that there was limited chance of UN troops achieving anything meaningful in Rwanda, especially given the withdrawal of the Belgian contingent and the near mutiny of the Bangladeshi troops; the force would not be able to stand between the RPF and FAR and enforce peace. Rather, the UN had the best chance of success by retaining a small force in the country to aid ceasefire negotiations and to provide a limited amount of security to civilians, without overly endangering the lives and safety of the blue-helmeted soldiers. As the basis hypothesis of this book suggests, it was perceived chance of success that led the FCO to respond to the crisis in this early period as it did; there was no chance of UNAMIR physically interceding to stop the violence but it could, at an acceptable cost, attempt to negotiate a settlement.

Summary

In Britain the first two weeks of the genocide were confused and misunderstood; Britain was in every respect an ignorant bystander. For these two weeks the UK looked on from the sidelines and completely failed to understand or appreciate the magnitude of the crisis or its true nature. Rwanda was a country with which the UK had very few links: trade was minimal, there were no historical links and Rwandans spoke French. Other than mountain gorillas, Rwanda was absent from the minds of media, Parliament and government. Even the minister at the FCO with responsibility for Africa admits that she knew little of the country. It was, as Edward Clay suggested, a 'small country far away of which we knew little'. It is not therefore a surprise that the FCO and journalists did not understand the history of Rwanda and failed to spot first the risk of massive human rights abuses and then the actual genocide. Rather than seeing the crisis for what it truly was – genocide – the Government and the media only saw what they expected, civil war, and therefore responded by calling for both sides to return to the negotiating table. The first necessary factor for humanitarian intervention to be considered – acknowledgment that there is a humanitarian emergency – had not at this stage been triggered. Instead the Government saw civil war and determined there was no chance of UN troops successfully intervening to stop the killing. Realistically the UN was in no position to interpose itself between the two armies; the risk of such a mission was far in excess of the acceptable costs given the very limited interests that Britain, and the wider international community, had in Rwanda. The killing would go on.

Notes

1 FCO, 'Rwanda: Annual Review 1994', 11 January 1995. Unless otherwise stated documents from UK government ministries, including the FCO, MOD and the Treasury, were obtained by the author using the Freedom of Information Act and are in the author's possession.
2 National Archives, London, FO 371/181953, Foreign Office note, 1 April 1965; FCO 31/291, FCO Annual Review 1968; FCO 31/1801, briefing note to Secretary of State, April 1974.
3 Hansard, HC Deb, 10 February 1964, vol. 689, cols 15–17.
4 G. Myers *et al.*, 'The Inscription of Difference: News Coverage of the Conflicts in Rwanda and Bosnia', *Political Geography* 15:1 (1996), p. 31.
5 S. Hayman, 'When Mother Went to the Mountains', *Independent* (25 March 1990), p. 45.
6 National Archives, London, FCO 31/291, memorandum attached to the 1968 Annual Report on Rwanda, January 1969.
7 National Archives, London, FCO 31/2183, R.J. Stratton's valedictory despatch, 5 September 1977.

8 National Archives, London, FCO 31/2183, Research Department memorandum, 6 September 1977.
9 T. Porteous, *Britain in Africa* (London: Zed Books, 2008), p. 6.
10 Cradock, *In Pursuit of British Interests*, p. 144.
11 Porteous, *Britain in Africa*, p. 11.
12 G.M. Khadiagala, 'Europe in Africa's Renewal: Beyond Postcolonialism?', in J.W. Harbeson and D. Rothchild (eds), *Africa in World Politics: The African State System in Flux* (Boulder: Westview, 2000), p. 100.
13 Hansard, HC Deb, 15 February 1993, vol. 219, cols 6–9w.
14 National Archives, London, FO 371/181953, untitled FO memorandum, August 1965.
15 Hansard, HC Deb, 18 January 1993, vol. 217, col. 17w.
16 C. Watson, 'Rwandan Guerrillas Advance on Capital', *Independent* (8 October 1990), p. 14.
17 C. Watson, 'Rwanda Invaded by Armed Refugees', *Independent* (3 October 1990), p. 16.
18 ITN Archive, Channel 4 News, 'Rwanda: French and Belgian Troops Go In'(5 October 1990).
19 G. Philo *et al.*, 'The Media and the Rwanda Crisis: Effects on Audiences and Public Policy', in G. Philo (ed.), *Message Received* (Harlow: Longman, 1999), p. 213.
20 L. Hilsum, 'Reporting Rwanda: The Media and the Aid Agencies', in A. Thompson (ed.), *The Media and the Rwanda Genocide* (London: Pluto Press, 2007), p. 176.
21 Michael Woods, 'Travel: Rwanda', *Guardian* (27 June 1992), p. 25.
22 R. Dowden, 'Africa's Uneasy Walk to Freedom', *Independent* (3 February 1992), p. 12.
23 Anon., 'The End of History', *Guardian* (31 December 1992), p. 16.
24 ITN Archive, ITV News, 'Rwanda: Civil War Refugees', (16 May 1993).
25 Department for International Development, Rwanda Project Listing 1989/90 to 1994/95.
26 FCO, 'Rwanda: Annual Review 1990', 23 January 1991.
27 FCO, letter from unnamed diplomat at British Embassy in The Hague to FCO London, 'Private Visit to Rwanda: 10–14 April', 23 April 1992.
28 FCO, memorandum from Edward Clay to FCO London, date redacted but likely to be early March 1994.
29 A. Mackintosh, 'Rwanda: Beyond Ethnic Conflict', *Development in Practice* 7:4 (1997), p. 466.
30 Amnesty International Library, Amnesty International, UA63/91, 'Legal Concern/Fear of Ill Treatment', 21 February 1991 (the Amnesty International Library can be accessed online at www.amnesty.org/en/library).
31 Amnesty International Library, Amnesty International, UA84/91, 'Rwanda: Possible Extrajudicial Executions', 11 March 1992.
32 Mackintosh, 'Rwanda', p. 470.

33 W. Madsen, *Genocide and Covert Operations in Africa 1993–1999* (Lewiston: Edwin Mellen Press, 1999).
34 Cameron, *Cat's Paw*, p. 81.
35 FCO, memorandum from Kampala to FCO London, 29 November 1990.
36 FCO, memorandum from Kampala to FCO London, 7 December 1990.
37 FCO, telegram from FCO London to High Commission Kampala, 13 December 1990.
38 Cameron, 'Britain's Hidden Role in Rwandan State Violence', *Criminal Justice Matters* 82:1 (2010), p. 75; A. Destexhe, *Rwanda and Genocide in the Twentieth Century* (London: Pluto Press, 1995), p. 46.
39 E-mail correspondence between author and MOD.
40 Interview with Lieutenant Colonel Mike Wharmby, London, 13 September 2010.
41 MOD, Defence Adviser to British High Commission in Kampala's Annual Report, 3 April 1990.
42 All CIA papers were accessed at www.foia.cia.gov. CIA, 'Support Cable: Briefing on Middle East and Africa', 5 October 1990.
43 CIA, 'Special Analysis of Libyan Activity in Africa: Reference: CPAS NID 90-288JX', 12 December 1990.
44 MOD, Defence Adviser to British High Commission in Kampala's Annual Report, 15 October 1991.
45 Letter from FCO to author in response to a Freedom of Information request.
46 S. Goose and F. Smyth, 'Arming Genocide in Rwanda', *Foreign Affairs* 73:5 (1994), p. 89.
47 H. Kissinger, 'Bureaucracy and Policy', *Washington Post*, 17 September 1973, p. A24.
48 Hansard, HL Deb, 10 March 1994, vol. 552, col. 19w; Hansard, HC Deb, 29 March 1994, vol. 240, col. 634w.
49 M. Huband 'Burundi Bloodbath Runs its Course as West Looks On', *Observer* (31 October 1993), p. 17.
50 Telephone interview with George Alagiah, 23 November 2011.
51 D. Hannay, *New World Disorder: The UN after the Cold War: An Insider's View* (London: I.B. Tauris, 2008), p. 166.
52 Interview with David Hannay, London, 23 April 2010.
53 US Department of State, report from US Mission to the UN to Secretary of State, 'Rwanda: Text of Proposed SC Res from 9/30', 1 October 1993.
54 Melvern, *A People Betrayed*, p. 192.
55 Kuperman, *Limits of Humanitarian Intervention*, p. 116.
56 L. Melvern, 'The Security Council in the Face of Genocide', *Journal of International Criminal Justice* 3 (2005), p. 850.
57 Cooke, *The Campaign Guide 1994*, p. 603.
58 Kovanda, 'The Czech Republic on the UN Security Council', p. 194.
59 Telephone interview with anonymous senior FCO official, 27 November 2011.
60 CIA, 'Global Humanitarian Emergencies Report', 1 October 1993.
61 Cameron, *Cat's Paw*, p. 24.

62 FCO, memorandum from Edward Clay to FCO London, undated but likely to be late February 1994.
63 *Ibid.*
64 *Ibid.*
65 *Ibid.*
66 Karel Kovanda does suggest that Dallaire's cables were shared with the US, France and Belgium with the General's knowledge; he makes no mention of the UK having access (Kovanda, 'The Czech Republic at the UN Security Council, p. 198).
67 Melvern, *Conspiracy to Murder*, p. 129.
68 Interview with David Hannay.
69 Interview with senior FCO official.
70 FCO, memorandum from Edward Clay to FCO London, 7 April 1994.
71 P. Smerdon, 'Belgian Troops Fly in for Rwanda Rescue', *Herald* (11 April 1994), p. 1.
72 FCO, memorandum from Edward Clay to FCO London, 12 April 1994.
73 Anon., 'Two African Presidents Assassinated', *The Times* (7 April 1994).
74 C. Adamsom, 'African Presidents Murdered as Jet is Shot Down', *Evening Standard* (7 April 1994), p. 1.
75 Anon., 'Rwanda to Halt Attacks on Peacekeepers', *The Times* (8 April 1994).
76 C. Adamsom, 'The Brutal Struggle in the Dreamland for Tourists', *Evening Standard* (8 April 1994), p. 5.
77 J. Landale, 'Foreigners Await Rescue from Rwandan Ordeal', *The Times* (8 April 1994).
78 K. Willsher, 'Paratroopers in Race to Rescue Westerners', *Mail on Sunday* (10 April 1994), p. 6.
79 ITN Archive, ITV News, 'Belgian Troops Flying to Rwanda' (9 April 1994); ITV News, 'Rwanda: Ceasefire Truce: Evacuation' (10 April 1994); Channel 4 News, 'Rwanda: Foreigners Flee' (11 April 1994); and ITV News, 'Rwanda: Evacuation Orphans' (12 April 1994).
80 J. Watson, 'Scientists Forced to Leave Gorilla Station', *Scotland on Sunday* (10 April 1994).
81 J. Palmer, 'Belgium Seeks Joint Force for Rwanda', *Guardian* (9 April 1994), p. 16.
82 R. Block, 'Rwanda and Burundi Straddle Perhaps Africa's Most Gory Faultline', *Independent* (8 April 1994).
83 N. Gordon, 'Angels Avenge Rwandan God', *Sunday Times* (9 April 1994).
84 ITN Archive, ITV News, 'Rwanda: Ceasefire Truce: Evacuation' (10 April 1994).
85 ITN Archive, ITV News, 'Belgian Troops Flying to Rwanda' (9 April 1994).
86 J. Landale, 'Foreigners Wait for Rescue from Rwandan Ordeal', *The Times* (9 April 1994).
87 S. Lambert, 'Rwandan Pillaging and Killing out of Control', *Independent* (9 April 1994), p. 10.
88 Anon., 'Thousands Die in Orgy of Bloodletting', *Daily Mail* (9 April 1994), p. 12.

89 M. Doyle, 'Reporting the Genocide', in A. Thompson (ed.), *Media and the Rwanda Genocide* (London: Pluto Press, 2007), p. 145.
90 R. Dowden, 'Rwanda's Twins Locked in Eternal War', *Independent* (10 April 1994), p. 12.
91 A. Hartley, 'Rwandan Refugees Shelled as Some UN Troops Pull Out'. *Herald* (20 April 1994), p. 6.
92 C. Adamsom, 'The Brutal Struggle in Dream Land for Tourists', *Evening Standard* (8 April 1994), p. 5.
93 ITN Archive, Channel 4 News, 'Rwanda: Foreigners Flee' (11 April 1994) and Channel 4 News, 'Rwandan Fighting: Belgians to Withdraw' (14 April 1994).
94 M. Woolridge, 'Reporting Africa', *Irish Quarterly Review* 84:336 (1995), p. 372.
95 M. Huband, 'French Lead Flight from Rwanda', *Guardian* (11 April 1994), p. 1.
96 C. Bond, 'Rebels Advance as Kigali Slaughter Goes on', *The Times* (12 April 1994).
97 M. Huband, 'UN Troops Stand by and Watch Carnage', *Guardian* (12 April 1994), p. 22.
98 T. Halpin, 'Caught in the Crossfire', *Daily Mail* (12 April 1994), p. 14.
99 Anon., 'Amid Stench of Death, Government Flees as Rebels Close in', *Independent* (13 April 1994), p. 1.
100 A. De Waal, *Evil Days: Thirty Years of War and Famine in Ethiopia* (New York: Human Rights Watch, 1991), p. 5.
101 Anon., 'Massacre as 650 Children Killed in Church', *Daily Mail* (16 April 1994), p. 2.
102 ITN Archive, Channel 4 News, 'Rwanda Fighting: Belgian Troops to Withdraw' (14 April 1994).
103 Jakobsen, 'National Interest', p. 206.
104 Anon., 'Carnage in Africa', *The Times* (11 April 1994).
105 Anon., 'Leading Article: Africa is Not a Lost Continent', *Independent* (11 April 1994), p. 15.
106 Anon., 'Leading Article: Blood at the Bottom of the Barrel', *Guardian* (8 April 1994), p. 23.
107 L. Hilsum, 'Rwandan Blood Flows as Foreign Forces Depart', *Guardian* (16 April 1994), p. 12.
108 Thirty-five letters relating to the Bosnia crisis were identified in the period 7 to 21 April 1994; this compares to thirteen relating to Rwanda.
109 W. Wanta and Y. Hu, 'The Agenda Setting Effects of International News Coverage: An Examination of Differing News Frames', *International Journal of Public Opinion Research* 3 (1993), p. 250.
110 United Nations, New York, UN S/Res 912, 21 April 1994.
111 Dallaire, *Shake Hands*, p. 323.
112 M. Albright, *Madam Secretary: A Memoir* (London: Macmillan, 2003), p. 149.
113 M. Heseltine, *Life in the Jungle: My Autobiography* (London: Hodder & Stoughton, 2000), p. 474.
114 Seldon, *Major*, p. 443.
115 Hurd, *Memoirs*, p. 546.

116 *Ibid.*, p. 541.
117 Interview with Baroness Chalker, London, 18 August 2010.
118 M. Barnett, *Eyewitness to a Genocide: The United Nations and Rwanda* (Ithaca: Cornell University Press, 2002).
119 Interview with Malcolm Rifkind.
120 Interview with Baroness Chalker.
121 Melvern, *A People Betrayed*, p. 371.
122 Interview with Malcolm Rifkind.
123 Belgian Senate, 'Parliamentary Commission of Inquiry Regarding the Events in Rwanda', 6 December 1997.
124 Hurd, *Memoirs*, p. 541.
125 Kovanda, 'The Czech Republic on the UN Security Council', p. 199.
126 B. Adcock, 'The UN and Rwanda: Abandoned to Genocide?', Radio National (Australia), 21 February 1999. Transcript available at www.abc.net.au.
127 Albright, *Madam Secretary*, p. 149.
128 United Nations, New York, UN S/Prst/1994/16, 7 April 1994.
129 I. Carlsson *et al.*, *Report of the Independent Inquiry into the Actions of the United Nations during the 1994 Genocide in Rwanda* (New York: United Nations, 1999), p. 22.
130 *Ibid.*, p. 21.
131 United Nations, New York, UN S/1994/470 'Special Report of the Secretary General on UNAMIR', 20 April 1994.
132 US Department of State, cable number 099440, Secretary of State to US Mission to the United Nations, New York, 'Talking Points for UNAMIR Withdrawal', 15 April 1994.
133 Carlsson, *Report of the Independent Inquiry*, p. 22.
134 Dallaire, *Shake Hands*, p. 272.
135 Interview with senior FCO official.
136 Hannay, *New World Disorder*, p. 167.
137 Albright, *Madam Secretary*, p. 150.
138 Curtis, *Ambiguities of Power*, p. 183.

3

The indifferent bystander?

If it can be demonstrated that Britain was not fully aware of the horrors occurring in Rwanda in April 1994, the same cannot be said of the position in the middle of May. Slowly, RPF victories in the war opened up some regions of the country to journalists, and more images and stories appeared in the British press. Then, when thousands of Hutu fled the war into neighbouring Tanzania the first of the refugee crises developed almost overnight and this received fairly extensive press coverage. But despite the increased awareness of what was happening in Rwanda, the British Government did little. At the United Nations, Britain supported the authorisation of UNAMIR II and then begrudgingly supported the French mission, Operation Turquoise and at home the Government made very few statements about the crisis and debate in Parliament was far from extensive. The Government and NGOs did start to send aid to the region in this period, but if in April Britain was the ignorant bystander, it could now be seen at best as the 'indifferent bystander'.[1]

This chapter explores the response in May and June. It begins with a review of how the press and Parliament responded to the decision to withdraw UNAMIR before looking at how the FCO continued to misunderstand the crisis throughout May. It then moves on to consider the three key events in these months - the refugee crisis in Tanzania, the decision to authorise UNAMIR II and then the French Operation Turquoise – and suggests that racial framing and bureaucracy had a significant influence on the British response.

Media disinterest

Although a few newspapers reported Oxfam and Christian Aid's concerns about UNAMIR's withdrawal, generally the media seemed content to suggest that once expatriates had been evacuated there was nothing more the international community could do to stem the 'orgy' of ethnic violence. There is no evidence of the media criticising or even really considering the Security Council's decision In the week immediately following UNAMIR's withdrawal; instead it was reported as inevitable, when it was reported at all. James Bones in *The Times,* for example, told readers that there 'was no end in sight to the wholesale slaughter'.[2] Bones reported, without question, a UN official's statement which suggested it was right for UNAMIR to be withdrawn when there was nothing that the force could meaningfully do. Similarly on 23 April the *Independent* front page included an article saying that the decision to withdraw UNAMIR had been condemned by Oxfam, but the paper itself made no further comment on the appropriateness or otherwise of the decision.[3] On 24 April, the *Sunday Mail* briefly reported ceasefire negotiations taking place in Tanzania, without even referring to the UN decision, let alone considering whether it was right or wrong.[4] On the same day the *Sunday Times* ran a shocking article that vividly recorded the horrors of Kigali: 'On the outskirts of the city the stream of refugees grew to a tide. Dozens of bodies lay piled up on the roadside. One twitched. In front of us, a uniformed man lifted his machete. We heard the skull crack. In three hours we saw more than 100 corpses.'[5] Yet despite the graphic nature of this report it did not even pause to consider how the world should or could have been responding. Despite making no reference at all to South Africa, the article was entitled 'White South Africa Watches Rwandan Bloodbath with Dread'; the editorial decision to go with this headline had the potential to leave the reader (especially those who skim headlines rather than read articles in full) with the impression that what was happening in Rwanda was less important than the first post-apartheid elections in South Africa that were due to be held just days later on 27 April and secondly presumed that once power was passed to black people in South Africa, there would inevitably be an outbreak of racially motivated violence like that ravaging Rwanda. The unstated insinuation in many of these articles from late April was that black Africans were naturally disposed towards violence and there was nothing that could be done to prevent it. Racial, or perhaps we should say 'continental' – after all, it was the fact that the killers and victims were African rather than black which was considered significant – stereotyping was dominating and indeed shaping the media framing in British newspapers and on British television.

As was the case in the first days of the genocide, it was only the *Guardian* and the *Observer* that questioned the international response. On 24 April Mark Huband wrote, 'Clearly there is little desire on the UN's part to stand up to such killers. Consequently it has insisted on portraying the slaughter as an armed conflict between the two sides in Rwanda's civil war ... To stop the slaughter the UN must send troops to confront the guilty civilians.'[6] Two days later in a *Guardian* parliamentary sketch reporting Labour MP Kim Howells' question to Douglas Hurd on whether there was one law for Europeans (referring to British involvement in Bosnia) and another for Africans, Simon Hoggart rather damningly suggested to readers that the Government's view was 'Yes'. He continued, 'Rwandans are thousands of miles away. Nobody you know has ever been on holiday to Rwanda. And Rwandans don't look like us.'[7] Then on 1 May the *Observer* condemned the decision to withdraw UNAMIR outright, suggesting that the reduced force was not sufficient to count the bodies let alone save lives.[8] However, although critical of the UN's failure to respond robustly, neither the

Guardian nor the *Observer* went as far as to call for actual intervention by the British Government.

Most of the media remained fairly uncritical of the decision to withdraw UNAMIR, but increasingly by late April, like Hoggart, a number of journalists did begin to comment on the difference in response to the Bosnian and Rwandan crises. Cameron Doudo in the *Independent* called on UN Secretary General Boutros-Ghali to resign and expose the 'racism of the Security Council';[9] Victoria Brittain in the *Guardian* spoke of 'double standards at the UN';[10] and an *Observer* leading article concluded, 'when it comes to blacks, the white-dominated world doesn't want to know'.[11] The question of whether race was influencing the response, as Boutros-Ghali would go on to suggest, was now being explicitly tabled. Although a minority of journalists asked the question, the majority of press reports continued to reflect the old clichéd images of the inevitability of African violence or added to the double standards in the treatment of Rwanda and Bosnia that were being criticised. For example, on the one hand the *Guardian* and its sister paper the *Observer* concluded the world was showing too little interest in Rwanda, on the other they themselves allowed Bosnia to dominate the foreign news sections. In the period 23 April to 17 May a search of the *Guardian* and the *Observer* identifies ninety-two articles on Bosnia and only fifty-five on Rwanda; in *The Times* and the *Sunday Times* the ratio was even more skewed at ninety-six to thirty-six. As one reader's letter to the *Herald* noted, 'It would appear that the fate of [Rwandan] people does not matter to either the UN *or the media* because they are black' (emphasis added).[12] These disparities suggest that the media considered Bosnia significantly more important than Rwanda and this would lead the public to reach the same conclusion.

Parliamentary debate

In *A People Betrayed: The Role of the West in Rwanda's Genocide*, Linda Melvern wrote, 'In the House of Commons there was no attempt to address the issue [of Rwanda]'.[13] She is correct that it was a number of weeks before Rwanda was discussed in Parliament but MPs' response was not quite as limited as she suggests. There was interest, especially amongst the Shadow Cabinet, but in these first few weeks of the genocide MPs were constrained by parliamentary procedure and the exigencies of domestic politics and as such Rwanda received less attention than perhaps it should.

Having been largely silent on Rwanda throughout the civil war period, a small number of MPs slowly started to demonstrate some interest in the crisis from the end of April. Even so, a search of Hansard shows that, despite being recognised by Foreign Secretary Hurd as the 'worst tragedy in the world in terms of quantity of suffering',[14] Rwanda did not command a huge amount of parliamentary attention. At the monthly questions to the Foreign Secretary on 25 April Hurd received just three questions on Rwanda. Kim Howells (Labour, Pontypridd) was the first to question the Government. Referring to the decision to reduce UNAMIR, and perhaps influenced by some of the above newspaper articles, Howells highlighted the issue of race, asking, 'Is there one level of compassion for our European friends in Bosnia and another for black Africans?' Brian Donohoe (Labour, Cunninghame South) continued the Rwanda questioning, asking, 'when will the Government put pressure on the United Nations to bring back its troops to prevent further slaughter?' Hurd's response side-stepped the question of race and reiterated the view that nothing could be done: 'I am not sure how', he responded, 'either honourable Gentleman supposes that maintaining a United Nations force on the original scale will help assuage these horrors.' In the only other question on the crisis at this session, Hurd received support from the Conservative backbencher James Lester (Conservative, Broxtowe), who suggested that the only viable response was for the Government to support the OAU in reaching a negotiated settlement.[15] Hurd agreed: as one of his predecessors had suggested in the House back in 1964, as the FCO had suggested in the memorandum to the First Secretary in Kampala in 1990 and as Edward Clay had suggested in his February 1994 reports, Rwanda was a problem for Africans, not the UK. Following this brief exchange, MPs would not have the opportunity to question Hurd in person again for another month.

In this period Labour MPs tabled a handful of written questions on the response to the crisis. It is notable that none suggested that the UK should be involved in Rwanda; instead MPs, like Hurd, thought it was for the UN and OAU to do something. For example, Tony Worthington (Labour, Clydebank), an MP with a significant interest in Africa, asked whether the Government would propose to the Security Council a strengthening of the UNAMIR mandate.[16] Similarly, in the only statement from the Labour front bench in the period to early May, John Reid, spokesman on defence, said during a debate on the British army:

> Earlier today I saw ... television pictures of what is happening in Rwanda. I was staggered by those photographs. I am also slightly staggered by the apparent indifference in the West to what is going on in Rwanda. I do not suggest that there is a racial element, but I and my party believe that the appalling slaughter of innocent people in Rwanda must be stopped. We believe that the United Nations and the OAU need to organise the immediate deployment of military forces to try to end the genocide.[17]

In the same debate Calum MacDonald (Labour, Western Isles) agreed, but was even blunter; he continued that those countries nearest trouble spots 'obviously had much greater' interest in intervening than those far away; Bosnia was a European problem, Rwanda an African one.[18] Of course, such a view was contrary to what MacDonald's future leader has since said; as we have seen,

Tony Blair, writing sixteen years later, drew no distinction between crises 'proximate or not', either way there was a responsibility to act.[19] At the time Blair made no such public comment.

Publicly there was little parliamentary opposition to the Government's inaction, but behind the scenes Labour was quietly discussing its response. At a meeting of the Shadow Cabinet on 4 May, Tom Clarke, Shadow Minister for Development, informed his colleagues that he 'was strongly pressing the ODA [Overseas Development Agency] for more decisive action to help with the humanitarian crisis on the borders of Rwanda'. Jack Cunningham, Shadow Foreign Secretary, at the same meeting expressed his disappointment that, despite Labour's requests, the Speaker, Betty Boothroyd, had refused permission for a Private Notice Question (PNQ) to be raised. Such an opportunity would have given the Labour front bench an opportunity to question the Government about Rwanda on the floor of the House.[20]

Members of the Shadow Cabinet also wrote to their opposite numbers in the Government. On 4 May, after the above meeting, Tom Clarke wrote to Baroness Chalker, Jack Cunningham to Douglas Hurd and David Clark to Malcolm Rifkind; all called for more action, but not by the UK. In his letter to Hurd, Cunningham wrote, 'I am writing to urge you most strongly to support the initiative of the Secretary General of the United Nations, who is seeking to establish a significant UN peacekeeping force in Rwanda'.[21] Again raising the issue of race explicitly, Cunningham continued by contrasting how Europe was responding to the events in Yugoslavia whilst seeming to show little concern for 'the future well-being of black African citizens'. David Clark, Shadow Secretary of State for Defence, wrote to Malcolm Rifkind a second time on 17 May. In this letter, Clark set out Labour's position: 'Labour believes that the situation in Rwanda is just as much a challenge to the authority of the UN as the situation in Bosnia. We must ensure that the international community acts to stop mass murder wherever it occurs. Above all as we strengthen the ability of the UN to bring peace we must be consistent in our process.'[22] Recalling how the RAF had assisted in the humanitarian crises in Ethiopia and Northern Iraq, Clark suggested that the Government should agree Labour's 'proposals to provide military *advice* to help end the killing' (emphasis added).[23] In a subsequent letter Clark clarified that he had not meant to suggest that British troops should be deployed to Rwanda, given the 'substantial contribution' they were already making to UN operations in Bosnia, but rather should make 'expertise and equipment' available to the UN.[24]

Was Parliament interested?

Given the limited number of questions asked in Parliament and the absence of public outcry from either Labour or Liberal Democrats, it is fairly easy to conclude that Parliament showed no interest in Rwanda. It is certainly true that few MPs spoke about Rwanda but that does not mean we can conclude, as Linda Melvern does, that there was no attempt to address the issue.

First of all we must note that there are in practice few mechanisms for backbench MPs to hold the Government to account over foreign policy. The main route available is asking questions of ministers, usually in writing. *Erskine May*, the politicians' handbook of parliamentary procedure, informs MPs that 'the purpose of a question is to obtain information or to press for action'.[25] By asking a question MPs are able to highlight subjects that they consider important and worthy of further Government explanation. Questions can then be considered a barometer of parliamentary interest in an issue. It is, though, only backbenchers who ask written questions, and when questions are intended to criticise Government action they come typically only from the Opposition. This is what happened in the case of Rwanda. Throughout late April and early May there were a small number of questions asked by a select group of Labour backbenchers on an almost daily basis.

The second avenue available to MPs is an adjournment debate. Such debates come at the end of a parliamentary day and provide an opportunity for a backbencher to question a minister in much more detail than is possible in normal questions. The right to lead an adjournment debate is made by ballot and as such each backbencher can expect to lead only one per year and then not at a time of their choosing. Therefore, when MPs win the right to an adjournment debate they typically select a topic likely to guarantee them coverage in their local newspaper rather than issues of foreign policy. For example, not untypical adjournment debates in late April 1994 included an MP raising the issue of a local police constable hounded from his job for failing to attend an 'improper all night party' at the police station[26] and a debate on the winding up of Livingstone's development corporation.[27] When Labour's Tony Worthington was finally able to raise the issue of Rwanda in an adjournment debate on 24 May, he himself noted that 'we are able to discuss the issue only because of my luck in a raffle'.[28] That there was not a fuller debate on Rwanda sooner is not necessarily evidence of lack of interest, but rather a demonstration of the inflexibility of the British parliamentary system.

It may be difficult for backbench MPs to bring forward a debate on foreign affairs, but it is within the power of the Opposition to do so. Certainly, one of the key roles of the Opposition is to 'bring to the public's attention aspects of the Government's policies and administration which would not otherwise be brought before Parliament'.[29] The Opposition could have done this either by dedicating one of the weekly Opposition Day debates to Rwanda or by a PNQ. However, as the Shadow Cabinet papers show, even the Labour front bench was not able to force the debate on Rwanda as long as the Speaker refused permission for such a question; privately Jack Cunningham accused the Speaker of 'colossal misjudgement' in refusing his requests for such a question.[30] Rwanda was eventually included in an Opposition Day debate of 22 June. It had been scheduled for an earlier date but was postponed due to Labour's leader John Smith's untimely death.

The other avenue available to the Opposition was to highlight Rwanda at what was then twice-weekly Prime Minister's Questions. PMQs each week was an opportunity for the Opposition hold the Government to account; almost certainly, questions asked by the Leader of the Opposition would receive media attention on the evening news and in the newspapers the following day. In this way the Opposition had the opportunity to potentially set the political agenda. One can of course argue that if Labour truly thought Rwanda important, it would have raised the subject at PMQs but this does in some ways misunderstand the dramatic nature of PMQs; in an ideal world, questions to the prime minister would focus on the key issues of the day, but in truth the Opposition will ask questions intended to embarrass the government. As no one was seriously criticising the Government for its failure to do more, Rwanda did not fall into this category and as such was an unlikely subject for PMQs.

In addition to these difficulties, there were a number of other domestic issues which affected how much attention Rwanda received in Parliament. First is the fact that the House was in recess twice in the period of the genocide; first from 1 to 11 April for Easter and then 27 May to 14 June for campaigning for elections to the European Parliament. In addition to these recesses, the Labour Party archives show that throughout April and May the Shadow Cabinet was heavily focused on campaigning for the European elections, as well as local elections and a number of by-elections. The second factor of note is the sudden death of Labour leader John Smith on 12 May. Smith's unexpected death clearly affected the Labour Party significantly, both at a personal level but also by refocusing much of Labour's attention inwards until Tony Blair was elected leader on 21 July. In this period Labour remained fairly quiet on most issues, not just Rwanda.

The various factors combine to mean that we should not be surprised that Rwanda did not receive more attention in Parliament. The recesses, the various elections and the difficulties of finding time on Parliament's agenda meant that there was little opportunity for debate. We do know, though, that behind the scenes Labour did try to force a debate and this was refused by the Speaker. Shadow Cabinet ministers also wrote to their opposite numbers questioning why more was not being done by the Government. MPs clearly could have campaigned more loudly for a response to Rwanda, but there were obstacles that prevented this and that MPs were more interested in domestic politics must not surprise us.

A slow and bureaucratic response from the Government

Like the media and Parliament, despite acknowledging that 'atrocious killings, on a much larger scale' were happening in Rwanda,[31] the Government's foreign policy attention remained on Bosnia. Reinforcing the idea that the media heavily influences foreign affairs, Douglas Hurd suggested, 'We are deeply moved and angered by what has been happening in Bosnia. Why? Because it is carried day by day and night by night in our newspapers and on our television.' But despite the newspaper headlines and stories of atrocities, Hurd made it abundantly clear that the Government was not focused on Bosnia just because of the media coverage. He continued:

> Anger and horror are not enough as a basis for decisions. It is a British interest to make a reasoned contribution towards a more orderly and decent world. But it is not a British interest, and it would only be a pretence, to suppose that we can intervene and sort out every tragedy which captures people's attention and sympathy. I have never found the phrase 'something must be done' to be a phrase which carries any conviction in places such as the House or the Government where people have to take decisions ... Decisions cannot be based either on false analogies or on a desire to achieve better headlines tomorrow than today.[32]

Contrary to the arguments of proponents of the CNN effect, British intervention in Bosnia was justified not on the grounds of television images but, as Hurd argued, on the grounds that as a European crisis it was relatively local to the UK and also, importantly, on the grounds that there was a belief that intervention would achieve something. Hurd told the House of Commons, 'From my slight knowledge of the former Yugoslavia, I do not believe that hatred and killing are inevitable, somehow irredeemably logged in the history books as something that has to happen. That is not the history of the former Yugoslavia. The killing and hatred will come to an end – perhaps not soon, but never too soon.'[33] The racially clichéd media coverage ensured the same conclusion was not being drawn about the war in Rwanda.

We can perhaps conclude that Hurd did not support, or even consider, intervention in Rwanda because it was far away and the killing was, as the press kept reminding politicians and public alike, inevitable and unstoppable. Whilst racial clichés suggested Bosnians, as rational Europeans, would someday put aside their issues and live in peace, the opposite was the implied future for Rwandans.[34] What Hurd and the FCO seemed to be missing was the realisation that the crisis in Rwanda, like the crisis in Bosnia, was as much political as it was ethnic or tribal; it was as much about holding onto power as it was about addressing years of perceived subjugation at the hands of the Tutsi. In the same way that racial stereotyping influenced media coverage, it also shaped the Government's understanding of and response to the crisis.

In the days and weeks after the decision to withdraw UNAMIR the Government continued to focus on the renewed civil war between the RPF and FAR rather than the genocide. The crisis was described by the FCO Minister Mark Lennox-

Boyd as a 'horrific and tragic civil war' on 9 May[35] and by the Prime Minister as a 'bitter civil war' on 17 May.[36] As long as the crisis was perceived to be civil war, as Graham Allison would have predicted, the FCO bureaucracy's response was to recall how it had responded to previous civil wars.[37] When the FCO looked through its 'repertoire of processes' it determined that the standard response to African civil war was to call for a ceasefire, look to others to manage the situation and donate aid; this was the line it pursued for the first six weeks of the genocide.

As responses to parliamentary questions demonstrated, the FCO continued to believe in late April and early May that the crisis would only be brought to an end by the warring parties returning to the negotiating table. Mark Lennox-Boyd said on 20 April, 'The priority for the moment is to establish a ceasefire',[38] and again on 21 April, 'The first priority is to try to bring about a ceasefire'.[39] The UN's successes in bringing an end to civil wars in Mozambique and Namibia through diplomatic means seemed to confirm to the FCO that diplomacy rather than intervention was the most likely way of ending the killing in Rwanda. Recent experience also suggested that UN troops intervening directly was not the solution; the deaths of Pakistani and American troops in Somalia in 1993 had certainly shown the risk of UN forces being dragged into a civil war. As Towle suggests, the analogies and histories of previous crises was shaping the response to the current crisis in Rwanda.[40]

If experience suggested that the first priority was to achieve a ceasefire other parliamentary answers show who the Government believed was responsible for trying to broker this: Alastair Goodlad on 5 May, 'We support the *United Nations'* efforts to promote a ceasefire';[41] Lennox-Boyd on 6 May, 'We also stressed the importance of retaining a *United Nations* presence in theatre to support ... their efforts to secure a ceasefire';[42] Douglas Hogg on 11 May, 'The *United Nations* Secretary General is still pursuing diplomatic efforts aimed at securing a ceasefire' (emphases added).[43] As far as the FCO was concerned, the responsibility for driving forward the ceasefire negotiations rested squarely with the UN Secretary General, not the UK. Consequently the Government's response in this period was far from proactive.

Beginning to question the inactivity

It would not be long before the media and the international community began to understand that passing the violence off as civil war was wrong. From early May there was an increasingly widespread realisation that there were genuinely two separate crises in Rwanda – the war and the genocide. On 2 May *The Times* described the events in Rwanda as 'genocide', making it the first paper to do so;[44] the *Guardian* then used the word three days later.[45] With this recognition that events in Rwanda constituted genocide, and after nearly four weeks of killing, there were suggestions in the media that something should be done; there was, however, no consensus on what that something should be. The *Herald* repeated the common line of 'If there is to be intervention in Rwanda it would be best under the aegis of the Organisation of African Unity';[46] the *Guardian* suggested that military intervention was unlikely to be successful, but continued, 'Yet non-intervention does not mean doing nothing. Diplomatic efforts at mediation must accelerate';[47] and the *Independent* recognised that 'If the moral case for intervention looks overwhelming, so do the practical difficulties'.[48] So at the same time as journalists became more supportive of some kind of intervention, they were not blind to the hurdles that would need to be surmounted: US objections to becoming involved, the opposition of the warring parties and logistical difficulties. Some in the media even questioned what a new mission would achieve. For example, Sam Kiley wrote in *The Times*, 'Look at the statistics, there were about two million Tutsi in Rwanda, some 80,000 have fled, a few thousand remain in camps. Where are the rest? Is there any point in coming when there is almost none left to save?'[49]

But if the press were less than certain about what should be done, British NGOs were much readier to call for action. In terms of lobbying, Amnesty International, ActionAid, Oxfam, Christian Aid, Survival International and Africa Aid all made efforts to raise politicians' awareness of the crisis by giving statements and interviews to the media and by contacting politicians directly. The NGOs were the first to publicly call the killing 'genocide' and were certainly less focused on the civil war element of the crisis than either the media or Government. For example, in a press statement of 26 April, Amnesty wrote, 'The international community misunderstands the cause of the killings. They are not solely ethnic. There is a campaign to eliminate any Hutu who are opposed to the campaign and to exterminate all Tutsi.'[50] Similarly, in a lengthy interview given to the *Independent* after being evacuated back to the UK, Anne Mackintosh, Oxfam's country coordinator for Rwanda, explained that the media misunderstood the situation, 'It is not nearly as simple or as mindless as tribal fighting. It is not neighbour turning on neighbour for no reason. It is elements of the presidential guard and the Rwandan army and hardline politicians – the people who stood to lose from the peace agreement – hanging on for grim death.'[51]

As well as trying to educate the public, media and politicians about what was happening in Rwanda, the NGOs lobbied for action. Amnesty International was at the forefront of these demands: 'Amnesty is urging the UN Security Council to immediately expand the capacity of UNAMIR to protect human rights'; 'Amnesty welcomes the meeting of the UN Human Rights Commission, but calls for stronger action'.[52] Oxfam also campaigned for a more robust response. On 3 May David Bryer, an Oxfam director, led a delegation of officials from Britain's leading NGOs to Downing Street to protest at the lack of international response to the genocide; and on 19 May Brendan Gormley, Oxfam's Africa director, wrote to the *Independent* calling on the Government to support the urgent deployment of UNAMIR II troops, but also noting the need to agree a ceasefire.[53] Alex De

Waal and Rayika Omaar are critical of the NGOs' lobbying. They highlight that the lobbying was preoccupied with the despatch of UN troops, something that was never going to be achieved quickly. NGOs such as Oxfam, they continue, did not express outrage at what was happening in Rwanda, or name the individuals alleged to be leading the genocide, or demand diplomatic measures such as economic sanctions. In this respect, they conclude, NGOs had a mistaken priority and through their naivety did nothing to stop the slaughter.[54]

In late May the Government also received its first public censure from an MP. On 24 May Labour's Tony Worthington won the right to lead the day's adjournment debate. At 11.42 p.m., in front of a nearly empty House of Commons, Worthington noted how little interest the House had shown in Rwanda before moving on to be, in his words, 'very critical' of a number of people. He began by claiming, like many others, that racism was affecting the response: 'It is inconceivable', he – probably accurately – suggested, 'that an atrocity in which half a million white people had died would not have been extensively debated in the House'.[55] He then criticised the media for their continued portrayal of the crisis as 'tribal' before moving on to 'condemn the members of the United Nations Security Council for their inactivity and ineptitude', suggesting that as the UK sat as a permanent member of the Council it must 'share in the blame'. He continued by questioning why, having described the crisis as 'genocide', the Government had not called for the provisions of the Genocide Convention to be enacted. (Worthington was incorrect here: no minister had at this point described the events as genocide. Mark Lennox-Boyd in a written response of 23 May had said, 'No representations have been made to the Rwandan government about genocide'; this was the first use of the word 'genocide' by a minister in connection with Rwanda, but was certainly not acceptance that genocide was occurring.)[56] This was the fiercest condemnation of the Government's response to date and the only one that openly criticised the Government for its inaction. Yet it must be put in perspective: this censure came from a lone Labour backbencher known for his interest in Africa; was played out to fewer than a dozen MPs; and was not reported in the press. This was not the sort of debate that would lead the Government to alter course.

The refugee crisis in Tanzania

At the end of April the crisis developed in a way that generated a new burst of media coverage but which distracted from the actual genocide. On 29 April over 250,000 Rwandan refugees fled into Tanzania in what *The Times* described as the largest 'exodus the UN has ever had to handle'.[57] Having been slow to call for action over the genocide, the media were quick to call for a response to this new refugee crisis. The *Independent,* the *Observer,* the *Herald* and the *Guardian* all called on the international community to provide at least emergency food, shelter and water to the refugees. Rather cynically, much of this increased coverage can be explained by the fact that although Rwanda remained unsafe and effectively closed off to journalists, reporters could quite easily travel to Tanzania. The crisis in Tanzania was logistically easy to cover; as Tom Walker described, 'planes crowded with journalists' arrived at the refugee camps in a very short space of time.[58]

As more journalists arrived in Tanzania and a few began to slip into the border regions controlled now by the RPF, suddenly more articles began to appear in the press, many focused on the work of British NGOs in the region. Such stories, as James Dawes points out, served both the media and NGOs.[59] From a media perspective NGO stories gave a British angle to the otherwise quite foreign crisis and also made it easier for the journalist to get a story in the first place; after all, it required less effort to quote an English-speaking nurse than to try to interview a Kinyarwandan-speaking local. The NGOs also benefited in terms of image and recognition of their own brand and also through heightened coverage and awareness of the actual crisis. Such reports are therefore fairly common in the reporting of news from Africa. The *Sunday Times* ran the first such article; entitled 'Momma Humanity', it followed a Scottish nurse, Sheila Wilson, who managed a Red Cross refugee camp in Tanzania.[60] The article completely failed to link the horror of the genocide with the unfolding refugee crisis. Wilson, for example, was quoted as saying, 'I was surprised the people were not in more of a bad state, some were traumatised and had sore feet'.[61] Of course, those that made it to Wilson's camp were the lucky ones; the half a million killed in Rwanda never had the opportunity to become refugees and were forgotten in this and most other articles. To concentrate on the refugees' blisters whilst failing even to mention the slaughter illustrates the nature of the media coverage throughout the crisis: it was much easier to fall back on cliché and stereotype, in this case white nurse helps black African orphan, than to try to understand what was happening in Rwanda. It was, to coin a phrase used by the BBC reporter George Alagiah, 'template reporting'.[62]

The refugee crisis did at last give British NGOs something practical to do in response to the events in Rwanda. The danger of the war zone had meant British NGOs had chosen not to operate in Rwanda, so until this point their activities had been restricted to campaigning for UN action. As De Waal and Omaar argue, 'relief organisations will always make charitable works their priority', and this was certainly the case in Rwanda.[63] Whilst human rights-focused groups, such as Amnesty and African Rights, continued to lobby for action, other groups quickly turned their focus towards the crisis in Tanzania rather than the on-going violence in Rwanda. Certainly the NGOs' efforts to stimulate a Government and public response were more effective in relation to the refugee crisis than the genocide and NGOs were quick to appeal to the British public to donate to the crisis. Initially individual NGOs, including the British Red Cross and Oxfam, ran their own appeals; then on 13 May the Disasters Emergency Committee (DEC – the umbrella organisation that brings together Britain's leading charities) launched a

Rwanda appeal that in the first two weeks generated over £2 million. By 16 June, and following a television appeal fronted by Helen Mirren and Michael Palin, the DEC had raised £4.25 million, four times the amount raised by a similar appeal for Yugoslavia earlier in the year.[64] Maybe here clichéd framing helped Rwandans; after all, the British public were familiar and comfortable with the idea of donating to starving and orphaned Africans. Ultimately the DEC appeal would raise £37 million before it closed in early 1995; making it the DEC's fourth most successful appeal of all time.[65]

In addition to the money received from the public, much of the aid promised by the Government – stage three of the FCO's standard responses to African crises, as we have seen, was to donate aid – was channelled through NGOs. On 21 April Mark Lennox-Boyd informed Parliament that £820,000 of emergency aid had been committed to the 'victims of the conflict in Rwanda'.[66] In the face of the mounting refugee crises in Tanzania and then Zaire, this amount gradually increased; by the start of May over £1.1 million had been promised, a further £2 million was then made available in the second week of May,[67] by 24 May the figure was 'more than £4.5 million'[68] and by the end of June the it was approximately £11 million.[69] Most of this funding was channelled through British NGOs, but the aid package did also include the donation of emergency food and equipment; for example, two mobile grinding mills were donated to the World Food Programme for the production of maize flour.[70] The Government, through the ODA, also provided a steel bailey bridge to improve access between the refugee camp at Benaco in Tanzania and the nearest town, Ngara, and an airbridge at Mwana which enabled relief supplies to be flown to the camps.[71]

The Government and public funding was used by NGOs predominantly in the refugee camps, with very little being used in Rwanda itself. The DEC funding paid for much of the infrastructure at the Benaco refugee camp, including the Red Cross shipping over thirty-eight tonnes of medical equipment to the camp,[72] Oxfam managing the water supply and Care International managing the warehousing and distribution of aid equipment and food.[73] But although the NGOs were resourced and quick to provide food, sanitation, water and shelter to refugees in Tanzania, there was still little they could do to ease or prevent the massacres in Rwanda other than continue to campaign for the UN to do more and sooner.

It is obviously hard to quantify whether the level of aid was sufficient, and it is of course easy to argue that any amount of aid is never enough, but one figure shows that the British Government was a comparatively major donor to the relief effort. When on 9 May it was announced in Parliament that £1.1 million had already been provided and a further £2 million made available to NGOs, it was noted that 'Other EU countries and the European Commission have announced nearly £2 million of assistance so far'.[74] Based on this figure, British aid outweighed that of the rest of Europe combined in the first month of the crisis. In addition to the cash, it is also apparent that without ODA expertise the operation of the

Tanzanian refugee camps would have been less successful; ODA funding of the airbridge, the bailey bridge and the secondment of logistical experts enabled relief efforts to operate and almost certainly saved many thousands of lives.

UNAMIR II

The growing refugee situation in Tanzania coincided with the climax of another African story that had been dominating world news for a number of weeks; on 10 May Nelson Mandela had been inaugurated as President of South Africa. Mandela's inauguration, which failed to spark the widespread violence that journalists and African experts had predicted, meant that journalists who had been reporting from South Africa for weeks were now free to cover other African stories. The ending of this story, combined with increased security in the border regions of Rwanda following RPF victories, meant that by late May more journalists were reporting directly from Rwanda and they appear to have been keen to shock. Rather than analysing or trying to explain the civil war and genocide, as is fairly typical of reporting of the global south, the media focused on the grotesque nature of the killings. The following extracts were not unusual: 'Next to a dead sow, bloated to bursting point, lay a woman. Her legs were splayed, her skirt pulled above her waist. Her throat had been slit';[75] '[the woman] said "I lost my child. When I refused to kill, the Government soldiers banged a gun on my child's head and she died."';[76] 'Many victims had their feet cut off and were left to die slowly. Pregnant women, still alive, slit open. Men tied, their genitals cut off and stuffed into their mouths.'[77]

One particularly gruesome aspect of the crisis that was widely but briefly reported in the UK was the washing up of corpses on the Ugandan shores of Lake Victoria. The descriptions of the scenes, as this example from the *Sunday Times* shows, were almost perversely sadistic:

> Swarms of flies gathered around the corpse, which was turning white after weeks in the river. The flesh appeared to have the same texture as raw chicken and was almost the same colour. The man's hair and flesh had come off his skull, exposing his cream-coloured cranium. The lips on his face were missing and he appeared to be smiling.[78]

The following day the *Guardian* ran a similar story describing how some of the corpses 'had their hands bound behind their backs. Others had been shot or had limbs or their heads chopped off.'[79] The *Independent* put the story on the front page, the *Daily Record* and the *Herald* both ran the story and even the *Daily Mail* had a short article (though only on page fifteen). Television images, despite being carefully edited, were also graphic. A Lindsay Taylor report for *Channel 4 News*, although shot from a distance, clearly showed bodies and mutilated limbs, bleached white by their time in the water, being removed from the lake.[80] Taylor, though, like many of the newspaper reporters, focused his report not on the cause of the bodies in the lake, but on the consequence. Only in the last few seconds of the four-minute report did he acknowledge that the risk of typhoid spreading to the Ugandan communities that depended on lake water and fish was, when compared to the massacres in Rwanda, 'relatively minor'.[81]

It was against this background of horror and growing refugee crisis that the Security Council, on the advice of the Secretary General, began considering reversing the decision to withdraw UNAMIR. In a report of 13 May, Boutros-Ghali proposed the deployment of an enlarged force – UNAMIR II. The report envisaged a force of approximately 5,500 troops, tasked with providing safe conditions for displaced persons, providing security to humanitarian organisations and monitoring Rwanda's borders, but it would not intercede in the war.[82] Notably in this initial report Boutros-Ghali made no suggestion that this mission was dependent upon a ceasefire. The Secretary General conceded the long-term need for a return to the principles of the Arusha Accords and called for there to be 'no delay' in the deployment of UN peacekeepers; he then called for the Security Council to consider what 'measures it can take before a ceasefire is achieved'.[83]

By the time Resolution 918 was agreed three days later on 16 May (and formally adopted the following day), it is clear that the Security Council had moved to a position of requiring a ceasefire to be in place at least before the bulk of UNAMIR II deployed. After the standard preamble, the Resolution's action points began, '[the Security Council] demands that all parties to the conflict immediately cease hostilities, agree to a ceasefire, and bring to an end the mindless violence';[84] the use of the word 'mindless' again demonstrating that the violence continued to be seen as tribal and savage rather than politically motivated and state orchestrated. It continued, 'the Secretary-General [is requested] to report as soon as possible on the next phase of UNAMIR's deployment, including inter-alia, on the cooperation of the parties [and] progress towards a ceasefire'.[85] Here was an indication that the Security Council would only agree to the deployment with a ceasefire in place and with consent from the warring parties.

There is evidence that the UK supported these preconditions and was probably instrumental in having them included in the mandate. In his formal statement given after the adoption of Resolution 918, David Hannay called on the UN to 'not lose sight of the need to achieve a ceasefire'.[86] More telling of British opinion, though, was Lennox-Boyd's statement to Parliament given on 24 May. He said that, despite supporting the passage of Resolution 918, 'there was no question of UNAMIR providing an interposition force in the civil war without a full ceasefire between the parties'.[87] UNAMIR, he explained, could only be successful if it had the consent and support of the opposing factions. Malcolm Rifkind similarly wrote to David Clark on 23 May that 'there is no support for any operation to enforce a peace in Rwanda'.[88] We can assume that Rifkind here was meaning there was no international support for a peace enforcement mission but he could equally have meant neither was there British support.

Britain, the US and UNAMIR II

Given the various claims of Melvern, Curtis and Des Forges that British policy at the UN was simply to support the US in its efforts to keep peacekeepers out of Rwanda, it is worth considering at this point how the British and American responses to the UNAMIR II plans differed.[89]

As Boutros-Ghali was drafting the report that would be released on 13 May, the US Government was already trying to influence the recommendations and the subsequent debate in the Security Council. In a memorandum to the US mission to the UN, the State Department wrote, 'As Vice President Gore has indicated [to Boutros-Ghali], we are interested in exploring the possibility of using an expanded force to create one or more secure zones in Rwanda along the border for the protection of refugees and displaced person in most immediate danger.'[90] It is this plan that Samantha Power subsequently named 'outside-in', as it was the opposite of General Dallaire's proposal to deploy new troops to Kigali and then work out across the rest of Rwanda ('inside-out').[91] Officially Washington argued that the outside-in option had proved successful in Operation Provide Comfort. In that mission US, British and French troops had deployed to the borders of Iraq to protect Kurds being persecuted by Saddam Hussein's government troops in the aftermath of the first Gulf War. If humanitarian zones on the borders of the state had proved successful in Iraq, surely, the logic followed, they could also work in Rwanda.

However, it is evident that any such arguments were merely cover for the fact that the US had significant reservations about deploying troops into Kigali itself as long as the civil war continued. The State Department noted in a memo to Madeleine Albright that a 'Kigali based operation in current circumstances would require a Chapter VII mandate'[92] (a Chapter VII mission being one authorised to enforce peace without the consent of the host state) and the US could not support such a mission. With the events in Somalia still fresh in the minds of the Clinton administration, there was significant opposition to enforcement missions generally; especially at the Pentagon, and especially to ones in Africa.[93] The proposed outside-in mission was a way of doing something in Rwanda, but at significantly less risk and with fewer troops than the proposed inside-out mission. Most importantly, it kept US troops out of the actual war zone.

The FCO supported the US mission's general principle that the UN should not deploy into Rwanda while the civil war continued, but opposed outside-in. As David Hannay described the situation, 'People were being killed inside Rwanda, not outside. You were not going to stop the genocide by operating in Uganda or Tanzania.'[94] A note written in early June similarly shows the FCO's view: 'We would hope to see resources concentrated in areas where there is a genuine risk to the civilian population, and not, for instance, on the border areas'.[95] For the FCO the solution was inside-out but only with the consent of the two parties and with guarantees for the safety of the UN troops.

That outside-in was not implemented seems to undermine the theory of Anglo-American collusion at the Security Council. The comments from Hannay show that the UK had real reservations over the efficacy of the proposal. It must also be fair to assume that if the UK had been supportive of the US plan it would most probably have been implemented. If two permanent members, both of whom were key providers of resources to UN missions, had supported outside-in, and made it known, as the US did, that they would provide troops or logistical support to such a mission, it is unimaginable that the remainder of the Security Council would have opposed it. And with the proposed outside-in mission being based in neighbouring countries (presumably with the authority of the host governments), it could not have been considered an infringement of Rwanda's sovereignty and would therefore most likely not have incurred the potential veto of China and Russia. Despite the fact that outside-in could probably have been approved, the FCO was clearly so opposed to the plan that, as it had with the decision to withdraw UNAMIR back in late April, it felt the need to stand up to the US and recommend an alternative course of action. The draft Resolution that came before the Security Council was then not the Resolution that the US would have preferred. Instead it proposed the plan that the FCO favoured. Resolution 918 was a compromise agreement - inside-out, but only once a ceasefire had been achieved. The FCO again appears to have directed the Security Council to adopt its favoured approach.

Despite Hannay's efforts, the UK must not be given too much, if indeed any, credit for pushing for an enhanced peacekeeping force. The Government's requirement that a ceasefire should precede the deployment of new troops effectively meant that any such deployment would not be immediate and the FCO most likely knew a ceasefire was unlikely to come any time soon. Throughout early May Edward Clay, Britain's High Commissioner in Kampala, continued to inform London that the chances of a ceasefire being negotiated were slim. In one undated telegram, Clay reported that although a ceasefire had been declared in Kigali it 'must continue to be exceedingly fragile, given that the RPF declared it unilaterally but subject to conditions which the RGF [Rwandan Government Forces] have not accepted'.[96] In another, Clay reported that the RPF appeared to be 'going for broke' and that 'our impression is increasingly that the RPF hope to establish themselves as the only organisation remaining in Rwanda capable of doing business with the outside world'.[97] In a third, Clay informed London of reports in the Ugandan press that the RPF would attack any UN troops who attempted to prevent an outright military victory.[98] The ODA assessment mission, operating in Tanzania from 21 to 26 May, also highlighted the low likelihood of an imminent cease fire, noting in its report that 'an early end to the civil conflict is not anticipated'.[99] With this intelligence coming from Clay and ODA staff, one can fairly conclude that by the end of May the FCO knew there was little chance of a ceasefire being agreed, the most likely outcome was military victory for the RPF; yet publicly a ceasefire was still what the British Government called for and was set as a precondition of UNAMIR II's deployment.

The Security Council's decision on 16 May to increase UNAMIR's size to 5,500 received a mixed response in the press; interestingly no newspaper particularly celebrated the decision. Having catalogued the problems facing any intervention only days before, *The Times*, *Independent* and *Guardian* all focused on, and criticised, the US's reluctance to actively support the proposed mission. The *Independent* called the debate one of the 'most shameful' in the UN's history before claiming that Rwandans were dying because 'the US messed up in Somalia'.[100] Reflecting the generally held sentiment that, following the collapse of the Soviet Union, the US was by 1994 the world's only remaining superpower and therefore had the potential to take the lead in what President Bush had called the 'new world order', the *Independent* concluded: 'If the United Nations is blocked from acting on Rwanda because Congress is picking over a few nickels and dimes for peacekeeping, what right has America to claim global leadership?'.[101] The *Guardian* was similarly critical, noting that 'the impact of the resolution was blunted by intense lobbying from the US'. The article rather accurately predicted that 'Despite a Security Council vote to send in the force to protect refugees and help deliver desperately needed aid, a hard-line stance by Washington has effectively ensured that the UN contingent will only dribble in over the coming weeks and months.'[102] Despite the criticism of the US, no one in the press questioned, or even raised, what role the UK had played in the Security Council debates. The FCO was neither chastised nor congratulated for the influential role that it played in implementing Resolution 918. Nor did anyone in the press suggest that now UNAMIR II had been authorised, British troops should be sent to Rwanda.

Britain's limited contribution to UNAMIR II

Despite having voted in favour of UNAMIR II, the Government seems to have given no consideration to deploying British troops. Instead the Government, in the words of David Hannay, 'actively encouraged African nations to contribute troops'.[103] The FCO appeared keen on pursuing this option for three reasons. First, there was no appetite amongst the press, the public, in Parliament or within Government for Britain to send troops. Secondly, the FCO did not feel that the UK had the resources to respond positively. Baroness Chalker, Minister of State at the FCO, explained the dilemma: 'How do you justify taking people off one valuable project to deal with another event'; the common view within the FCO, she suggested, was that 'we cannot take that on as well'.[104] It should be noted that at the time Britain was the fourth largest troop-contributing nation to the UN (after Pakistan, France and India) and was heavily committed to Bosnia. Finally, as Hurd had told Parliament, within Government Rwanda was still held to be an African problem that required an African solution.

The Government did, though, agree to make a contribution to UNAMIR II. On 15 June, nearly a month after Resolution 918 had been authorised, Hannay was instructed to inform the UN of Britain's 'readiness in principle to provide fifty British Army trucks for UNAMIR'.[105] Variously it has been suggested that these four-wheel-drive trucks, each capable of carrying twenty soldiers, did not arrive in Rwanda, that they were not fit for purpose or that they were a mere gesture by the British Government. Certainly the vehicles did arrive in theatre, but it appears that they did not impress General Dallaire. He recalls:

> Not to be outdone by the Americans [who had offered to lease the UN fifty armoured personnel carriers (APCs)] the British offered fifty Bedford trucks – again for a sizeable amount to be paid up front. The Bedford is an early Cold War-era truck, which in 1994 was fit only to be a museum relic ... The British later quietly withdrew their request for payment and provided some of the vehicles, which broke down one at a time until there were none left.[106]

Dallaire is certainly correct that the trucks were initially offered to the UN 'for a sizeable amount'. The Secretariat was first told that the 'MOD were prepared to sell the trucks at a cost of 4,500 pounds per vehicle'; on top of this, refurbishment costs – including spraying the vehicles white – would add an estimated £1,500 per vehicle.[107] A fax from David Hannay to Whitehall suggests agreement was reached to pay for the vehicles no later than 31 March 1995; there is no public evidence either way of whether this amount was ever paid.[108]

However, Dallaire's suggestion that these vehicles were fit only to be placed in a museum would seem unfair. It is true that generally the Bedford was a Cold War-era vehicle (in 1994 the MOD was in the process of replacing the Bedford with new Leyland DAF vehicles and the fifty Bedfords were being withdrawn from service as part of this process) but these particular vehicles were on average fourteen years old. The FCO memo sent to New York records, 'MOD have advised that the Bedford trucks have been well maintained ... Their average mileage is of the order of 60,000 ... since they have been operational until the last minute MOD believe that a full service should be sufficient for most'.[109] It is important to note that if these vehicles had not been offered to UNAMIR they would have remained in front line service with the British army for at least another year.

Lieutenant Colonel Mike Wharmby, who commanded the British contingent deployed to Rwanda in August, also disputes Dallaire's claims. In response to the question 'Was Dallaire's criticism of the trucks provided by the UK fair?' Wharmby answered, 'No – the same trucks were still in service with the British army. They weren't the newest, but they were what was available ... my soldiers managed to drive them everywhere.'[110] It seems rather that it was not the Bedfords themselves that were the problem, but instead the fact that they were being driven in a very harsh and unforgiving environment, initially by soldiers with little experience of driving or maintaining that particular vehicle and that spare parts were not available. One senior FCO official recalls, for example, that before the British troops arrived in Kigali in August 1994, UNAMIR did not even have the capability to repair punctures.[111] Certainly, these vehicles were not the newest or the best, but once the British contingent arrived in Rwanda they were able to maintain and service the vehicles and provided experienced, well-trained drivers. At that point the vehicles began to make a valuable contribution to UNAMIR.

Dallaire's cynical suggestion that the British Government only offered the trucks so as not to be outdone by the American offer of APCs is also slightly unfair, though in some ways not too far from the truth. Rather than to avoid being outdone by the Americans, it appears to have been the French announcement, made on 18 June, that France was planning to send troops to Rwanda that had more influence on the British decision to offer the trucks. In a memorandum to London, the mission in New York wrote

> The latest French initiative seems to strengthen further the case for issue of an early press release announcing our offer. If for any reason the offer is not followed up by the UN, we will have lost nothing by announcing it. If we have not announced it, we will have nothing at all to say about UK help to UNAMIR.[112]

The FCO made such an announcement on 17 June, a couple of days before the French mission became public. Given that the FCO and MOD had been considering the UN's request for equipment since late May,[113] one could cynically conclude that the offer of the trucks was only made in response to the announcement of France's plans. However, FCO documents suggest that the timing of the announcement was certainly influenced by the French, but the actual decision to offer the trucks was made independently of this if for no other reason than to encourage other nations to contribute to UNAMIR II. As David Hannay explained, the UK was actively trying to encourage African nations to provide troops to UNAMIR II; Britain had to be seen to be making a contribution itself, hence the offer of the trucks.[114]

Nor are suggestions that the trucks were merely gesture politics correct. At this point in the crisis the UK had not been asked by the UN to provide personnel for the operation. As Malcolm Rifkind wrote to his Labour counterpart David Clark, 'We have, along with several other nations, been asked by the UN whether we can provide *vehicles* for the expanded force and we are investigating this possibility' (emphasis added).[115] African nations had offered to provide troops to the mission but they were incredibly poorly equipped and would be reliant on Western countries to provide logistical support. The offer of trucks was exactly what had been requested by the UN. As Lennox-Boyd responded to a parliamentary question about the trucks, 'The hon. Gentleman grossly underestimates our contribution to assistance in Rwanda. The fifty trucks that he dismissed so contemptuously are precisely what the Secretary General asked us to supply.'[116] Neither should one forget that logistical support and expertise were also exactly what the media and Labour Party had been suggesting the Government should offer.

Operation Turquoise

By late June, weeks after the approval of UNAMIR II, still no new troops had arrived in Rwanda. Expressing public frustration about this delay, President Mitterrand announced on 18 June that French troops would deploy to Rwanda to establish a humanitarian safe haven in the south-west. Operation Turquoise received UN backing and arrived in Rwanda on 23 June. The launch of France's mission generated another of the sporadic surges of media interest in the crisis; on 21 June, for example, the *Independent* alone ran five separate articles on Rwanda and a further four two days later, including the front page. The media response to the French mission, though, was almost universal condemnation; and the opposition of the RPF, aid agencies and some members of the Security Council received significantly more attention than the American support for the mission.

France's historical involvement in Rwanda, particularly its support for President Habyarimana and its supplying of weapons to FAR were the main reasons that most of the press opposed Turquoise. The *Independent*, for example, stated, 'No country is less well placed for such a mission' before continuing, 'The French should think hard before sending troops to Rwanda ... a French intervention is likely to do more harm than good.'[117] *The Times* agreed with this last sentiment. One consequence of the French deployment was that UNAMIR was forced to withdraw any French-speaking troops that remained in the force for fear of antagonising the RPF; *The Times* therefore pointed out that although French troops offered security only in the largely Hutu western third of Rwanda, Tutsi in Kigali were now being protected by a smaller UNAMIR force.[118] Noting this same issue, the *Guardian* concluded, 'the right strategy is to despatch a mainly African force, with strong logistical support from Europe and North America ... For French troops to barge in from eastern Zaire would only compound the disaster.'[119]

It was not just France's previous involvement in Rwanda and the impact on UNAMIR that led to criticism of the mission. The majority of the print media accused President Mitterrand of opportunism. In an article entitled 'The Unofficial Motives Behind a Perilous Plan', the *Scotsman* questioned whether this was genuinely a humanitarian mission. It went on to suggest that the mission was as much driven by a French desire to 'cut a dash on the world scene' and to show 'French speaking Africa that it had not been abandoned' as by genuine humanitarian concern for Rwanda.[120] As Asteris Huliaras argues, in the early 1990s, with the end of the Cold War and the emergence of a more powerful neighbour with the reunification of Germany, France's historical feeling of self grandeur and status was being undermined. Flexing its muscles in Africa was, then, a way of demonstrating its position as a great power.[121] The *Guardian* suggested that Mitterrand launched Turquoise to score a 'public relations coup'; it was a demonstration to the French public of France's unique power to intervene in African crises.[122] In a similar vein *The Times* acknowledged entirely sarcastically on the first day of the mission 'tonight's television screens will at last bring good news, footage of Tutsi infants cradled in the arms of French soldiers'.[123] Overall the press was not impressed by France, seeing the whole operation as foolhardy, hypocritical and politically motivated. Only the *Herald* called the mission 'worthy'; the newspaper certainly did not ignore the risks associated with the mission, but it concluded that if no one else was willing, France should at least be allowed to 'try' to save lives – not an overly ringing endorsement.[124]

On 22 June in the House of Commons the Opposition day debate focused on overseas aid and for the first time since the crisis began a member of the Shadow Cabinet raised Rwanda on the floor of the House. Tom Clarke began the debate by noting the Government's 'failure to respond adequately to emergencies such as the current holocaust in Rwanda'.[125] He went on to describe the crisis as a 'genocidal war' before, albeit two months too late, saying that it was 'disgraceful that Britain agreed to the withdrawal of most of the United Nations force'. For Clarke, Britain and the wider international community lacked the political, not the military, will to bring the crisis to an end: 'If only we had a fraction of the will which we saw in the Gulf War and the Falklands, the British people could hold their heads up high.'[126]

Clarke then moved on to speak about the French mission. '[L]et me make it plain', he began, 'on behalf of the Opposition that we regard the French initiative as being fraught with difficulty, if only because there are clearly grave questions about their neutrality in Africa'.[127] He continued, 'What we require now ... is not the dispatch of troops from Western Europe; we need full logistical support for the African troops by the United Nations and a more substantial British contribution to humanitarian aid ... We want the United Nations' impact to be effective, worthwhile and supported by Great Britain and the Western nations in terms of the necessary equipment.'[128] This was Labour saying quite categorically that it believed genocide was taking place and that the British Government should be doing something practical in response, and this response should not simply be supporting the misguided proposed French mission.

The Government's reluctant support of Operation Turquoise

The Government's response to the announcement that France would deploy troops to Rwanda unilaterally, albeit with Security Council support, was not entirely consistent; publicly the FCO and ministers expressed support for the proposed mission but there is evidence that privately they were less enthusiastic.

Various British newspapers reported that whilst on a scheduled visit to the UN on 21 June Hurd had expressed his support for the French mission: '"I think the French are acting courageously, obviously at some risk, to fill a gap in time, while the UN force gets itself together," Hurd said', the *Evening Standard* reported.[129] Correspondence between the FCO and the UK's mission in New York reflects less than wholehearted support for the proposal. In a telegram to Hannay on 21 June the FCO wrote: 'Ready to support a resolution backing the French plan, but remain concerned about its effect on UNAMIR and on the credibility of UN peacekeeping generally'.[130] (That this telegram had to be sent to Hannay when the Foreign Secretary was already in New York suggests that at this stage it was not Hurd who was leading policy on Rwanda.) The FCO appears to have had two linked concerns: first, the fact that the French military had actively supported FAR throughout the Rwandan civil war, and secondly, the RPF was indicating that it opposed the French mission, believing it to be a veil for fresh French support of the interim Government. The telegram to Hannay continued, 'the French will in practice have difficulty in maintaining impartiality'.[131] The FCO was therefore aware that the French mission would most likely lead to military, logistical or political support being given to FAR and also would almost certainly lead to RPF hostility towards the UNAMIR force proper; in fact the 21 June telegram references General Maurice Baril's statement that the RPF had already begun to view French-speaking troops in UNAMIR as legitimate targets. In the FCO, the private view was that Turquoise was a high-risk and unwelcome mission.

However, against this was the clear acceptance of the unfortunate truth that, due to difficulties in finding troops and logistical support, UNAMIR II would not be deployed any time soon. In the meantime, massacres would continue in Rwanda in the face of the Security Council's call for something to be done; the genocidal government of one of the world's smallest countries was biting its thumb at the organisation tasked with maintaining international peace and order. Resolution 918, which had authorised UNAMIR II, had 'under[lined] the urgent need for coordinated international action to alleviate the suffering of the Rwandan people and to help restore peace in Rwanda',[132] yet still six weeks later nothing had been done, making the UN seem quite impotent. The FCO concluded that this continued failure of the UN to do anything jeopardised the whole concept of UN peacekeeping. In the telegram to Hannay the FCO wrote, 'UN credibility would be badly affected by an operational fiasco in Rwanda on top of last year's problems in Haiti and Somalia'.[133] This left the FCO in the position of not genuinely supporting the French mission, but on the other hand having to agree to it because there was no other viable option. For most governments such a dilemma would have in reality been of little significance, but as a permanent member of the Security Council, the British, through economic and diplomatic pressure, wielded a remarkable amount of power or at least influence with fellow Europeans, the US and those states dependent on the UK for aid or trade. This diplomatic footprint made the UK particularly powerful at the UN in 1994 and its support, or lack of support, could potentially influence the vote of others.

It is clear that the Security Council was split on the idea of the mission, with some members, New Zealand in particular, opposed on the grounds of France's historical role in Rwanda. In an interview with the author, Hannay, also highlighting the fear of retaliatory attacks by the RPF, summed up the British position:

> No we were not enthusiastic about it at all ... We identified some of the subsequent problems that would arise; people with blood on their hands would be saved. But we feared there could be massive loss of life amongst ordinary Hutus not just people involved in the killings if something was not done ... If we had abstained, I think the resolution would have failed.[134]

The documentary evidence suggests that Hannay was instructed to neither openly oppose nor endorse the mission, but privately to caution other members of the Security Council of the perceived risks. Hannay was instructed to 'continue to question the proposal' and to 'not discourage others [redacted] from pressing for further briefing orally or in writing on the implications for UNAMIR'.[135] The instructions also contain the intriguing part sentence '... and we do not wish to be associated with any attempts to sabotage it'; the first half of this sentence has been redacted and we can therefore only speculate at Hannay's full instructions, though they clearly relate to Turquoise. However, that the instructions conclude 'if the French look like getting the votes, you should support' seems to indicate that although the FCO did not support this proposal, it did not want Britain to be seen as the country that prevented something being done in Rwanda, and it was also conscious that the UK would not want to be seen openly disagreeing with its close ally France.

The British reluctance to support the mission wholeheartedly, though, is reflected in the fact that despite requests from the French, the Government did not provide British troops or logistical support to Operation Turquoise.[136] Douglas Hogg, Foreign Office Minister, confirmed in the House of Commons that France had approached the UK and other European allies for logistical support, but 'in the event [the French] supported their operation nationally'.[137] The British press seemed to suggest that the French request had been refused by the FCO. The *Guardian* wrote of Douglas Hurd that when '[a]sked why Britain had not contributed any troops, as France requested, he said: "We don't contribute troops to every peacekeeping initiative.'"[138] *The Times* was fairly blunt in its coverage, suggesting that Hurd had 'rebuffed a personal appeal' from Alain Juppé, France's Foreign Minister, to provide troops. It went on to claim that a FCO spokesman had suggested that, 'for historic and practical reasons, it was unlikely that Britain would offer troops'.[139]

What more could the British Government have done?

In this period, despite the donation of fairly considerable amounts of aid, the British did little to address the underlying issue of genocidal violence in Rwanda: at the UN, Hannay effectively prevented outside-in and also argued for clauses in Resolution 918 that would delay the deployment of UNAMIR II; and, when asked directly by the French, Hurd refused to send British troops to help establish safe zones. However, rather than simply highlighting what Britain did not do, if we are to judge Britain's responsibility for the crisis, we must again turn to the question of what the Government could have done; we must, as Daniela Kroslak suggests, measure its capacity and capability to respond.[140]

The diplomatic effort

As the British focus throughout May and June was on achieving a ceasefire, it could be suggested the Government could have played a more active role in this process, rather than delegating it to the UN. In this scenario it is hard to see what role the UK would have performed. As we have seen, the FCO did not have any meaningful relationship with the members of the Rwandan interim Government (remember the British ambassador to Rwanda had spent only one weekend in the country in three years and aid to the country before April 1994 was minimal). The FCO was not therefore positioned to compel the interim Government to move towards a ceasefire. It would also have been aware that France maintained links with the Government in Rwanda and we can reasonably assume that the FCO was happy to leave negotiations with the Rwandan leaders to the French. Nor does it seem that the UK's relationship with the RPF was sufficiently close to have been influential in encouraging that party to the negotiating table. Numerous reports from Edward Clay in Uganda show that he did not have free access to the RPF and keeping close to the UK was not a RPF priority; Clay wrote in one telegram in early May, 'We have tried but failed to contact RPF spokesman in Kampala', before continuing, 'Like you, we rely largely on Reuters and press reports about the situation in Rwanda'.[141] Certainly the British Government continued to call publicly for a ceasefire, but there is no reason to believe that it was in any way well placed to have had any more success in achieving a negotiated end to the fighting than anyone else.

A second diplomatic avenue would have been to condemn the violence more openly. Sending home diplomats is a standard way of expressing objections to the policies of a particular government and in the case of Rwanda would have demonstrated the isolation of the interim Government from the international community. A number of authors, including De Waal and Omaar of African Rights,[142] for example, have criticised the US Government for not dismissing the Rwandan ambassador to Washington and his staff sooner (this was eventually announced on 14 July). No such course of action was available to the UK as at the time there was no Rwandan embassy in London. The UK could have argued for the Rwandan ambassador to the UN to be dismissed from the Security Council, to which, in one of those ironies of history, the country had been elected on 1 January 1994 (Tony Worthington indeed suggested this in Parliament on 24 May). This move would have had two effects: it would have firstly indicated that the international community did not condone the actions of the Rwandan Government and secondly would have stopped Rwandan officials having access to and attempting to influence the private discussions of the Security Council about how the UN should respond to the crisis. In one telegram to London, David Hannay expressed his frustration that the Rwandans were able to use the Security Council as 'a mouthpiece for their faction'. Hannay wrote, 'Highlights, and low points, of the Council debate on Rwanda. Rwandan Foreign Minister makes offensive speech blaming four centuries of Tutsi domination, and Ugandan interference, for Rwanda's problems. Puts responsibility for the massacres on the RPF. New Zealand reacts sharply, questioning Bicamumpaka's right to sit at the Council table.'[143] However, whilst some individuals within the FCO would have liked to have taken some form of action, Hannay explains that such a move would have been almost impossible to achieve:

> [Rwanda] had been elected [to the Security Council] by the General Assembly. No provision exists to expel a member. Personally I felt strongly that they should at least have been suspended, but the Russians were desperately opposed to this and the Americans were not keen. There was concern over the precedent this would have set. Remember, we were not too far from the end of the Cold War. There was some fear that such a precedent could be abused.[144]

Hannay was clear that, despite behind-the-scenes discussions of Security Council members, the Russians feared such a move would create a precedent that the Western allies would at some point abuse and would therefore have vetoed any move to expel Rwanda.[145] Dismissal was thus not a viable option.

Other diplomatic measures that were not properly considered were economic sanctions, the public naming and condemnation of the leaders of the genocide or the public threat of indictment of perpetrators. Given the limited nature of trade and aid between the UK and Rwanda, unilateral economic sanctions would have been worthless. There was, though, no reason why the British Government could not have brought these potential measures to the UN or European Union for discussion; there is no evidence that British diplomats did do this. It seems that instead British diplomats, like other members of the UN, the media and NGOs, got caught up in the calls for a ceasefire or the discussions of the need for a UN force. The misinterpretation of the crisis as civil war made this approach almost inevitable and meant that other diplomatic measures, which may have had more impact, were not considered. In this respect, then, it can be said that the British Government could have done more, but its failure to do so is explained by a fundamental misunderstanding of the crisis and the oft-stated belief that Rwanda was someone else's problem.

Military intervention

Looking at military intervention, what more could the UK have done? First is the question of whether front line British troops could have been deployed as part of UNAMIR II. Linda Melvern correctly suggests that in 1994 the UK had two military units that could have been rapidly mobilised for deployment overseas – the 5 Airborne Brigade and the Special Air Service (SAS);[146] there were, though, other units that could have been deployed. The SAS, the army's special forces unit, was not really suited to the proposed peacekeeping mission if for no other reason than the fact that it did not have the necessary manpower: the SAS consists of only one regiment (at the time approximately four hundred men) and at least one quarter of the force was on permanent stand by in an anti-terrorist role. The SAS is also known to have been committed in Bosnia and Northern Ireland. Any suggestion that it could have been sent to Rwanda should be dismissed. On the other hand, elements of the 5 Airborne Brigade could have been deployed. The brigade was made up of two battalions from the Parachute Regiment and various support units (a battalion being approximately 550 men). In 1994 some of 5 Airborne's units, including one of the Parachute Regiment battalions, were maintained on a state of readiness of five days (meaning that from receipt of orders deployment in theatre could be achieved in under a week). There are reasons why deployment of this brigade was unlikely. First it cannot be ignored that when British troops did eventually deploy to Rwanda in August 1994 they depended on the US Air Force for airlift capability; without this support the deployment of 5 Airborne Brigade would have been much slower, if not impossible. And in May and June 1994 the US adamantly opposed deployment of any of its troops in Rwanda. Secondly, 5 Airborne Brigade was in 1994 the army's rapid response force. Given the British involvement in Bosnia, which at any time may have required reinforcement to ensure the troops' safety, the MOD would have been less than keen to send a combat element of this force to Africa; to do so would have increased the risk faced by British troops already deployed elsewhere.

In addition to 5 Airborne Brigade there were a further eight infantry battalions that were not already on active service (including Northern Ireland), training for imminent deployment, or recently returned from active service , which could potentially been sent to Rwanda.[147] Additionally two of the three Royal Marine Commandos were available to deploy (42 and 45 Royal Marine Commando). The Royal Marines particularly had experience of peacekeeping operations, having served as part of Operation Provide Comfort, and as would be shown in October 1994, when 45 Commando deployed to Kuwait to deter a threat of another Iraqi invasion (Operation Driver), were able to deploy overseas on very short notice.

The question of practical ability to deploy to Rwanda must be addressed before simply accepting that British troops as they were available could have been sent. As Melvern notes, 5 Airborne Brigade was on five day movement orders, and certainly when British troops did deploy to Rwanda in July at least some units were in country within a matter of days, though it must be acknowledged that this movement was largely reliant on the US Air Force. Other units would certainly have taken longer than 5 Airborne. Major General Andrew Farquhar, in 1994 the commanding officer of the infantry battalion The Green Howards (one of the eight battalions that on paper were available for deployment), believes that – assuming airlift capability was immediately and freely available – his battalion would have been able to deploy a command group within forty-eight hours, a lead company within seven days (a company being around 120 men) and the whole battalion within thirty days. He continues that, given their experience in Northern Ireland, British soldiers were more experienced in peacekeeping than most other armies and as such would have required little special training or reorganisation; but still it would have been a month before his troops were fully operational.[148]

The inland situation of Rwanda would mean that the deployment of any troops would have been entirely dependent upon airlift capacity. Airlift capability rather than manpower was in many ways the limiting resource. The eventual deployment of British troops to Rwanda in August and the Royal Marines to Kuwait in October 1994, in response to the Iraqi threat to again invade Kuwait, both demonstrated that the Royal Air Force (RAF) did not have the capacity to move large numbers of troops and equipment on its own. In October 1994 over one thousand Royal Marines deployed to Kuwait as part of Operation Driver in just ten days but, as in Rwanda, this move was partly facilitated by the US Air Force. One should also assume that a deployment to Kuwait would have been much quicker than one to Rwanda, given the differences in infrastructure. In the case of Rwanda US Air Force support was unlikely; in May and June, as we have seen, the Pentagon remained adamantly opposed to any role for the US military in Rwanda. We must therefore assume that even offered, British troops would not have arrived in Rwanda in meaningful numbers until at least a month after the order for deployment was given.

Despite their availability, in this period no British troops were volunteered to either UNAMIR or Operation Turquoise. As we have seen, Malcolm Rifkind informed his Opposition counterpart that the UN did not make any request to the UK to provide front line troops; instead the UN requested Britain provide logistical support. This may be true (Melvern suggests it is not[149]) but alone it does seem a rather unconvincing explanation of why Britain did not send troops to Rwanda. Britain may not have been asked directly to provide troops, but the Government was certainly aware that the UN was desperately trying to find 5,500 soldiers; Britain had after all supported the enlargement of UNAMIR. If there had been the will amongst the British political elite to do something practical in Rwanda, infantry troops were available and could have been volunteered even if they had not been requested. Such a deployment, even if at less than battalion strength, would have had a massively positive impact on UNAMIR II; the British troops would have been well trained, well equipped and certainly some were able to deploy relatively quickly. A British deployment might also have encouraged other nations to provide troops. We must acknowledge that the speed and scale of the genocide meant that a deployment of troops in early June would probably have been too late to save the majority of Tutsi,[150] but if Britain had sent troops at this time, some lives, possibly running into the tens of thousands, would almost certainly have been saved.

Even without British troops being deployed it has to be questioned whether the Government could have done more to speed up the deployment of UNAMIR II. First it could have been less stringent about deployment being conditional on a ceasefire and secondly it could have accelerated the offer of the fifty trucks. Looking first at the need for a ceasefire it is easy to see why the British Government was so adamant about this precondition. As we have seen, the British were concerned about the reputation of UN peacekeeping generally should the mission to Rwanda fail. The Government was genuinely concerned that the deaths of more UN troops, so soon after the Somalian fiasco and the Belgian deaths in Rwanda back in April, would have seriously undermined the credibility of neutral peacekeeping. The Government also continued to believe that there was nothing that could meaningfully be done while the war continued. The UN mission, it reasoned, would only be successful once fighting stopped; Somalia had shown that the UN could not stand in the middle of a war. The insistence on there being a ceasefire in place was then not just a way of delaying the deployment of UNAMIR II but was the Government's genuine belief on how the crisis would best be solved. Neither should it be forgotten that the US would have, and did, oppose any attempts to deploy without a ceasefire being in place first. Therefore, even if the British had removed this precondition UNAMIR II still would probably not have deployed any sooner.

With regard to the second issue of why it took so long for the UK to approve the offer of the Bedford trucks there appears to be no obvious explanation and the British Government must face some criticism for this procrastination. The

UK, like other countries, was formally asked what equipment it could provide on 16 May (and possibly informally even earlier), yet the offer of the vehicles was not made to the Secretariat until 16 June, a whole month later; even then the UN did not accept the offer immediately. Instead the Secretariat responded that it required some time to consider the offer whilst it awaited final equipment requests from the troop-contributing nations. It would seem a safe assumption that these various delays were driven largely by bureaucratic inefficiency, as the UN's request passed from the mission in New York to the FCO in London to the MOD and back through the same long and tortuous chain – an indication perhaps that there was no senior figure in the British Government, at this stage, championing a quick and positive response that could have bypassed these steps. If the vehicles had been made available sooner it is possible that at least one of the African battalions that would eventually serve with UNAMIR II could have deployed sooner; there is no way of telling what the impact of this would have been but we can reasonably assume that some Rwandan lives would have been saved.

Summary

In May and June the nature of the crisis changed. The horror of the killing was truly evident in the press for the first time, the images from Lake Victoria were particularly harrowing and the refugee problem in Tanzania developed almost overnight. Yet the British response remained muted. NGOs and a handful of MPs campaigned for some form of response; but quite resolutely throughout the period the FCO's response was characterised by bureaucratic management. The FCO continued to wrongly understand the crisis as an African tribal civil war stoked by historical hatred. The response was therefore drawn straight from what Graham Allison would call the FCO's 'bounded repertoire of processes':[151] call for a ceasefire, expect someone else to respond to the crisis and donate aid. It was only when the refugee crisis developed in Tanzania, and then received such media and international attention, that Britain was spurred into action: the NGOs sent nurses and established refugee camps, the public donated cash and the Government provided aid.

The Government certainly could have done more in this period to address the genocide happening in Rwanda, especially diplomatically or by providing logistical support to UNAMIR II sooner; but the misinterpretation of the crisis, bureaucracy and a belief that this was someone else's problem explain why it did not. Parliament could have been more vocal, but the inflexibility of the parliamentary system and the lack of media criticism of the Government both meant Rwanda was marginalised. Rather than falling back again and again on cliché, the media could have paid more attention to the crisis, been more critical of Government policy or tried harder to educate the public. The media coverage, though, fits into a pattern of reporting Africa that had been seen time and time before. But in all these respects Britain was no different from other Western nations; as we have seen, Britain in this period was one of the leading aid donors. Britain still did not understand the crisis in Rwanda and responded as if it was just another African war. Was Britain the indifferent bystander? Not really, it was instead the bystander that allowed racial framing and bureaucracy to dictate its response; as late as mid-June it still remained fairly ignorant of what was happening in Rwanda.

Notes

1 L. Melvern and P. Williams, 'Britannia Waived the Rules: The Major Government and the 1994 Rwandan Genocide', *African Affairs* 103 (2004), p. 2.
2 J. Bones, 'Retreating UN Leaves Token Force in Rwanda', *The Times* (22 April 1994).
3 A. Savill, 'UN Slashes Rwanda Force', *Independent* (23 April 1994), p. 1.
4 Anon., 'Rebels Sign Ceasefire', *Sunday Mail* (24 April 1994), p. 17.
5 A. Heseltine, 'White South Africa Watches Rwandan Bloodbath with Dread', *Sunday Times* (24 April 1994).
6 M. Huband, 'UN Leaves Rwanda in Grip of Killers', *Observer* (24 April 1994), p. 16.
7 S. Hoggart, 'Policy and Politics', *Guardian* (26 April 1994), p. 6.
8 Anon., 'It's Not Too Late for Rwanda', *Observer* (1 May 1994), p. 26.
9 C. Duodo, 'Dear Boutros Boutros-Ghali', *Independent* (25 April 1994), p. 19.
10 V. Brittain, 'Aid Agencies Condemn UN Pull out,' *Guardian* (23 April 1994), p. 12.
11 Anon., 'It's Not Too Late for Rwanda' *Observer* (1 May 1994), p. 26.
12 G. Murray, 'Letters to the Editor: UN Double Standards', *Herald* (27 April 1994), p. 16.
13 Melvern, *People Betrayed*, p. 231.
14 Hansard, HC Deb, 25 April 1994, vol. 242, col. 26.
15 Hansard, HC Deb, 25 April 1994, vol. 242, col. 16.
16 Hansard, HC Deb, 28 April 1994, vol. 242, col. 263w.
17 Hansard, HC Deb, 4 May 1994, vol. 242, col. 755.
18 *Ibid.*
19 Blair, *Journey*, p. 61.
20 Labour Party archive, People's History Museum Manchester, minutes of meeting of the Shadow Cabinet, 4 May 1994.
21 FCO, letter from Jack Cunningham to Douglas Hurd, 4 May 1994.
22 MOD, letter from David Clark to Malcolm Rifkind, 17 May 1994.
23 *Ibid.*
24 MOD, letter from David Clark to Malcolm Rifkind, 24 May 1994.
25 P. Silk, *How Parliament Works* (London: Longman, 1998), p. 176.

26 Hansard, HC Deb, 18 April 1994, vol. 241, cols 613–20.
27 Hansard, HC Deb, 20 April 1994, vol. 24, cols 1013–20.
28 Hansard, HC Deb, 24 May 1994, vol. 244, col. 309.
29 R. Blackburn *et al.*, *Parliament: Functions, Practices and* Procedures, (London: Sweet & Maxwell, 1998), p. 338.
30 *Ibid.*
31 Hansard, HC Deb, 29 April 1993, vol. 223, cols 1175–6.
32 *Ibid.*
33 *Ibid.*
34 Myers *et al.*, 'The Inscription of Difference,' p. 43.
35 Hansard, HC Deb, 9 May 1994, vol. 243, col. 28w.
36 Hansard, HC Deb, 17 May 1994, vol. 243, col. 671w.
37 Allison, *Essence of Decision*, p. 88.
38 Hansard, HC Deb, 20 April 1994, vol. 241, col. 538w.
39 Hansard, HC Deb, 21 April 1994, vol. 241, col. 613w.
40 P. Towle, *Going to War: British Debates from Wilberforce to Blair* (Basingstoke: Palgrave Macmillan, 2009), p. 67.
41 Hansard, HC Deb, 5 May 1994, vol. 242, col. 615w.
42 Hansard, HC Deb, 6 May 1994, vol. 242, col. 675w.
43 Hansard, HC Deb, 11 May 1994, vol. 243, col. 161w.
44 J. Bones, 'Shamed UN Asks West to Intervene', *The Times* (2 May 1994).
45 L. Hilsum, 'Refugees from Terror Scratch out Existence under Plastic', *Guardian* (5 May 1994), p. 14.
46 Anon., 'Intervention in Rwanda', *Herald* (2 May 1994), p. 10.
47 Anon., 'The Orphan of Africa', *Guardian* (4 May 1994), p. 19.
48 Anon., 'Peace Making: A Task for Africans', *Independent* (12 May 1994), p. 19.
49 S. Kiley, 'I Saw Hills Covered with Bodies', *The Times* (14 May 1994).
50 Amnesty International Library, Amnesty International News Service, 26 April 1994.
51 C. Dodd, 'Rwanda: Have my Friends Survived?', *Independent* (22 April 1994), p. 22.
52 Amnesty International Library, Amnesty International News Service, 3 May 1994 and 26 May 1994.
53 B. Gormley, 'Letter: The Killing in Rwanda', *Independent* (19 May 1994), p. 21.
54 A. De-Waal and R. Omaar, 'The Genocide in Rwanda and the International Response', *Current History* 94:591 (1995), p. 158.
55 Hansard, HC Deb, 24 May 1994, vol. 244, cols 308–16.
56 Hansard, HC Deb, 23 May 1994, vol. 244, col. 43w.
57 J. Adams, 'Rwanda Exodus Overwhelms UN', *Sunday Times* (1 May 1994).
58 T. Walker, 'Hutu Refugees Loot Food Lorries after Press Keeps them Waiting', *The Times* (4 May 1994).
59 J. Dawes, *That the World May Know: Bearing Witness to Atrocities* (Cambridge: Harvard University Press, 2007), p. 2.
60 R. Steiner, 'Momma Humanity', *Sunday Times* (22 May 1994).
61 *Ibid.*

62 D. Clark, 'The Production of a Contemporary Famine Image: The Image Economy, Indigenous Photographers and the Case of Mekanic Philipos', *Journal of International Development* 16 (2004), p. 699.
63 De Waal and Omaar, 'The Genocide in Rwanda', p. 161.
64 R. Dowden, 'Britons Donate £4.25 million to Appeal', *Independent* (16 June 1994), p. 13.
65 According to Disasters Emergency Committee, www.dec.org.uk/appeals/appeals-archive. The larger appeals were: Tsunami earthquake appeal, 2004 (£390m); Asia quake appeal, 2005 (£59m); and Kosovo crisis appeal, 1999 (£53m).
66 Hansard, HC Deb, 21 April 1994, vol. 241, col. 614w.
67 Hansard, HC Deb, 9 May 1994, vol. 243, col. 28w.
68 Hansard, HC Deb, 24 May 1994, vol. 244, col. 314.
69 Hansard, HC Deb, 15 June 1994, vol. 244, col. 618.
70 Hansard, HC Deb, 14 June 1994, vol. 244, col. 389w.
71 ODA, undated internal report, 'Rwanda and Burundi Refugees and Displaced: Humanitarian Aid Assessment and Monitoring Mission 21–26 May 1994'.
72 S. Wilson, 'British Aid is Flown out to Hell on Earth', *Scotsman* (27 June 1994).
73 J. Gibbon, 'Rwandan's Secret Lifeline', *Independent* (30 June 1994), p. 35.
74 Hansard, HC Deb, 9 May 1994, vol. 243, col. 28w.
75 S. Kiley, 'Desolate Village Bears Witness to Rwandan Carnage', *The Times* (19 May 1994).
76 M. Huband, 'I Killed my Brother', *Guardian* (30 May 1994), p. 20.
77 R. Dowden, 'The Graves of the Tutsi are Only Half Full', *Independent* (24 May 1994), p. 1.
78 M. Wanendeya, 'Rwanda's Deadly Tide Pollutes Lake Victoria', *Sunday Times* (22 May 1994).
79 Anon., 'Rwandan Rebels Seize Key Installations', *Guardian* (23 May 1994), p. 24.
80 ITN Archive, Channel 4 News, 'Lake Victoria Health Risk' (23 May 1994).
81 *Ibid.*
82 United Nations, New York, UN S/1994/565, 13 May 1994.
83 *Ibid.*
84 United Nations, New York, UN S/Res (1994) 918, 16 May 1994.
85 *Ibid.*
86 FCO, telegram from David Hannay in New York to FCO London, 17 May 1994.
87 *Ibid.*
88 MOD, letter from Malcolm Rifkind to David Clark, 23 May 1994.
89 Melvern, 'Security Council in the Face of Genocide', p. 850; Curtis, *Ambiguities of Power*, p. 183; Des Forges, *Leave None*, p. 603.
90 US State Department, memorandum from State Department in Washington to US mission to UN in New York, 13 May 1994.
91 Power, 'Why the US Let the Rwanda Tragedy Happen'.
92 US State Department, memorandum from State Department in Washington to US mission to UN in New York, 13 May 1994.

93 S. Power, *A Problem from Hell: America and the Age of Genocide* (London: Flamingo, 2003), p. 350; Burkhalter, 'The Question of Genocide', p. 45.
94 Interview with David Hannay.
95 FCO, memorandum from FCO London to UK mission to UN in New York, 'Rwanda: Secretary General's Report', 3 June 1994.
96 FCO, telegram from Edward Clay in Kampala to FCO London, undated. The RPF declared a ceasefire a number of times so it is not possible to date the telegram accurately; however, it was most likely written in early May.
97 FCO, telegram from Edward Clay in Kampala to FCO London, undated but stamped by the FCO 12 May 1994.
98 FCO, telegram from Edward Clay in Kampala to FCO London, 20 May 1994.
99 ODA, internal report, 'Rwanda and Burundi Refugees and Displaced: Humanitarian Aid Assessment and Monitoring Mission 21–26 May 1994'.
100 R. Dowden, 'Don't Blame the UN for an American Mess', *Independent* (18 May 1994), p. 16.
101 *Ibid.*
102 L. Elliot, 'Fury Greets US Block on Peace Force', *Guardian* (18 May 1994), p. 11.
103 Interview with David Hannay.
104 Interview with Baroness Chalker.
105 FCO, telegram from FCO London to UK mission to UN in New York, 15 June 1994.
106 Dallaire, *Shake Hands*, p. 376.
107 FCO, telegram from FCO London to UK mission to UN in New York, 15 June 1994.
108 FCO, fax from UK mission to UN in New York to FCO London, 2 August 1994.
109 *Ibid.*
110 Interview with Lieutentant Colonel Mike Wharmby.
111 Interview with senior FCO official.
112 FCO, telegram from UK mission to UN in New York to FCO London, 17 June 1994.
113 MOD, letter from Malcolm Rifkind to David Clark, 23 May 1994.
114 Interview with David Hannay.
115 MOD, letter from Malcolm Rifkind to David Clark, 23 May 1994.
116 Hansard, HC Deb, 22 June 1994, vol. 245, col. 245.
117 Anon., 'Leading Article: A Rash French Venture in Rwanda', *Independent* (21 June 1994), p. 15.
118 Anon., 'Rwanda Francais', *The Times* (23 June 1994).
119 Anon., 'The French in Rwanda', *Guardian* (21 June 1994), p. 23.
120 Anon., 'The Unofficial Motives behind the Perilous Plan', *Scotsman* (22 June 1994).
121 Huliaras, 'The Anglo-Saxon Conspiracy', p. 598.
122 A. Gumbel, 'French Aim in Rwanda is "To Save Lives"', *Guardian* (20 June 1994), p. 9.
123 Anon., 'Rwanda Francais', *The Times* (23 June 1994).

124 Anon., 'Worthy French Initiative', *Herald* (21 June 1994), p. 12.
125 Hansard, HC Deb, 22 June 1994, vol. 245, cols 243–6.
126 *Ibid.*
127 *Ibid.*
128 *Ibid.*
129 Anon., 'Rebels Battle for Rwandan Capital', *Evening Standard* (22 June 1994), p. 24.
130 FCO, telegram from FCO London to UK mission to UN in New York, 21 June 1994.
131 *Ibid.*
132 United Nations, New York, UN Res 918, 17 May 1994.
133 FCO, telegram from FCO London to UK mission to UN in New York, 21 June 1994.
134 Interview with David Hannay.
135 FCO, telegram from FCO London to UK mission to UN in New York, 21 June 1994. Three or four words have been redacted from this sentence in the document that has been released.
136 In response to a Freedom of Information request the FCO confirmed that an approach was received from the French Government to provide troops but refused to release any of the documents relating to this request.
137 Hansard, HC Deb, 28 June 1994, vol. 245, col. 521.
138 M. Huband, 'Militiaman Claims France Trained Rwanda's Killers', *Guardian* (22 June 1994), p. 14.
139 J. Bone, 'UN Ready to Back French Intervention in Rwanda', *The Times* (21 June 1994).
140 Kroslak, *Responsibility of External Bystanders*, p. 4.
141 FCO, telegram from Edward Clay in Kampala to FCO London, 3 May 1994.
142 De Waal and Omaar, 'The Genocide in Rwanda', p. 158.
143 FCO, telegram from Sir David Hannay in New York to FCO London, 18 May 1994.
144 Interview with David Hannay.
145 *Ibid.*
146 Melvern, *People Betrayed*, p. 232.
147 These were: The Royal Scots, The Green Howards, the Cheshire Regiment, The King's Own Scottish Borders Regiment, the Queen's Own Highlanders, The Gordon Highlanders, The Argyll and Sutherland Highlanders and the UK-based battalion of the Ghurkha Rifles.
148 E-mail correspondence with Major General Andrew Farquhar, 5 October 2011.
149 Melvern, *People Betrayed*, p. 232.
150 Kuperman, *Limits of Humanitarian Intervention*, p. 120.
151 Allison, *Essence of Decision*, p. 88.

4

The bystander who did too little, too late?

Having approved UNAMIR II back in May, the international community, with the exception of France, was not quick to do much more. As June came to an end, the war continued. The Hutu extremists continued to murder Tutsi wherever they retained control and in the west French troops controlled a large portion of the country. In the UK, trucks had been offered to the mission and aid was being donated to the refugee camps in Tanzania but there was still, in late June, little serious consideration of doing much more. By late July the situation on the ground would be quite different: the RPF finally defeated FAR and the crisis in Rwanda shifted from being genocide to become the world's worst refugee crisis. As the nature of the crisis changed so too did the West's reluctance to become involved; from late July Britain, and other Western nations, significantly increased the level of aid flowing to the region and finally sent troops. The professor of international relations Sir Adam Roberts describes this response as 'too little too late';[1] as he points out, nearly a million people had already died before the West decided to actively intervene. This chapter explores the change in policy in July and August, in order firstly to address Tony Blair's suggestion that the UK did not respond to the crisis and secondly to try to understand the motivation and mechanics of the foreign policy decision-making process; how and why did the UK change from being the passive bystander to the second largest contributor to UNAMIR II?

Reacting to the crisis in Goma

By early July Rwanda was almost fully open to journalists. In the north and east, reporters were able to travel relatively freely, albeit accompanied by RPF guides. In the west, the French-controlled zone was now reasonably safe and the refugee camps in neighbouring Tanzania and Zaire continued to provide newsworthy stories without the need to enter a war zone. Only the north-west of Rwanda, which the interim Hutu Government continued to hold, remained unsafe and inaccessible; it was of course in this area that genocide continued.

The easing of access meant that media coverage of the crisis grew in quantitative, if not qualitative, terms throughout July, but the sudden explosion of journalists covering Rwanda in no way helped clarify or better explain the crisis to the public. Instead, as Mel McNulty argues, 'the Western news consumer was fed a series of unlinked reports about seemingly unrelated crises, which generally fitted into the typical African mould of biblical catastrophes'.[2]

In the first two weeks of July, journalists benefiting from the security provided by French troops switched media attention from the refugee crisis in Tanzania to the situation in western Rwanda. This led, for a short period at least, to fairly extensive coverage of the RPF's continuing advance and the potential for a standoff between French and RPF troops when the two finally met. Because of France's history of supporting Habyarimana's regime, the RPF continued to object to the presence of French troops in Rwanda; the RPF viewed Operation Turquoise not as a humanitarian mission but as an attempt by the French Government to prevent the RPF securing outright victory in the civil war. In early July a war of words developed, with both France and the RPF demanding that the other not interfere in its mission. The media, sensing the potential for actual conflict between the two, reported this mini-crisis enthusiastically. Notably, despite the media cynicism of Operation Turquoise only a few weeks earlier, it was the French who the press now portrayed as the heroes in this drama; French soldiers were suddenly lauded for their attempts to protect refugees from what was quite incorrectly implied to be the advancing and villainous RPF. For example, Sam Kiley wrote in *The Times*, 'French forces came under attack from the Rwandan Patriotic Front yesterday during an operation to rescue the Front's own Tutsi supporters'.[3]

This particular angle was part of a noticeable shift in reporting that suddenly started presenting the Hutu as victims and the Tutsi-dominated RPF as the aggressor. Whether this was because journalists in the west now saw first hand the suffering of Hutu refugees, without having previously been inside Rwanda to see the treatment of Tutsi over the last few months, or because of deliberate media efforts to achieve some level of objectivity in reporting the crisis is not clear; the eminent journalist Martin Bell suggests it may have been the latter.[4] Either way, having reported the atrocities committed by the Hutu militia since April, the media now seemed desperate to identify and report examples of Tutsi violence, almost as if editors could not believe that only one side was committing atrocities. Mark Doyle, who reported for the BBC, for example recalls, 'I used to take regular calls from BBC editors in London asking me to make sure that I "put the other side". The implication, of course, was that the RPF must be killing as many as the Interahamwe and the Government army and I should be reporting this.'[5] The print media similarly assumed that the RPF must either be carrying out revenge atrocities or would do so as soon as it reached areas where Hutu control had been strong. Robert Block, on the front page of the *Independent*, for example, was not exceptional in portraying the Tutsi as vengeful killers:

> To the east an angry rebel army pressed ahead with its offensive ... The speed of the assault on Butare [Rwanda's second city] led to a daring French mission yesterday to evacuate 600 Rwandan orphans and displaced children, and 100 nuns and priests ... Hutus in Government controlled areas say the RPF is killing Hutus in retribution for attacks on the minority Tutsi population ... Desperate [Hutu] men begged rides from journalists and French troops as they left the city.[6]

The specific mention of orphans and nuns – the clichéd epitome of innocence – was surely deliberate on Block's part and acted only to reinforce in the reader's mind the victim status of the Hutu and the inhumane barbarity of the RPF. As a whole the press seemed to be salivating over the prospect of further violence that they would be on hand to witness; there seemed an almost delightful anticipation that 'If Kigali falls there will be massacres'.[7] Of course this reporting was largely responsible for why, only a few weeks later, the public would so fundamentally misunderstand the refugee crisis. Remembering this reporting, most people would assume the Hutu were the victims of the genocide, not the perpetrators.

This was heightened further by the media's sudden sympathy for the suffering of the Hutu refugees that were beginning to flee westwards. Newspapers continued to depict Rwanda as war ravaged and unstable but there was a definite shift in the second week of July away from reporting the war to reporting the impending refugee crisis: 'Hundreds of thousands of people are fleeing a rebel offensive in northwest Rwanda, creating a fresh humanitarian crisis';[8] 'The first wave of refugees stripped the crops from the fields. Those following behind must often make do with roots, bulbs and leaves that make them sick.'[9] Suddenly, and for the first time, the more empathetic word 'refugee' became more prevalent in the press than 'rebel', 'troops' or 'soldier'.[10] This change in language reminded readers of the humanity of the Hutu victims. The reporting of the refugees' suffering demonstrated that Hutu were more like us, they were somehow less foreign and their suffering and hunger could be understood – all factors which would make some form of bystander response more likely.[11] It also gave the reader the impression that the Hutu were in no way responsible for the position they found themselves in, another factor which increased the likelihood of people back in the UK empathising with the suffering.[12] The change in language implied that the Tutsi, who had been murdered in April to June at the height of the civil war, were responsible for their own fate; the Hutu refugees, on the other hand, demanded sympathy as the trauma they were experiencing was not of their making. Of course, the absolute opposite was the truth.

This shift added to the confusion of the reporting of the overall crisis. As McNulty suggests, in the eyes of the Western media consumer, Rwanda was a collection of separate crises: there had been a civil war, a massacre, refugees were in Tanzania, then bodies washed up on the shores of Lake Victoria, then in July the war was being won by the rebels and there were yet more refugees.[13]

Newspaper readers, and television viewers even more so, could be easily excused for not really understanding the crisis and whether it was the Hutu or Tutsi who were the victims, or indeed both or neither – maybe they were as bad as each other. As both Mike Woolridge and Fergal Keane suggest is typical of reporting of Africa,[14] journalists failed to contextualise the various elements of the crisis in their reporting; instead the media consumer was presented with unlinked 'snapshots' and the dominant snapshot by the middle of July – and the one that would have the most impact on the public – was of the suffering Hutu. Over the next few weeks this became even more apparent as the Goma refugee crisis unfolded.

From around 17 July the reporting of Rwanda changed completely, the focus was now entirely on the refugee crisis in the Zaire border town of Goma. Fearing the advance of the RPF, huge swathes of the Hutu population, including the genocidal militia and the army, moved westwards en-masse, stopping first in the French safe zone and then travelling further west into Zaire, particularly to Goma. As many as one million Hutu became refugees in the second half of July. This mass movement of people again made Rwanda front-page news in the UK; in the week 18 to 24 July the crisis appeared on the front page of the *Guardian* five times, the *Independent* three times and even the *Evening Standard* once (the first time that the *Standard* led with Rwanda since the first week of genocide back in April).[15] The refugee story was also extensively covered on television news, partly because it was so easy for journalists to travel to the refugee camps and also because the images of refugees struggling to survive in the barren volcanic landscape of east Zaire made strikingly good television. The influx of journalists to the region was also, as Mark Colvin of the Australian Broadcasting Corporation points out, facilitated by aid agencies who practised a policy of actively encouraging journalists to cover the story so as to generate public awareness.[16] The academic Susan Moeller acknowledges the same point; she recalls one television image that demonstrated the sudden influx of journalists to Goma: 'One showed Rwandans dying somewhere near Goma. The camera panned out toward ten other cameras surrounding and filming the dying.'[17] There would eventually be over five hundred journalists of various nationalities based in Goma, whilst the number in Rwanda remained very low, never rising much above a couple of dozen.

Two particular aspects are evident in the reporting of this period; both fall into what can be described as the media's tendency to report Africa through 'ready recourse to cliché'.[18] First is the frequent description of the crisis as being biblical, which rather unhelpfully is fairly typical of reporting Africa. *The Times*, for example, described the crisis as being an exodus of 'biblical proportions' on 20 July;[19] on 23 July the *Guardian* in a leading article wrote, 'The hell fires are burning in Goma';[20] and the *Daily Mail* employed perhaps the most exaggerated of the biblical clichés with the headline 'Exodus of Lost Tribe: Refugee Scenes of Biblical Proportions Overwhelm Aid Effort'.[21] Such language had the potential to distort the public, and indeed politicians', understanding of the crisis. Words such as 'exodus' and 'lost tribe' were far from neutral; instead they portrayed one side as the innocent victims and the other as aggressors. The choice of words recalled the story of Moses leading the Israelites to freedom pursued by their former Egyptian enslavers – this kind of reporting easily led to the incorrect assumption that the Hutu were the wronged party fleeing the murderous Tutsi. To represent the movement of Hutu across Rwanda, escaping the pursuing RPF as being in any way similar to the Moses story was, of course, to ignore the previous months of history when the Hutu had been enacting savage genocide on the Tutsi minority. The media ignored this immediate history and projected the Hutu refugees very much in the role of innocent and powerless victims suffering their own hell. Ibrahim Seaga Shaw also argues that describing events in these biblical terms, which he points out was also the case in the reporting of the 1984 Ethiopian famine, strips the human responsibility from the crisis.[22] Such a differentiation is incredibly significant in terms of stimulating some form of public response: the public consistently shows itself more willing to respond to natural disasters, or 'acts of God' (such as droughts, famines, earthquakes) than to manmade disasters such as civil war. Rather than being a self-inflicted disaster Rwanda had become one that must have divine causes and one therefore likely to stimulate a bystander response.

The second aspect of the reporting in this period is entirely in line with the findings of the report by the charity VSO, *Live Aid Legacy* (written in 2001 and therefore partly informed by events in Rwanda). The main conclusion of the report was headed 'starving children with flies in their eyes' and found that 'the British public strongly associate the developing world with doom-laden images of famine, disaster and Western aid ... these images are still top of our minds and maintain a powerful grip on the British psyche'.[23] It was these doom-laden images of starving children that were to dominate the reporting of Rwanda in late July. The coverage started with stories of families separated in the flow of refugees; one article in the *Independent* was fairly typical of the heart-wrenching stories that journalists were witnessing in Goma and choosing to report:

> Children ran screaming in terror, tears pouring down their cheeks. Women desperately cried out the names of the children they had lost in the pandemonium ... A man wandered hopelessly in the crowd with a piece of paper mounted on a stick. It gave his name and said: 'Reward of 500 Rwandan francs offered for anyone who finds my eight-year-old son, Gashore.'[24]

Despite being written three months after the start of the genocide, this was one of the first articles in which a journalist quoted a Rwandan's name; if coverage of the genocide was completely depersonalised, the reporting of the refugee crisis was evidently more human. This focus on the dead and the dying soon completely dominated the Rwanda coverage and in many reports the focus was on children or babies. Two articles from the *Daily Mail* were fairly representative: '[M]ore than 100 lay dead in the dust. One baby slept beside the bloodstained body of her mother';[25] and 'One young boy had a baby strapped to his back who was clearly close to death. A flicker of life appeared in the infant's eyes after a Red Cross nurse went along the row of seven children, slowly pouring water into their mouths.'[26] The almost inevitable outbreak of cholera in the camps, when it came, around 20 July, only heightened the lack of balance in the reporting. For example, one article in the *Independent* ran, 'Out of a refugee population of 1 million [a cholera epidemic] would mean 5,000 to 10,000 deaths within days. Cholera can kill in hours. One refugee family said their son died within two hours of falling ill'[27] – there was no mention in any article of the fact that the average *daily* death toll during the genocide had in some weeks exceeded 10,000. This reporting, that time and time again centred on the suffering of the children, heightened the empathy readers felt for the Hutu refugees and reinforced the status of Hutu as victims. Only a handful of times did the press recall, or try to explain, the horror of the genocide in which many of these same Hutu, children included, had participated.

Television coverage was not much different. A study by the Glasgow Media Group focuses on the portrayal of the refugee crisis on television in late July. The study shows that television reports from Central Africa were double in July what they had been in April and May at the peak of the genocide. More significantly the study notes that, although a lack of context in the coverage of wars and humanitarian crises is not unusual, there was an almost *complete* failure of the television news to contextualise and explain this particular crisis. The study concludes:

> The media were drawn to the images of chaos and death in Goma, which were so compelling for their audiences, but there was much less coverage of what had caused the exodus to Goma and what had happened to Rwanda's Tutsi people ... Many British viewers – who had no previous knowledge of Central Africa – saw little or nothing of the genocide, but were given very extensive coverage of the refugee crisis.[28]

Drawing on his own experience, George Alagiah, the first BBC journalist to report from Goma, reaches similar conclusions. He recalls working eighteen-hour days in order to 'feed the beast that is the newsroom on a headline story' and of deliberating whether to present the 'exodus as primarily a humanitarian or political problem';[29] he opted for humanitarian. Unlike most in the media, Alagiah accepts that with hindsight this decision was wrong; he publicly admits that he 'lost the plot' when from 20 July he began for a week to concentrate on the risk of cholera in the camps. For at least a week in the print media and on television, Alagiah says, 'the genocide was forgotten, and cholera became the story. That was all the newsroom wanted to know about. How were they treating it? How did it spread? What could Britain do to help?'[30] Like the newspapers, television news gave the impression of Hutu as victims, without much regard for the recent past.

Due to the shift in emphasis, the coverage of the refugee crisis, unlike that of the genocide, did indeed very quickly fall into the CNN effect model, or at least its first two stages: coverage of suffering led to media criticism of government, which led to widespread calls for actions. Greg Philo records, for example, that in the six days to 21 July the British television news contained twenty-eight references which were critical of the Western relief effort, far in excess of the total number seen during the whole of the genocide period.[31] Newspaper coverage was similarly critical and demanding of some form of response with all the majors calling for more to be done and most also providing readers with details of how to donate to the various charitable appeals. The press also reported calls from Labour and the Liberal Democrats for Britain to do something. In response to this change in media coverage, for the first time ministers found themselves having to publicly defend Government policy. Baroness Chalker informed journalists that Britain had offered support to Operation Turquoise and was providing financial aid,[32] and Malcolm Rifkind told the press, 'Britain could "hold its head high" over its contributions to alleviate the suffering'.[33]

Whilst the same could not have been said of the genocide, the press was unanimous in calling for a response to the refugee crisis; as the *Independent* suggested, 'The moral imperative to help is clear'.[34] The refugee crisis, and its media coverage in particular, raised public awareness of Rwanda as nothing had before. Douglas Hurd may argue that this coverage did not force Britain to respond as it eventually would, but by late July and for the first time, the Government was being held accountable for its action, or inaction. Press coverage and the public response meant Rwanda could no longer be ignored. However, although there was of course a humanitarian imperative to alleviate the suffering of the Hutu refugees, the public and media calls for action were based on a misinformed understanding of the crisis. The months of ignorance of what was happening in Rwanda led to the widespread belief that Hutu were the victims and Tutsi the aggressors.

Parliament

It would be misleading to claim that Rwanda was a major issue in either the Commons or the Lords in July (Parliament went into summer recess on 21 July, around the time cholera was beginning to spread in Goma), but it was debated orally more than it had been previously and it did receive more attention than Bosnia in late June and into July.[35] The crisis was raised at questions to the Foreign Secretary, questions to the Secretary of State for Defence and Prime Minister's questions, as well as in the House of Lords. Despite, or possibly because of, this level of debate, the Labour front bench continued to be refused permission from the Speaker 'on an almost daily basis' to demand a formal statement on Rwanda from the Government.[36] During these first three weeks of July the nature of the parliamentary discussion also changed slightly; as in the media, there was a noticeable increase in MPs now calling for more to be done in response to the crisis.

The parliamentary debate can be split into two separate categories: first calls for the UN response to be speeded up; and, secondly suggestions that the UK itself should be responding more robustly. In respect of the UN mission the dominant view in the Commons continued to be that the UN had prime responsibility for the crisis. There was clear frustration that despite the approval of UNAMIR II nothing seemed to be happening in terms of troop deployment. Tony Worthington asked in a written question on 20 July, for example, 'what are the principal causes of the further delay in the deployment of UN troops in Rwanda?'[37] A week earlier Jack Cunningham, the Shadow Foreign Secretary, had similarly asked at the monthly FCO questions:

> The United Nations agreed a force for Rwanda, but did not agree its deployment. Now that its deployment has been agreed, we are told that it has been held up because of lack of logistical support from Western countries. Why is further delay occurring? ... We want to know from Foreign Office Ministers whether it is lack of capability or lack of political will that is preventing the United Nations from getting its act together.[38]

Implicit in Cunningham's question was the suggestion that the Government should be providing more logistical support than the fifty trucks already offered. In the same debate Worthington made Labour's point explicit: 'Surely the Minister realises that fifty trucks are wholly inadequate as supplementary logistical support'.[39] Conservative MPs were also frustrated by the UN, but as would be expected were less critical of the Government's record. Peter Luff (Conservative, Worcester), for example, suggested responsibility for resourcing UNAMIR II lay with countries with closer links to Rwanda, 'Does he [the Secretary of State for Defence] also understand that, against the background of the many demands on British forces around the world, there is general support for the view that Francophone countries should take prime responsibility for the situation in Rwanda?'[40]

The second aspect of the debate, suggestions that Britain should be more involved in the response to the crisis, was less evident and generally fell into three categories: Britain should provide more logistical support; Britain should press for those committing genocide to be punished; and Britain, through NGOs, should provide more aid to Rwandan refugees. Labour backbenchers continued to press the Government on the issue of logistical support; Worthington alone asked questions on five occasions on logistics in the three weeks to 21 July. In terms of calls for justice these came from both Houses and were led by the Liberal Democrats. In the Commons, Simon Hughes (Liberal Demomcrat,

Southwark) asked, 'Given the [UN's] finding that genocide has been perpetrated in Rwanda, can [the Foreign Secretary] assure the House that all responsible for it will speedily be brought to justice by the relevant international authorities?'[41] In the Lords, Hughes' colleague Lord Avebury went further by suggesting the Government call upon the UN to invoke the Genocide Convention to punish those responsible for the genocide.[42]

It was the final area of increasing aid to Rwanda and Rwandan refugees that received most cross-bench support and also most support from the front benches of both Labour and Liberal Democrats. Andrew Rowe (Conservative, Mid-Kent), for example, called for assurances from the ODA that NGOs working in Zaire would receive 'every possible assistance as quickly as possible'.[43] It was Labour and the Liberal Democrat MPs who seemed most attentive to the refugee crisis. Simon Hughes recalled the Government's donations to other crises before calling for money for Rwanda to be 'forthcoming';[44] Paddy Ashdown (Leader of the Liberal Democrats) on 19 July used the opportunity of PMQs to ask about Rwanda;[45] and Shadow Cabinet member Tom Clarke reminded the Government that tens of thousands of lives were at risk in Zaire and that 'humanitarian intervention on a massive scale is now absolutely necessary'.[46] In private correspondence with the Foreign Secretary, Jack Cunningham repeated these calls, writing, 'I urge the British Government to take the lead in actively and generously supporting the humanitarian effort'.[47]

The number of questions relating to the refugee crisis is indicative of how MPs generally interpreted the overall Rwandan crisis. Parliament, like the media, emphasised the refugee crisis over the genocide, the humanitarian over the political. As one MP suggested, MPs thought the response needed to be through aid, rather than focused on trying to solve the region's political problems.[48]

The aid community's response

Given the close relationship between the ODA and NGOs in this period and the fact that much of the ODA's funding was channelled through British NGOs, it is appropriate here to explore the response of both together. Through the ODA the British Government continued in July, August and September to be heavily involved in addressing the humanitarian crisis both in Rwanda and in neighbouring countries. In terms of pure financial aid, on 27 July Peter Burton, head of the disaster unit in the ODA, informed contacts at the US Embassy in London that UK aid to Rwanda at this stage stood at £18 million bilaterally, as well as £22 million of assistance being channelled through EU programmes.[49] During her visit to Rwanda on 29 July, Baroness Chalker announced a further £10 million of aid, bringing the total British contribution to £50 million since the beginning of April. By the end of August, this had increased by a further £10 million to £60 million.

The British Government can rightly claim to have done more than most to relieve the suffering of Rwandans. This nevertheless does not stop Melvern and Williams from dismissing the Major Government's claims that 'it was doing more [in Rwanda] than many states, with the inference that it was therefore somehow absolved of guilt' for failing to stop the genocide. For a permanent member of the UN Security Council to justify its response by comparison 'to the lowest common denominator', they suggest, 'is patently absurd'.[50] This claim sadly ignores the fact that Britain was far from the lowest common denominator; all told the UK would be the fourth largest aid donor to the crisis in Rwanda, behind the US, EU (to which the UK was again one of the largest contributors) and Japan.[51] To dismiss this funding, which undoubtedly saved many thousands of lives, is absurd.

In terms of using the donated monies, on 16 July three chartered planes left the UK carrying aid for refugees in Zaire. The first, a huge Antonov 124, carried eleven trucks; the other two carried eighty tons of plastic sheeting, tents and blankets for use in the growing refugee camps.[52] The ODA continued to fund the hire of two of these planes for the United Nations High Commissioner for Refugees (UNHCR) to use for a period of one month. Additionally, ODA logistics experts travelled to Zaire to assist UN staff with the distribution of food and equipment, and the team that had been managing the airport in Mwanza (Tanzania) also redeployed to Goma in response to the crisis there. At the request of UNHCR, a second ODA airfield cargo-handling team was also deployed to Entebbe (Uganda) in late July.

By mid August the ODA increasingly believed that the best solution to the crisis was for the refugees to return to Rwanda and British aid was refocused towards achieving this aim. The US ambassador to London reported a conversation he had with Baroness Chalker, who by this time had travelled to Rwanda herself:

> [she said] she had visited many refugee camps throughout the world but had never seen anything as horrendous as the Rwandan refugee camps at Goma. It was 'like the middle ages' with thousands of bodies wrapped in blankets left along the roads. She returned to London even more determined to take action to encourage refugees to return to Rwanda.[53]

Consequently, the British bilateral aid effort shifted its focus to Kigali rather than Goma; this was a deliberate attempt to improve conditions in Rwanda itself so as to encourage refugees home. Chalker also remained conscious of the potential for the refugee situation to worsen once Operation Turquoise withdrew from south-west Rwanda at the end of August. Therefore, £3.5 million of ODA funding was targeted at supporting NGO and UN programmes in that region.[54] As well as funding emergency relief – food, water and sanitation – the ODA's activities in Rwanda were concentrated on three broad priorities: encouraging reconciliation through the use of mass media, mainly radio (broadcasting equipment was purchased from the BBC to assist with this); providing a kick start to the economy; and supporting the new administration's structure and systems. In terms of the third area an ODA assessment team, for example, recognised that the new Rwandan Minister of Health was working out of a hotel room with no equipment or transportation; £120,000 of ODA money was therefore channelled into purchasing office equipment and vehicles for the Minister.[55]

The ODA was clear that it did not intend to become involved in long-term reconstruction or development work in Rwanda.[56] By the end of September the ODA concluded that the emergency crisis was over in Rwanda and therefore the provision of aid could be wound down. Of course at this stage many thousands of Rwandans were still either refugees in Zaire or internally displaced in their own country but, as ODA officials told American diplomats, '[the] ODA has no plans at this point to engage in rehabilitation programs since it has never had a country program in Rwanda'.[57] Once the emergency humanitarian crisis was over, Rwanda, for a while at least, slipped back to being the small country far away.

Compared to the ODA's rather structured view of how to assist and rebuild Rwanda, the NGO response as a whole was a lot more frantic and certainly more influenced by media coverage and public interest. The head of the charity Feed the Children recalled, 'By early July our supporters were calling to say what were we doing? We are responsive to the wishes and intentions of our supporters. We don't want to let them down.'[58] What ensued was what can best be called the 'Scramble for Rwanda', as thousands of aid workers flocked to the region, mainly to Zaire. Over one hundred separate NGOs would eventually turn up to 'help' in Goma. Nicholas Stockton describes Goma as being 'awash with the modern symbols of international aid: T-shirts, car stickers and flags'. With so many NGOs in Goma, he continues, they 'all clamoured for television coverage and made claims about what could be achieved, some of which were indeed outrageous'.[59] In such a crush of aid workers, NGOs fought to ensure they did not miss any opportunity for publicity; Oxfam, for example, had its name painted six feet high on water tanks in one refugee camp and ensured they were used as a backdrop for television reports. CARE UK acknowledges that it 'had never received media coverage like that before'.[60]

The extensive coverage of NGOs combined with ongoing and sympathetic media reporting certainly appears to have influenced public donations to the aid campaigns. The level of donations to the DEC demonstrate this: donations peaked twice, first in May at the height of the refugee crisis in Tanzania (£1.8 million) and then in August at the height of the Goma crisis a massive £5.1 million was received.[61] By November, when immediate interest in Rwanda had dropped and media coverage was negligible, donations reduced to a mere £0.3 million. Similarly John Grain, who logged credit card donations for Oxfam, noted that donations 'mirrored almost exactly the ebbs and flows of TV and tabloid coverage of Rwanda: May 1,000 calls, June 134, July 6,000 (the largest ever response to an appeal in a month), August 2,500, September 100'.[62] As Feed the Children was also to recall, after some weeks the media lost interest in

Rwanda and 'the money dried up immediately. It was like turning off a tap.'[63] The evidence from Rwanda is that public awareness and media coverage are linked. As Knecht and Weatherford acknowledge, 'there is solid research evidence showing that national news coverage heavily influences citizens' perceived salience of political issues'.[64] It also demonstrates a weakness in the existing CNN effect model: images of atrocities alone are not sufficient to move the public, there must also be sympathy for the victims. Clearly, the public actively responded to the suffering refugees yet largely ignored the victims of genocide.

The fairly substantial funding channelled through them by the ODA on top of the generosity of the public meant British NGOs were able to play a significant role in the humanitarian relief in the region. The following is a description of just some of the many and varied activities performed by British NGOs. In July, fearing the imminent flow of refugees, Oxfam used £400,000 of its own reserve funds to preposition water pumps and pipes in Goma. The Oxfam infrastructure was sufficient to provide water to 50,000 people, and therefore quite inadequate in terms of the eventual exodus of refugees to Goma, but it did provide emergency relief in the first few days until more equipment could be shipped over from the UK and thus averted many deaths.[65] Also in Goma, ActionAid responded to the difficulties of the rather mundane but absolutely vital task of digging toilets in the volcanic rock by shipping heavy plant from Scotland and operating this in the camps. Seeing the overload of agencies in Goma, Save the Children UK unusually decided to operate only in Rwanda and developed a role in two very specific areas. Firstly, it worked with UNICEF to support the Ministry of Family and Rehabilitation in Rwanda with regard to protecting women's rights; traditionally women were not able to own land in Rwanda and therefore the death of their husbands in the genocide led to many women having their claim to property questioned. Secondly, Save the Children took the lead role in reuniting parents and children separated during the genocide and refugee exoduses. Save the Children also provided training to Rwandans so this work could be carried on once its involvement reduced.[66]

Despite their efforts, there have been numerous criticisms of the NGO community's response to the crisis. For example, some have question whether aid should have been given so freely to the perpetrators of genocide; but as a CARE UK spokesperson articulated 'Our remit is to provide humanitarian assistance [to anyone who needs it]. That is what we do'.[67] There has also been criticism that NGOs did not understand the history of Rwanda and this ignorance of the political dimensions of the crisis meant many aid workers gave misleading and misinformed interviews to the media. Comments by one aid worker, for example, about how his daily routine involved helping hungry Hutu who faced the dilemma of remaining in the refugee camp and risking cholera, or returning to Rwanda and the prospect of a being killed by the Tutsi army, simply misrepresented the crisis.[68] Finally, NGOs have been criticised for focusing overly on Goma and therefore having the dual effect of locking Hutu into a life of dependency on foreign aid and also of prolonging the conflict by giving aid to FAR soldiers, who continued to launch cross-border attacks for a number of months. As Andy Storey highlights, in 1994 only '35.3 per cent of all aid had been allocated for use within Rwanda ... By September 1995, twenty times more aid had gone to refugees outside the country than to support refugee resettlement within Rwanda'.[69] Save the Children UK, which as noted above chose to work in Rwanda, argued the availability of aid in Goma deterred ordinary Hutu refugees from returning home, something that the British Government considered key if the crisis was to be solved rather than simply fixed with the temporary sticking plaster of emergency food and water.[70] These criticisms, though, are far from unique to British NGOs. Clearly there were weaknesses in the response, the NGOs did become overly media focused and there was no overriding strategy on how to solve the crisis rather than simply manage it; like the media and Parliament, NGOs ignored the political issues. But that said, British aid and British NGOs also clearly saved very many lives.

The Government's military response

In the same way that media and parliamentary debate picked up in July, consideration of Rwanda also increased within Government – but there is limited evidence that the latter was a result of the former. In addition to the financial aid that the Government had been donating by now for a number of months, in late July the Prime Minister, some would say finally, authorised the deployment of British troops. The military deployment would become known as Operation Gabriel and British troops would, at their peak, make up the second largest contingent within UNAMIR II, with some six hundred troops deployed out of UNAMIR's total strength of just over five thousand. The troops were to prove essential to the UN mission, providing much-needed logistical, engineering and medical support which UNAMIR simply did not have. As the FCO recognised, the British soldiers 'filled in the gap until UN contractors [Brown & Root] were able to come on line'.[71]

The decision in principle to deploy troops was taken on 28 July and the formal directive issued three days later; the first troops deployed within hours of this directive, on 1 August. The exact chronology of the decision-making process is slightly unclear. UNAMIR II had been approved by the Security Council on 16 May; at that stage the UK, and other Western states, were asked only what *equipment* they could provide. On 18 May the UN Secretary General made requests for *troops* to African states only.[72] A month later, on 15 June, when Britain offered the fifty Bedford trucks, the UN had still not requested the British Government provide actual soldiers.[73] The first mention of a UN request for British troops, in the documents made available to the author under Freedom on Information, appeared a month later still in a letter from Douglas Hurd's private secretary to Malcolm Rifkind's military secretary at the MOD. It was dated 12 July and read:

> There has been no response to the UN Secretary General's request for logistical support, so the UN propose to award a contract to the US contractors, Brown and Root ... The Foreign Secretary proposes that, in response to the UN's request, the UK should offer a REME [Royal Electrical and Mechanical Engineers] company and workshop to UNAMIR for about 8–10 weeks to cover the gap before the UN contractors are brought in.[74]

Unfortunately, there is not any publicly available evidence to support this, but presumably the UN would have made an approach to the British Government a few days before the 12 July letter. Notably the MOD did not initially agree with Hurd, and a letter was sent to Hurd rejecting his proposal. But just a week later, Hurd and Rifkind met. At the meeting the Foreign Secretary questioned whether his original 'REME idea should be shelved' as 'life has now moved on' and it was agreed by both Ministers that the possibility of doing something in Rwanda should be investigated. It was decided that a military official, posing as a civilian, would therefore accompany Baroness Chalker on her visit to the region departing on 24 July.[75] Between 10 and 24 July the Government's position had effectively moved from giving no thought to an actual troop deployment to actively evaluating options – a week clearly is a long time in politics.

At the same time as Chalker departed for Uganda on Sunday 24 July, the MOD's Current Operations Group met in Whitehall. Chaired by Rear Admiral Brian Goodson (Assistant Chief of Defence Staff) and attended by Brigadier Simon Pack (Director of Defence Commitments – Middle East and Africa) and Glyne Evans (Head of the UN Department at FCO), the group met to 'develop an outline list of military options for the provision of assistance in Rwanda'.[76] The fact that the committee met on a Sunday is an indication that the plan to deploy British troops was really picking up momentum, suggesting it had support, or at least interest, at senior levels of Government. It is also noteworthy that a section of the record of this meeting was redacted before release under the Freedom of Information Act 'as it contains information supplied by the Security Services'.[77] Given the redacted section runs to no more than two sentences, the conspiracy theorists' claims that MI6 was actively engaged in the Rwandan conflict, discussed earlier, again seem questionable. After a meeting, which the minutes suggest was fairly brief, the Current Operations Group concluded that a recommendation should be made to the Chief of Defence Staff that British troops be deployed to Rwanda with a stipulated date for withdrawal; a caveat that, given other military commitments, was central to the proposal. The recommendation was then discussed at a meeting between the Chief of Defence Staff and the Secretary of State Malcolm Rifkind at 8 a.m. on Monday 25 July, where it was agreed that, pending a formal request from the FCO, the MOD would approve the deployment of troops.[78] Lieutenant Colonel Mike Wharmby, who would command the British element, was informed of the possible deployment at 1.30 that same day. On 27 July, following discussions with the UN and reports back from Colonel Joscelyne (presumably the officer who, in disguise, had accompanied Chalker to Rwanda), Glyne Evans wrote to the Foreign Secretary advising that the 'UN are enthusiastic about a possible British offer to UNAMIR. We now need to make a formal response.'[79] The following day, 28 July, the Foreign Secretary received approval from the Cabinet Subcommittee on Overseas Policy and Defence, to make the formal offer to the UN;[80] the first British troops deployed to Rwanda just three days later.

The evolution of the decision

As this chronology shows, the decision to deploy troops evolved very quickly. The Government moved from a position of not considering any form of troop deployment in late June, to actually deploying over six hundred just a few weeks later. To understand how this decision evolved, we need to look separately at the two ministries involved.

The Foreign Office

From the FCO's perspective the key question is why ministers and officials suddenly on 12 July recommended a deployment of British troops – why did they want the UK to move from being an almost passive bystander to suggesting some form of humanitarian intervention? A clear understanding of why the position changed would after all go a long way to explaining the general question of what motivates intervention. Unfortunately, despite numerous Freedom of Information requests by the author, none of the documents released to date fully and adequately explains this shift, perhaps underlining Paul Williams' claim that the foreign policy making 'process remains among the most secret in government',[81] or alternatively demonstrating not all decisions are fully documented. From interviews and the documents that have been made available we are, though, able to piece together an understanding of the key changes in policy makers' thinking that led to the shift.

The first point of note is that the decision seems to have been made in the FCO without serious discussion with its subsidiary organisation the ODA. In 1994 the ODA was an agency of the FCO rather than an independent department in its own right, as it would become in 1997 under Tony Blair's Labour Government. The ODA, and its minister Baroness Chalker, was generally responsible for Britain's relations with sub-Saharan Africa, with the exception of South Africa; the FCO retained responsibility for British relations with the UN, including all peacekeeping missions. Given its interest in, and knowledge of, Africa, an outsider would perhaps expect the ODA to have been consulted about the decision to send troops to Rwanda; this does not appear to have been the case. Instead bureaucratic parochialism meant the FCO took responsibility for decision making with limited, if any, recourse to the ODA, an organisation that on-paper at least should have been more knowledgeable about Rwanda. The report by the Joint Evaluation of the Emergency Assistance to Rwanda Committee, for example, records that 'On 25 July, the Head of the Emergency Aid Department in the ODA informed his counterpart at the OFDA [the US Office for Foreign Disaster Assistance] in Washington that the UK was *not planning* to send a military contingent to Rwanda' (emphasis added).[82] Given the close military links between the US and UK it seems unlikely that this demonstrates a deliberate reluctance to share information with the Americans. It might not be a surprise that an ODA official, albeit a fairly senior one, was not aware that that very morning the Secretary of State for Defence had approved the mission, but the claim that the UK was not even *planning* to send troops suggests a remoteness from the decision-making process and the discussions that had already taken place within the FCO and MOD. Notably, no one from the ODA attended the MOD's Current Operations Group meeting of 24 July, again suggesting a remoteness from the decision-making process. As further evidence of the ODA's lack of involvement, a telegram of 22 July from David Hannay in New York to Baroness Chalker includes a paragraph that begins, 'Separately we have received an informal request [from the UN Secretariat] to examine the possibility of making available to UNAMIR a company sized REME unit'.[83] It would seem odd for Hannay to inform Chalker of this a whole ten days after Douglas Hurd had written to Malcolm Rifkind about the same UN request, unless Chalker had not up to this point been involved in the decision. Despite this evidence, Chalker does suggest that she tried to influence some sort of Government response. She recalls, 'I kept saying privately in the Foreign Office "Can't we do something, they are mad with killing"'.[84] It seems, though, that the decision to recommend sending troops to Rwanda was ultimately made in the FCO proper, and therefore presumably by Douglas Hurd, rather than in the ODA.

The second point of note is that, despite the arguments of proponents of the CNN effect, in this case the media do not appear to have been a major influence on FCO policy making. Clearly, politicians and FCO officials will have been aware of the media coverage and it was against this backdrop that decisions were taken; however, it seems highly unlikely that it was news coverage that triggered the decision to propose sending troops. Whilst John Major was reputedly shocked into responding to the Kurdish crisis in 1991 after watching the Sunday morning news,[85] there seems to have been no such identifiable turning point in respect of Rwanda. A review of the ITN archive, for example, shows that there was only one story on Rwanda on the ITV news in the week prior to Douglas Hurd's 12 July letter.[86] Although it has not been possible to confirm all the coverage that appeared on the BBC news, the research by Georgina Holmes on *Newsnight*'s coverage of the genocide suggests that Rwanda was covered on the programme on

4 July (when Hurd was in Geneva)[87] and then next on 15 July, three days after the letter was sent.[88] BBC's *Panorama* programme on 27 June had been a half-hour special report by Fergal Keane on Rwanda;[89] this programme went on to win the prestigious Royal Television International Current Affairs Award but at the time of airing it received no contemporary newspaper coverage. It would again seem hard to draw a direct line from this programme to Hurd's letter, written over two weeks later. Nor is there anything of particular note in the print media in the week preceding Hurd's letter to Rifkind; indeed, it was only after Hurd's letter that media coverage of Rwanda again picked up, this time focused on Goma. There was, then, no one obvious trigger media story that outraged politicians into action and nor, as we have seen, is Hurd – opposed to the general idea of intervention as he is – the sort who would have responded to the few stories in the media which predicted the imminent Goma crisis.

If it was not the media that influenced the decision to send troops, what then did? In response to the author's question of why there was a change of heart about sending troops, Malcolm Rifkind replied, 'It was not so much a change of heart, but by that time the full horrors had become evident ... When it became clear that it was not just killing but genocide there was a realisation that we should do something to assist.'[90] He continued that if there was to be a significant intervention it was likely that the UK, given what the Conservative Party called '[Britain's] unique place in the world's affairs',[91] would not have wanted to be outside of that: 'We would probably have looked to be involved in a major initiative in some way'.[92] Hurd might have regularly suggested that the UK was not going as far as to 'volunteer to be an international policeman'[93] but Rifkind's comment supports the view, widely held in the Conservative Party, that Britain's position as a permanent member of the Security Council, as a prominent member of NATO and as a leading industrial nation gave it some responsibility to be part of major international interventions. This claim is of course contradicted by the UK's initial reluctance to contribute to UNAMIR II and the refusal to become involved in Operation Turquoise (though, as we have seen, this can be explained by suspicion of French motives), but it does suggest that the Government's decision to support intervention was partially driven by a perception of duties incumbent upon Britain given its position on the international stage.[94] David Hannay makes a similar point when he claims, 'we actively encouraged African nations to contribute troops [to UNAMIR], but how would this have looked if we offered nothing – we had to do something ourselves.'[95]

The Hurd letter of 12 July looks most likely to have been triggered by a direct request from the UN for British troops. Although there is no direct evidence of this, the 12 July letter makes reference to a request and we do know just a few days later a public Security Council presidential statement called 'upon Member States to provide the necessary contributions in order to ensure the deployment of the expanded UNAMIR in the immediate future'.[96] The view within the FCO that the UK ought to be involved in major humanitarian interventions and the private and public requests for contributions to UNAMIR look the most likely catalysts for Hurd to write his letter to Rifkind. It was, then, less moral obligation to help needy Rwandans that influenced decision making and more a belief within the FCO that the UK, as a key member of the international community, had a responsibility, perhaps driven by the permanent seat on the Security Council or by some historical perception of Britain's place in the world, to contribute to the international response when asked.

The Ministry of Defence

If the change in policy happened in the FCO around 12 July, it was not until 24 July that the MOD moved to a position of supporting the deployment, having originally dismissed the suggestion ten days earlier. First of all we must acknowledge that the bureaucratic nature of government meant the MOD was unlikely to have considered a deployment to Rwanda before it was approached by the FCO. Malcolm Rifkind and William Hague, both of whom have been Foreign Secretary, agree that the FCO, not the MOD, takes the lead on any decision to offer British troops to UN missions.[97] The BBC documentary which charted the deployment of British troops to Angola in 1995 similarly demonstrates that when it comes to UN missions the MOD very much responds to the FCO, and in the case of Angola did not even anticipate the FCO's offer of troops.[98] It therefore seems reasonably certain that no one at the MOD, at least at a senior level, had seriously considered sending British troops to Rwanda until the Foreign Secretary's proposal of 12 July was received.

In a MOD minute responding to Hurd's first proposal, a number of practical and political arguments against the deployment were listed. The practical objections included firstly the fact that the deployment of a self-supporting REME company, once force protection and logistical support were factored in, would be much larger in terms of military personnel than the Foreign Secretary envisaged; secondly the observation that the REME was already overly committed; and thirdly a suggestion that it would take so long for equipment to arrive in Rwanda that it would make the mission useless.[99] In terms of political objections, the memorandum demonstrates that MOD civil servants, understandably, had less of a concern about the UK's international standing than their colleagues at the FCO. It suggested, 'The gravity of the situation in Rwanda is quite clear. It is also true that a suitable contingent of technicians could do a very useful job in maintaining vehicles ... It does not, however, follow that it is necessarily for the UK to fill this breach.'[100] The minute continued that Britain was already shouldering a heavy burden in other UN missions and that there were other countries with closer links to the region currently less committed than the UK. At the time the UK was already providing 3,668 of the UN's 73,210 deployed peacekeepers, making the UK the fourth largest troop contributor (3,240 were deployed in Bosnia, 413 in Cyprus and 15 in Kuwait).[101] A draft letter accompanying the minute, meant for Rifkind to send to the Foreign Secretary, therefore ended, 'The Secretary of

State has to conclude, with regret, that he cannot accept the Foreign Secretary's proposal'. In the final version sent to Hurd on 19 July this closing sentence was softened to 'The Defence Secretary sees significant problems with the Foreign Secretary's proposal'.[102] Despite the change in wording, this was a fairly serious disagreement at the heart of government and, as Thomas Weiss and Cindy Collins suggest, such institutionalism demonstrates how intervention does not automatically follow, even when it is the preferred option of the political decision makers, in this case the FCO.[103] It also demonstrates how cost/benefit analysis does feature significantly in bystander decision making; at this stage the MOD deemed the cost of intervention to be too high and to justify their decision MOD officials listed numerous reasons why intervention was not possible. Many of these reasons, such as the over-commitment of the REME, remained unchanged just days later when the MOD reversed its decision.

With the initial plan rejected, Hurd and Rifkind met face to face on 19 July to discuss both Rwanda and the crisis in Haiti. The official record of the meeting recalls Rifkind as having said the proposed mission to Rwanda 'would be controversial, it would put pressure on our own resources, and it would not be all that relevant to the problem as it now stood. We should only proceed if it were clearly seen to be in our national interest';[104] whether he meant 'seen' by the public and media or the Government is not clear. Something clearly would have to change before the MOD altered its position. Two things did change between 19 and 24 July that meant the MOD's cost/benefit calculation altered sufficiently that officials could support the proposed deployment.

The first, made clear at the meeting of the Current Operations Group on 24 July, was that '[in the last week the] climate for an offer of help had improved, due to a change in the security situation in Rwanda'.[105] The change in security situation referred to was the apparent and maintained peace that followed the RPF's declaration of a ceasefire on 18 July following victory in the war. Prior to 18 July Western militaries saw the situation on the ground as too dangerous. A CIA briefing paper which was exploring the possibility of some US involvement in Rwanda, for example, as late as 13 July stated, 'We believe that the military capabilities of the RPF and rogue Hutu military units could potentially pose serious threats to air operations in to Kigali'.[106] Following the downing of President Habyarimana's plane it was, of course, known that at least one side in the war had access to anti-aircraft weapons and the RPF had publicly made it clear that it would consider the UN or Western countries involving themselves in Rwanda legitimate targets if they were believed to be siding with the Hutu Government. With a ceasefire in place and the Hutu army and militias having crossed into Zaire, as well as the French forces stabilising the south-west of the country, the situation had changed. Rwanda suddenly appeared a relatively safe environment into which peacekeepers could be deployed. This removed the fear within the MOD of being 'sucked into someone else's war'.[107] The effective victory of the RPF had two other consequences. First, it meant the reopening of Kigali airport, thereby removing one of the logistical problems that the MOD had foreseen in the note of 19 July. Secondly, it meant that the Pentagon's objections to becoming involved in Rwanda reduced. Although US troops would not deploy into Rwanda in any large numbers (the US Operation Support Hope operated in Zaire, outside of UN control), the US was now willing to authorise flights into Kigali; as Operation Gabriel would be dependent on US airlift capability this was an enabling factor for the British mission. The suggestion that bystander intervention becomes more likely when the perceived costs of intervention are lower seems in this case to be accurate.

The second change was that there was suddenly political will within the British Government to support some form of deployment, or, as it was worded in one MOD letter, 'there is a growing political imperative [to act]'. Whether the MOD felt this was being driven by Parliament, the media, public opinion or the Government is not made clear in the letter[108] but at the meeting of the Current Operations Group this factor was described as 'The Government require a visible and actual presence in area'.[109] Rifkind also spelled this out to the Chief of Defence Staff, 'Presentational gestures were not on the agenda'.[110] If the British Government was going to authorise the deployment of troops, which by 24 July seemed likely, it was to be a meaningful deployment focused on providing UNAMIR with the resources that it most needed. From where this 'political will' was suddenly emanating is not clear; presumably, given that the MOD had refused the FCO's request to authorise troops on 12 July, it had to be coming from somewhere other than just the FCO. Although there is not yet publically available evidence to confirm this, nor anything in his autobiography or subsequent biographies – which all remain quiet about Rwanda – one can assume that Prime Minister John Major was now suggesting that some form of British involvement was desirable; the MOD clearly felt comfortable in rejecting a request coming from the FCO but it would be unlikely that it would so easily dismiss a request that came from Number 10. Writing generally about how the Government works, Williams, Kavanagh, Seldon and Coles all dismiss the idea that pressure on the MOD to support intervention would have come from anywhere else, other than possibly the Cabinet Subcommittee on Overseas Policy and Defence, which the Prime Minister himself chaired.[111] As has been the case in numerous interventions, there seems a high likelihood that the direct involvement of the political leader therefore positively contributed to the decision to intervene. What caused John Major suddenly to show an interest in Rwanda we do not yet know; the only evidence we have to explain the shift is Baroness Chalker's recollection that she spoke privately to John Major at some time in July.[112] Maybe hearing from the only person in government with first hand knowledge of the crisis was what moved Major, or alternatively the fact that the Current Operations Group first mentioned the change in political will at their meeting on a Sunday afternoon is *maybe* evidence, as in the case of the Kurdish crisis, that Major simply saw Rwanda on the Sunday morning news.

Operation Gabriel – financing, make up and orders

Once the decision had been made to deploy Gabriel, much of the FCO's attention shifted towards the practicalities of funding the mission. As both Rifkind's military secretary, Commander Timothy Laurence (later Vice-Admiral and Princess Anne's husband) and Douglas Hurd suggested in a BBC documentary aired in 1996, agreeing the funding of peacekeeping missions and winning the support of the Treasury was typically the hardest part of deploying troops.[113] This appears to have been no different in 1994; the difficulty is highlighted in an undated internal FCO document: 'I need hardly say that the FCO has no financial provision for this and, if the UN are not to pay within this financial year, we would have to put a case to the Chief Secretary [of the Treasury] for access to the Reserve. We are very far from being able to take his agreement for granted.'[114]

There was in the case of Rwanda a potential issue regarding the UN reimbursing Britain's costs, meaning that a drawdown of the government reserve may have been needed – by July the funds authorised by the Security Council and assigned to UNAMIR back in April had been exhausted. The cost of withdrawing the bulk of the force, and then resupplying Dallaire's rump headquarters by air meant that UNAMIR's budget was fully spent.[115] Cost and bureaucratic inertia again risked stalling British involvement even though it now had the support of the FCO, the MOD and we presume the Prime Minister. In New York, Hannay therefore pressed the UN Secretariat to schedule an emergency meeting of the Advisory Committee on Administrative and Budgetary Questions to authorise an additional contingency to cover UNAMIR's costs from July through to September. He also suggested the FCO contact other governments, particularly France, the US and Belgium, to encourage support for such an extension.[116] Without such authority it would not be possible for the UN to authorise reimbursement of the UK for the costs of Operation Gabriel. This extension was eventually given, in what Hannay described as a very poorly attended meeting. The UN did not formally agree to reimburse the British costs until September and even then only after the FCO had submitted justification of why money was needed for rations (the supplies available in Rwanda did not provide sufficient calories), why there was a need for replacement uniforms (no laundry facilities were available in theatre until the British sent a mobile bath unit) and why the force would need petrol (diesel was available in Rwanda but the British ambulances ran on petrol).[117]

In spite of the UN's procrastination, the British deployment was not significantly delayed. As the UN bureaucracy considered the reimbursement, Gabriel was funded from the Treasury's emergency reserve – something that officials at the Treasury did not seem overly happy about, as one internal note records: 'I'm afraid the Chancellor agreed to a Reserve claim at Cabinet. Good start to our campaign!!'[118] The use of the double exclamation mark clearly demonstrates the Treasury mandarins' frustration at the Chancellor. Having seen the Chancellor agree to fund the British deployment, in what appears to have been a bit of a shock to officials, the Treasury was quick to determine whether this could be included in Britain's official aid figures. The Treasury wrote to the ODA a number of times questioning why if the mission had predominantly humanitarian aims the cost could not be included in the aid figures; from the Treasury perspective this was particularly relevant as the Government had set an annual aid target of 0.7 per cent of GNP, which looked unlikely to be met; including the costs of Gabriel in the figures went some way to meeting that target. Perhaps confirming that intervention after all is about promoting national interest, in this case defined as receiving international recognition, the Treasury was also conscious of 'securing proper credit in international circles' for the effort that it was making.[119] As might be expected, officials at the Treasury were keen for some return on what they saw as their investment in Rwanda.

Funding agreed, if somewhat begrudgingly, the British force that ultimately deployed to Rwanda was far in excess of the REME company that had initially been envisaged by Hurd back at the start of July. Instead it consisted of not only a REME contingent, but also engineers, medics, logistics specialists, signallers, headquarters staff and a platoon of infantry. This force seems to have been built up in response to a UN wish list; General Dallaire recalls meeting Baroness Chalker in Uganda in the last week of July during her visit to the region:

> I met up with her at Kilometre 64, and we carried on northward, crossing into Uganda at the Gatuna bridge, while I pointedly explained why we needed the promised British trucks, engineers, maintenance platoon, field hospital, small headquarters and UNMOs [United Nations Military Observers]. She sent the colonel who was travelling with her to do a recce in Kigali and told him to forward a list of our needs to the British Ministry of Defence.[120]

This real need for logistical support was noted by other British officials who visited the region. As one senior FCO official who visited UNAMIR in late July recalled, 'by that time UNAMIR only had one operational armoured vehicle and was required to somehow transport vehicles back to Uganda for even the simplest repairs'.[121]

Given the requirement for a full range of logistical and support resources, the force that deployed to Rwanda was drawn from a range of units, both army and RAF. Table 1 shows troop numbers by unit over the period of the deployment.

Compared to the 5,000 British troops deployed to northern Iraq in 1991 or the 3,000 in Bosnia in 1994, a deployment of 600 non-combat troops may not seem that significant, it was nonetheless the single largest contribution of troops by a Western nation to a UN mission other than UNPROFOR in Yugoslavia (the US sent a larger contingent, but as noted above this remained under national command). By comparison Australia sent 313 medics to Rwanda, Canada 367 soldiers and Austria 16 military observers. Other Western nations including

1: British troops deployed to Rwanda, 1994

	Troop numbers:			
Unit	*13 Aug*	*13 Sep*	*13 Oct*	*13 Nov*
10 Airborne Workshop, REME	98	196	182	171
9 Parachute Squadron, Royal Engineers	84	150	144	122
23 Parachute Field Ambulance, Royal Army Medical Corps	88	160	157	149
29 Movement Control Regiment, Royal Logistics Corps (RLC)	6	6	6	19
30 Signals Regiment, Royal Corps of Signals	33	30	29	29
UK Mobile Movements Squadron, RAF 91 Squadron, 9 Supply Regiment, RLC 160 Provost Company, Royal Military Police	27	10	8	8
A Company 2 Battalion, Princess of Wales Royal Regiment	–	45	44	35
Others	–	9	6	6
Total	336	606	576	539

Source: MOD.

Denmark, Italy, Ireland, Finland, Germany (along with Italy, a member of the G7), Holland, Norway, New Zealand (whose representative at the Security Council had argued for a more robust response), Portugal, Spain and Sweden sent no troops.[122] The British were not, though, willing to offer Dallaire everything he wanted. On 23 August, the UN 'urgently' requested a military helicopter unit to provide additional logistic support and assist in airborne surveillance and reconnaissance; the request was rejected without serious, or indeed any, consideration.[123]

The forces, which within UNAMIR were known as BRITFOR, were commanded by Lieutentant Colonel Mike Wharmby, who in 1994 was the Commanding Officer of the Combat Service Support Battalion, part of 5 Airborne Brigade, the UK's out-of-area rapid response brigade. Wharmby's orders were very much to fit into UNAMIR. The British troops, unlike the Americans, wore the UN blue beret, and the directive issued to Wharmby stated, 'You are to carry out the tasks given to you by the Force Commander UNAMIR ... BRITFOR will deploy in accordance with the Force Commander UNAMIR's orders. BRITFOR will provide engineering, maintenance, repair and medical support to UNAMIR.'[124] Wharmby's orders continued to include more specific tasks that each element of the force was to achieve. The Royal Engineer element were to 'repair and drill wells for the provision of water; open 2 routes north of Kigali as directed; repair roads, bridges etc; be prepared to clear mines'.[125] The Engineer contingent also included a mine-clearing capacity which, on-paper at least, was not to be used for general mine clearance, but only where mines or booby traps impacted on BRITFOR's capability to achieve its mission; in practice this restriction was somewhat stretched. The REME workshop was to provide 'repair and recovery' support to UNAMIR, prioritising first BRITFOR's own vehicles, secondly the fifty 'UK gifted 4 Tonne vehicles' and then other UN vehicles. The field ambulance unit was directed to establish treatment centres ready to give medical treatment both to UN personnel and returning Rwandan refugees.

Wharmby recalls that during his briefings two things were made quite clear to him by senior officers. First, that the British deployment was to be a humanitarian deployment and that the specialists under his command must not be used for other roles, such as general peacekeeping.[126] Although there was a platoon of infantry forming part of the Gabriel force, this was to be used purely as protection for the other British troops, particularly the medics; peacekeeping was to be left to other contingents, such as the Ghanaians and the Ethiopians. The rules of engagement (RoE) under which Gabriel operated also made this clear; for example, the British troops were authorised to 'carry personal weapons (pistols, rifles and light machine guns)' but these were to be carried unloaded and were only to be used in self-defence and after a verbal warning had been given in French and English (troops were provided with phonetic instructions on how to issue the French warnings) and warning shots fired into the air.[127] Although these rules seemed quite clear on paper, Wharmby admits in practice that was not quite the case:

> The RoE did cause us some confusion and we did have a number of discussions over the satellite phone late into the night. Essentially we were there for humanitarian reasons and not to intervene. If people under our protection were attacked, for example if they were in one of our medical facilities and that came under attack, we would have been justified to use lethal force. But if we saw someone being attacked in a field as we were driving down the road, we would not. It would at the end of the day be up to the individual soldier to justify their actions. We were never there to intervene, we were there to defend ourselves and fulfil our humanitarian mission.[128]

Secondly, as noted above, it was made clear to Wharmby that he was to fall under the tactical command of General Dallaire, commander of UNAMIR. However, even this was not as clear cut as the order may have seemed:

> There was some uncertainty amongst the UN staff. This was partly because of the French Operation Turquoise and party because of the US mission. Also they had seen the Belgians fly into Rwanda and assume command of their units that were supposed to be part of UNAMIR. Amongst Dallaire's staff there was an institutional uncertainty and suspicion about national missions

> and national control. I'm not sure that Dallaire ever recognised that we were fully his.[129]

Operation Gabriel in Rwanda

When the order was given to deploy British troops, Wharmby and his soldiers were on exercise on Salisbury Plain. Ironically, the format of the exercise was that the brigade had deployed on a UN Chapter VII mission in Africa and was keeping the peace in a border dispute between the 'Hutu' and 'Tutu'; the exercise had been scheduled many months previously and Wharmby believes any such similarity to the mission in Rwanda was purely coincidental (though the choice of names is incredibly coincidental).[130] In terms of speeding up the deployment, it did mean that the units were already assembled and equipped. The first elements of Operation Gabriel, fifty men, deployed on the morning of 1 August, many of them initially having to put up with tented accommodation due to war damage across Kigali.[131] It was hoped that the remaining troops and the associated heavy equipment would deploy very soon after, but in fact this was delayed due to 'transportation difficulties'.[132] The particular difficulty was that, despite the US Government agreeing with the UN Secretariat that it would make a C5 transport plane available to the British, no C5 had arrived in the UK. Whether this was due to further deliberate delays by the US military, genuine technical faults with the plane or because the US Air Force was giving priority to assisting the deployment of the Ethiopian battalion joining UNAMIR is not clear. The impact, though, was that the deployment of the British mission temporarily stalled until 5 August. Operation Gabriel was considered operational on 17 August and was fully deployed by the 21st. At this stage the bulk of the force was deployed in Kigali; the field ambulance unit (178 men and women in total) was deployed in Byumba (near the border with Uganda) and the Engineers (forty-four soldiers) were in Kitabi (in the south-west).

The speed of the deployment and more significantly the reconnaissance, which was completed in less than thirty-six hours, were to limit the effectiveness of the deployment for the first weeks. For example, the first detachment arrived in Rwanda without adequate vehicles, which severely hampered their ability to move around Kigali, let alone the country as a whole. There was also a lack of clarity over the role of the medical contingent; namely whether they were there to treat UN personnel or refugees. This resulted in the medics lacking medicines suitable for treating the local population who would make up most of their patients throughout the three-month deployment. As one army medic recalls, 'we had to beg, borrow and steal' equipment and medicine from NGOs nearby, including ironically a consignment of machetes shipped to the country by one Irish NGO.[133]

Once in theatre, much of Gabriel's work was aligned with the general FCO belief that 'the key to tackling the humanitarian crisis lies in creating conditions within Rwanda which will attract refugees and displaced persons back to the homes'.[134] In fact the mission statement drawn up by the Commanding Officer of 23 Parachute Field Ambulance was initially 'to provide humanitarian assistance in northwest Rwanda in order to encourage refugees to return to the country from Zaire'.[135] The unit therefore reopened the abandoned hospital at Ruhengeri in the north-west of Rwanda, which was on the route home for many returning refugees. The operation of this hospital also demonstrates how the army and NGOs worked together in Rwanda; the army doctors provided the health care at Ruhengeri and the distribution of food and water was managed by a British NGO. After ten days of operating the hospital, the field ambulance unit was moved south as part of Dallaire's plan to prevent a further exodus of refugees following the planned withdrawal of the French Operation Turquoise troops. Once relocated to the south the unit split into eight mobile treatment sections. The mobile teams, each made up of a doctor and six paramedics, travelled daily to the camps for internally displaced persons, providing immediate aid and also, they hoped, encouraging people to remain in Rwanda where they were receiving care. Wharmby sees the medics' performance in the south-west as a key achievement of Operation Gabriel: 'Our presence fixed several hundred thousand people in the region in what would have been an exodus once the French withdrew – so this prevented the situation in Zaire worsening. Our presence drew NGOs in and they were able to provide water and food. So the medics kept people in the region.'[136]

Meanwhile the Royal Engineer detachment was heavily involved in road repair and the provision of clean water. In Gatuna, the main bridge linking Uganda and Rwanda had been destroyed in the fighting and replaced by tree trunks covered in earth; not surprisingly this makeshift bridge was collapsing under the weight of traffic. To ensure the continued flow of aid from Uganda the tree-trunk bridge was replaced by the Engineers. In Kitabi a reverse osmosis plant was set up to provide clean water to the British field hospital. In the towns of Mukarange, Manuyagiro, Gikore, Shangasha and Bushara water pumps or storage tanks, damaged during the war, were repaired; this alone had a massive impact on public health, reducing the risk of both cholera and dysentery. And in Kigali the Engineers cleared roads of unexploded ordinance and reinstated the refuse tip in order to remove major health hazards from the city.

Overall, during the three months that Gabriel was deployed, the troops carried out 132,605 medical treatments, vaccinated 95,453 children against meningitis and measles, produced 5.4 million litres of clean water, repaired 98 culverts, built 12 bridges, made safe 3,308 mines and unexploded ordnance, repaired 467 vehicles, delivered 1,500 tonnes of aid and transported 20,000 refugees home.[137] Additionally, British soldiers worked in Dallaire's headquarters, providing communications across the country and also logistical support to various other UN contingents and NGOs. The British troops also voluntarily assisted in the reconstruction of Rwanda. For example, soldiers refurbished five orphanages;

during their rest periods the units based in Kigali helped rebuild the Missionaries of Charity Orphanage where 300 children were being cared for. The troops rebuilt the walls, refitted the electrics and repaired the water supply and sanitation. The wives and families of those serving in Rwanda also led a fundraising appeal back home; the money they raised was used to buy cooking, cleaning and kitchen equipment for the orphanage and also paid for a new play area to be built.[138]

Rwanda forgotten

The deployment of British troops led to an increase in newspaper coverage of the crisis, if only briefly. The reporting, though, was often more dramatic than accurate; the BBC's Mark Doyle recalls how the MOD and Pentagon were both keen to get positive coverage of the deployment: 'The US and British army media relations staff promptly announced to the world, in keeping with the usual image of Western troops arriving in Africa, that they had "taken control" of the airport ... the airport had been in the control of the RPF for weeks'.[139] Wharmby similarly notes the pressure he was placed under to 'sell' his mission to the media. 'All countries that get involved in this sort of mission want to get maximum credit out of it. I received some criticism from superiors for not getting more media coverage of what we were doing,' Wharmby explained before continuing, 'but there were no journalists for me to speak to – there was no one there.'[140] Wharmby's point is borne out by the fact that whilst there were some 500 journalists in Goma, newspaper by-lines suggest that throughout July and August fewer than a dozen British journalists reported from Rwanda itself, and even then some of those relocated to Goma after only a brief visit to Rwanda. The similarities in coverage across the various newspapers demonstrates that most of the coverage of the work of British troops was not first hand reporting but instead relied on MOD press releases issued almost exclusively from Whitehall, as opposed to briefings from officers in the field.

Despite the deployment of British troops, this renewed media interest in Rwanda, like the cholera outbreak in Goma, proved to be short lived. Whereas the *Guardian* ran twenty-eight articles about Rwanda in the week ended 31 July, there were only nine in the week ended 21 August. The crisis was replaced on the front page by stories of more domestic interest: British athletes failing drugs tests at the Commonwealth Games, threats of a train-drivers' strike and fresh calls for an IRA ceasefire. Even the fear in mid-August of a second wave of refugees, following the departure of Operation Turquoise's French troops, did not rekindle anywhere near the same level of interest the initial exodus to Goma had. This story, like most foreign news stories, had run its natural course and moved first to the inside pages, before slowly vanishing from the press almost completely; as Germaine Greer suggested in the *Guardian*, 'when the dying stops' media interest simply vanishes.[141] Like the ODA, which was quick to disentangle itself from

Rwanda as soon as the humanitarian emergency appeared to be under control, journalists, Greer suggested, desperate for a good picture or a Pulitzer Prize, deserted Rwanda as quickly as they had arrived. Rwanda had been forgotten as quickly as it had come to the media's attention back in early April. The small country far away, once again slipped from the British consciousness.

Summary

July and August were the months during which the British Government moved from being an ignorant and passive bystander to an active participant in the relief of the humanitarian crisis. The combination of aid and military resources meant that overall the UK became one of the largest contributors to the Rwanda relief effort; though, like that from most of the international community, this aid did not arrive in the country until the civil war, and genocide, had ended – hence, Adam Roberts' claim of too little, too late. The argument that the UK did eventually do more than most other countries may not be enough to appease the critics, such as Linda Melvern or General Dallaire, but it is a fact. The British Government, British NGOs and the British public responded to the humanitarian crisis – eventually – in a way that most other countries simply did not. Of course that is not to say the UK must be absolved of all criticism.

The media in particular must be held up for rebuke. The press coverage throughout the whole crisis was responsible for a gross misunderstanding of what was happening in Rwanda, and the focus on Goma and cholera in July and August without the historical perspective of the genocide was an insult to the memory of the nearly one million murdered during the genocide. This media misrepresentation, a result of poor research, a misguided attempt to achieve balance in reporting the two sides of the conflict and a focus on shocking rather than educating, led the public and NGOs to focus on Goma while the situation in Rwanda itself received little attention. The British public and British NGOs responded to this coverage by donating huge amounts of money and performing valuable work in the region. The Hutu in Goma certainly benefited from this aid, and the response to the crisis contradicts any suggestion that the British public were suffering from compassion fatigue in the early 1990s. But the outpouring of generosity did little for those left suffering in Rwanda itself and in reality prolonged the violence in the region, which continues even now. In terms of the Government's response, it is impossible to quantify the exact benefit of the deployment of Operation Gabriel, but as the statistics above demonstrate, the contribution of British troops was impressive and far outweighed anything offered by most other Western nations.

It is, of course, impossible to argue that Sir Adam Roberts is wrong to suggest that Britain did too little. Clearly more could have been done – it always can. But the UK's resources are not limitless; increasing aid to Rwanda would have meant diverting resources from other worthy causes. The facts, as we have seen in this chapter, though, are that Britain did do something in Rwanda; Tony Blair is simply wrong to suggest otherwise.

Notes

1 A. Roberts, 'The United Nations and Humanitarian Intervention', in J. Welsh (ed.), *Humanitarian Intervention and International Relations* (Oxford: Oxford University Press. 2006), p. 71.
2 M. McNulty, 'Media Ethnicization and the International Response to War and Genocide in Rwanda', in T. Allen and J. Seaton (eds), *The Media and Conflict: War Reporting and Representations of Ethnic Violence* (London: Zed Books, 1999), p. 270.
3 S. Kiley, 'Rwanda Rebels Fire on French Force', *The Times* (4 July 1994).
4 M. Bell, 'TV News: How Far Should we Go?' *British Journalism Review* 8:1 (1997), p. 10.
5 Doyle, 'Reporting the Genocide', p. 154
6 R. Block, 'Entire City Flees the Rwandan Rebels', *Independent* (4 July 1994), p. 1.
7 Anon., 'Rebels Fire on Evacuation Convoy', *Herald* (4 July 1994), p. 1.
8 G. Dimore, 'Rwandans Flee Big Rebel Push', *Independent* (11 July 1994), p. 12.
9 C. McGreal, 'Rwanda's Latest Nomads Flee Advancing Gunfire', *Guardian* (13 July 1994), p. 11.
10 In the week 11 to 17 July, 'refugee' appeared 131 times in articles also mentioning Rwanda; this compares to 62 mentions of the word 'rebel', 29 of 'troops' and 26 of 'soldier'.
11 P. Robinson, 'The News Media and Intervention: Triggering the Use of Air Power during Humanitarian Crises', *European Journal of Communication* 15 (2000), p. 138.
12 H. Bierhoff, *Prosocial Behaviour* (New York: Psychology Press, 2002), p. 196.
13 McNulty, 'Media Ethnicization', p. 270.
14 Woolridge, 'Reporting Africa', p. 371; F. Keane, 'Mediating Africa', public lecture at Northumbria University, 10 June 2011, www.northumbria.ac.uk/sd/academic/sass/about/humanities/history/historynews/4758996?view=Standard&news=archive (accessed 11 June 2014).
15 *Guardian*: 18, 20, 22, 23, 24 July. *Independent*: 20, 23, 24 July. *Evening Standard* 19 July. The database used does not record which page articles from *The Times* appeared on.
16 M. Colvin, 'Letter: Reality and Rwanda', *Guardian* (6 August 1994), p. 24.
17 S. Moeller, *Compassion Fatigue: How the Media Sell Disease, Famine, War and Death* (London: Routledge, 1999), p. 295.
18 McNulty, 'Media Ethnicization', p. 270.
19 Anon., 'Devastated Rwanda', *The Times,* (20 July 1994); I. Gilmore, 'World Agencies Helpless as Refugees Pour out of Rwanda', *The Times* (20 July 1994).

20 Anon., 'Leading Article: The Hell of Reproach that is Goma', *Guardian* (23 July 1994), p. 24.
21 Anon., 'Exodus of Lost Tribe', *Daily Mail* (20 July 1994), p. 12.
22 Shaw, 'Historical Frames and the Politics of Humanitarian Intervention', p. 359.
23 VSO, *Live Aid Legacy*, p. 3.
24 Anon., 'Mayhem as Rwandans Stampede into Zaire', *Independent* (18 July 1994), p. 9.
25 Anon., '100,000 in Death Run from Rwandan Haven', *Daily Mail* (19 July 1994), p. 11.
26 Anon., 'Exodus of Lost Tribe', *Daily Mail* (20 July 1994), p. 12.
27 G. Dinmore, 'Cholera Fear for Rwanda Refugees', *Independent* (21 July 1994), p. 13.
28 Philo *et al.*, 'The Media and the Rwanda Crisis', p. 226.
29 G. Alagiah, *Passage to Africa* (London: Abacus, 2007), pp. 123–5.
30 *Ibid.*, p. 127.
31 Philo *et al.*, 'The Media and the Rwanda Crisis', p. 217.
32 C. McGreal, 'Rwandan Refugee Crisis Deepens', *Guardian* (19 July 1994), p. 12.
33 Anon., 'Exodus of Lost Tribe', *Daily Mail* (20 July 1994), p. 12.
34 Anon., 'Leading Article: Rwanda's Moral Call on the West', *Independent* (23 July 1994), p. 10.
35 Hansard records 46 mentions of Bosnia in June 1994 and 60 in July; against 101 and 88 for Rwanda in the same periods.
36 Labour Party archives, minutes of meeting of the Shadow Cabinet, 20 July 1994.
37 Hansard, HC Deb, 20 July 1994, vol. 247, col. 233w.
38 Hansard, HC Deb, 13 July 1994, vol. 246, col. 971.
39 *Ibid.*
40 Hansard, HC Deb, 19 July 1994, vol. 247, col. 168.
41 Hansard, HC Deb, 13 July 1994, vol. 246, col. 970.
42 Hansard, HL Deb, 21 July 1994, vol. 557, col. 43w.
43 Hansard, HC Deb, 18 July 1994, vol. 247, col. 16.
44 *Ibid.*
45 Hansard, HC Deb, 19 July 1994, vol. 247, col. 172.
46 Hansard, HC Deb, 18 July 1994, vol. 247, col. 16.
47 FCO, letter from Jack Cunningham MP to the Foreign Secretary Douglas Hurd MP, 20 July 1994.
48 Confidential telephone interview.
49 US State Department, cable from US Embassy London to State Department Washington, 'Britain Increases Rwandan Aid', 27 July 1994.
50 Melvern and Williams, 'Britannia Waived the Rules', p. 15.
51 Joint Evaluation of Emergency Assistance to Rwanda (JEEAR), *The International Response to Conflict and Genocide: Lessons from the Rwanda Experience, Volume III: Humanitarian Aid and Effects* (Copenhagen: Joint Evaluation of Emergency Assistance to Rwanda, 1996), p. 25.

52 US State Department, cable from US Embassy London to State Department Washington, 'UK Increases Humanitarian Aid to Rwanda', 15 July 1994.
53 US State Department, cable from US Embassy London to State Department Washington, 'Ambassador's Courtesy Call on Minister for Overseas Development', 19 August 1994.
54 US State Deptartment, cable from US Embassy London to State Department Washington, 'British Aid for Rwandan Refugee Crisis', 17 August 1994.
55 *Ibid.*
56 *Ibid.*
57 US State Department, cable from US Embassy London to State Department Washington, 'Britain Winding Down Emergency Aid to Rwanda', 29 September 1994.
58 Hilsum, 'Reporting Rwanda', p. 178.
59 N. Stockton, 'In Defence of Humanitarianism', *Disasters* 22:4 (1998), p. 358.
60 Hilsum, 'Reporting Rwanda,' p. 182.
61 JEEAR, *Volume III*, p. 116.
62 Hilsum, 'Reporting Rwanda,' p. 176.
63 *Ibid.*, p. 178.
64 T. Knecht and S. Weatherford, 'Public Opinion and Foreign Policy: The Stages of Presidential Decision Making', *International Studies Quarterly* 50 (2006), p. 714.
65 JEEAR, *Volume III*, p. 70.
66 *Ibid.*, pp. 62–3.
67 N. Middleton and P. O'Keefe, *Disaster and Development* (Cambridge: Pluto Press, 1998), p. 115
68 Anon., 'After 25 Wars, I've Never Had a More Disgusting Day', *Herald* (30 July 1994), p. 4.
69 Storey, 'Non-Neutral Humanitarianism', p. 386.
70 Hilsum, 'Reporting Rwanda', p. 177.
71 US State Department, cable from US Embassy London to State Department Washington, 'More on British Troops and Aid to Rwanda', 1 August 1994.
72 Carlsson *et al.*, *Report of the Independent Inquiry into the Actions of the United Nations*, p. 26.
73 Hansard, HC Deb, 15 June 1994, vol. 244, col. 594w.
74 FCO, letter from J. Smith at FCO to J. Pitt-Brooke at MOD, 'UNAMIR in Rwanda', 12 July 1994.
75 MOD, minutes of meeting, 'Meeting with the Foreign Secretary: Rwanda and Haiti', 20 July 1994.
76 MOD, minutes of meeting of Current Operations Group, 24 July 1994.
77 MOD, written correspondence with the author in response to a Freedom of Information request.
78 MOD, minutes of a meeting on 25 July 1994.
79 FCO, letter from Glyne Evans to Foreign Secretary, 27 July 1994.
80 Members of the subcommittee were: the Prime Minister, Foreign Secretary (Douglas Hurd), President of the Board of Trade (Michael Heseltine),

Chancellor of the Exchequer (Ken Clarke), Defence Secretary (Malcolm Rifkind) and Attorney General (Nicholas Lyell).

81 P. Williams, 'Who's Making UK Foreign Policy?', *International Affairs* 80:5 (2004), p. 909.
82 JEEAR, *Volume III*, p. 67
83 FCO, telegram from UK mission to UN in New York to FCO for attention of Lady Chalker, 'Rwanda: Provision of Logistical Support', 22 July 1994.
84 Interview with Baroness Chalker.
85 Seldon, *Major*, p. 161.
86 ITN archive, 'Rwanda: French Forces Establish a Haven', *News at Ten* (6 July 1994).
87 M. Binyon, 'Fears Grow that Bosnia Will Slip back into War', *The Times* (5 July 1994).
88 G. Holmes, 'Did *Newsnight* Miss the Story? A Survey of How the BBC's "Flagship Political Current Affairs Programme" Reported Genocide and War in Rwanda', *Genocide Studies and Prevention* 6:2 (2011), p. 191.
89 http://news.bbc.co.uk/1/hi/programmes/panorama/3585473.stm (accessed 11 June 2014).
90 Interview with Malcolm Rifkind.
91 Cooke, *The Campaign Guide 1994*, p.v.
92 Interview with Malcolm Rifkind.
93 Conservative Party archive, Douglas Hurd speech to the Conservative Central Council Meeting in Harrogate, 5 March 1993.
94 White, *Democracy goes to War*, p. 68.
95 Interview with David Hannay.
96 United Nations, New York, S/PRST/1994/34, 14 July 1994.
97 Interview with Malcolm Rifkind, and interview with William Hague, Northallerton, 10 July 2009.
98 BBC Television, *Mission Angola: Defence of the Realm* (aired BBC One, 29 August 1996).
99 MOD, memorandum on Rwanda written by C. Gordon, 18 July 1994.
100 *Ibid.*
101 United Nations, 'Summary of Contribution to Peacekeeping Operations by Countries as of 31 July 1994', available at www.un.org/en/peacekeeping/resources/statistics/contributors_archive.shtm, accessed 11 June 2014.
102 MOD, letter from Private Secretary to Malcolm Rifkind to FCO, 19 July 1994.
103 T. Weiss and C. Collins, 'Politics of Militarised Humanitarian Intervention', in S. Totten and P. Bartrop (eds), *The Genocide Studies Reader* (New York: Routledge, 2009), p. 367.
104 MOD, minutes of meeting with the Foreign Secretary, 20 July 1994.
105 MOD, minutes of the meeting of the Current Operations Group, 24 July 1994.
106 CIA briefing paper, 'Rwanda: Security Conditions at Kigali Airport', 13 July 1994, accessed at www.foia.cia.gov.
107 Interview with Malcolm Rifkind.
108 MOD, letter from Malcolm Rifkind's Private Secretary to FCO, 25 July 1994.

109 MOD, minutes of the meeting of the Current Operations Group, 24 July 1994.
110 MOD, minutes of a meeting between Malcolm Rifkind and Chief of Defence Staff, 25 July 1994.
111 Williams, 'Who's Making UK Foreign Policy,' p. 918; Coles, *Making Foreign Policy*, p. 92; D. Kavanagh and A. Seldon, *The Powers behind the Prime Minister* (London: HarperCollins, 1999), p. 202.
112 Interview with Baroness Chalker. Chalker could not recall exactly when she had this conversation with Major and did not comment on his response.
113 BBC Television, *Mission Angola*.
114 FCO, internal memorandum sent to Resource and Finance Department, undated.
115 FCO, telegram from UK mission to UN New York to FCO London, 'UNAMIR: Budget', 17 August 1994.
116 *Ibid.*
117 FCO, letter to Kofi Annan from FCO, 'UK Participation in UNAMIR', 1 September 1994.
118 Treasury, internal memorandum, 'Rwanda: British Contribution', 28 July.
119 Treasury, letters from Treasury to ODA, 9 August 1994 and 16 August 1994.
120 Dallaire, *Shake Hands*, p. 486.
121 Confidential interview.
122 United Nations, 'Summary of Contribution to Peacekeeping Operations by Countries as of 30 September 1994', www.un.org/en/peacekeeping/resources/statistics/contributors_archive.shtml (accessed 11 June 2014).
123 FCO, telegram from UK mission to UN New York to FCO London, 23 August 1994.
124 MOD, internal memorandum, 'Operation Gabriel – Directive to Commander British Forces UNAMIR', 31 July 1994.
125 *Ibid.*
126 Interview with Lieutenant Colonel Mike Wharmby.
127 MOD, internal memorandum, 'Operation Gabriel – Directive to Commander British Forces UNAMIR', 31 July 1994.
128 Interview with Lieutenant Colonel Mike Wharmby.
129 *Ibid.*
130 *Ibid.*
131 M. Whittle, '10 Airborne Workshop Deploys to Rwanda', *Craftsman*, September 1994, p. 69.
132 US State Department, cable from US Embassy London to State Department Washington, 'UK Rwanda Assistance', 3 August 1994.
133 Confidential interview with Royal Army Medical Corps officer, 4 May 2012.
134 Treasury, letter from FCO to Treasury, 'Rwanda: British Contingent', 2 August 1994.
135 A. Hawley, 'Rwanda 1994: A Study of Medical Support in Military Humanitarian Operations', *Journal of Royal Army Medical Corps* 143 (1997), p. 79.
136 Interview with Lieutenant Colonel Mike Wharmby.

137 Hawley, 'Rwanda 1994', p. 78.
138 MOD, Army News Release 124/94, 30 August 1994.
139 Doyle, 'Reporting the Genocide', p. 155.
140 Interview with Lieutenant Colonel Mike Wharmby.
141 G. Greer, 'Media Duty Begins When the Dying Stops', *Guardian* (8 August 1994), p. 18.

5

The responsible bystander?

Despite the ODA's claims in September 1994 that it had no intention of developing a long-term relationship with Rwanda, that is exactly what has happened. Britain's relationship with Rwanda could not now be more different from it was before the genocide.[1] Whereas before 1994 politicians would have struggled to find Rwanda on a map, now each summer Kigali airport arrivals hall teems with visiting MPs. Since the genocide all-party parliamentary groups have visited Rwanda almost annually, and trips to the country have been *de rigueur* for ministers with responsibility for overseas aid (indeed Clare Short visited the country within just three months of taking office as the new Secretary of State for International Development in 1997). Since 2007 a group of Conservative MPs and party members has volunteered in Rwanda each summer; as part of Project Umubano, over 230 volunteers have worked in the country on health, legal and building projects. Senior politicians have also visited the country: in 2007 David Cameron (then leader of the Opposition) visited Kigali; in 2009 Tony Blair (by then the former prime minister) spent two days in the country; and in 2014 Foreign Secretary William Hague visited Rwanda to mark the genocide's twentieth anniversary. This newly formed relationship has been cemented by visits by Rwandan politicians to the UK; President Kagame, for example, has visited Downing Street, met the Queen at Buckingham Palace, been the guest of honour at the Conservative Party annual conference and addressed the Oxford Union. Quite a change in stance from 1966 when the FCO informed the British ambassador to Rwanda that there was no prospect whatsoever of an official, let alone a state, visit by President Kayabanda to the UK.[2]

Beyond the reciprocal visits, the Anglo-Rwandan diplomatic relationship has changed markedly. In 2009 (forty-four years after it first enquired about membership) Rwanda became only the second country to join the Commonwealth that had not formerly been a British colony; in 1995 the first British Embassy was opened in Kigali; and for a number of years Britain has been Rwanda's largest bi-lateral aid donor.[3] Untainted by any relationship with the former genocidal government, the UK has become a genuine and good friend to post-1994 Rwanda.

The crisis has also had an impact on British political rhetoric that continues to this day. Senior British politicians regularly recall the 1994 crisis and have generally been quick to suggest more should have been done. Tony Blair, for example, in his annual conference speech of 2001 said, 'And I tell you if Rwanda happened again today as it did in 1993 [sic], when a million people were slaughtered in cold blood, we would have a moral duty to act there'.[4] Similarly the Conservative Party has, since 1997 at least, suggested that if another Rwanda-style crisis was to happen then Britain should intervene. William Hague, at the time Shadow Foreign Secretary, made this point explicitly in a 2009 speech entitled 'The Future of British Foreign Policy', saying, 'We are all agreed we would try to intervene if another Rwanda was predicted'.[5]

The crisis is also frequently recalled in the House of Commons and since 1994 every time MPs debate intervention, Rwanda is inevitably drawn upon as an analogy. For example, in 2004 John Maples (Conservative, Stratford) implored the House to ensure the UN did not fail in Darfur as it had done in Rwanda;[6] in 1999 Tess Kingham (Labour, Gloucester) argued, 'For the sake of basic humanity, the genocide in Rwanda should have been stopped', before continuing that the Government must not similarly prevaricate in the case of Kosovo;[7] and in 2004 in a debate on the war against Iraq, Barbara Roche (Labour, Hornsey and Wood Green) used the international failure to act against the Nazi Holocaust and the Rwandan genocide as justification for why action was needed against Saddam Hussein.[8] In political shorthand 'Rwanda' has become a metaphor for the terrible consequences of failing to act.

The most significant medium-term legacy of the crisis was not, though, the change in rhetoric or diplomatic relations; the events in Rwanda were also a major driver of change in Britain's, and the wider international community's, attitude toward humanitarian intervention. In 2005, following the publication of a report commissioned by the Canadian Government in response to the events in Rwanda and Yugoslavia, the UN General Assembly approved the policy of 'Responsibility to Protect' (R2P). R2P argues that if a state fails or is unwilling to exercise its prime responsibility of protecting its citizens, the international community has a responsibility to intervene. R2P also goes further than the Genocide Convention by authorising intervention in cases not just of genocide, but in cases where civilian populations are at risk from war, ethnic cleansing, famine or any other humanitarian crisis. Ramesh Thakur summarises the general conclusion of the report, 'Where a population is suffering serious harm, as a result of internal war, insurgency, repression or state failure, and the government in question is unwilling or unable to halt or avert it, the norm of non-intervention yields to this international responsibility to protect'.[9] This policy, which had (or maybe it is still correct to say 'has') the potential to completely shift the international community's response to humanitarian crises, was later endorsed by the Security Council in Resolution 1674. Whilst the crises in Yugoslavia, East Timor and Haiti undoubtedly contributed to this change, as one FCO official described the birth of R2P, '[in the British mind at least] there is a clear and direct link between what happened in Rwanda and R2P; one most certainly led to the other'.[10]

If the genocide has so evidently changed the Anglo-Rwandan relationship, why then did it take so long for Britain to respond back in 1994? It is easy to argue that it was simply lack of national interest; this argument may fit neatly into the realist school of foreign policy but it ignores that fact that there was a British response, albeit too late to stop the killing. We should remember that in May 1994 Britain argued for an increase in UNAMIR troop levels and opposed the American outside-in mission; that from May onwards the Government donated huge sums of money, eventually becoming one of the relief effort's largest contributors; that in July the Government approved the deployment of some six hundred troops to UNAMIR, far in excess of what the UN had originally requested and making the UK the mission's second largest contributor; and, when asked, the British public donated millions of pounds to the Rwandan aid appeal. The more interesting question is, then, not why did Britain fail to intervene sooner, but why did it intervene quite so robustly?

Explaining the public response

As we have seen, the public response to the genocide was muted; there were generally no calls for 'something to be done' and sympathy for the victims was not particularly obvious. Instead comments such as 'why not let them get on with settling their differences in their own traditional way'[11] were common in the letters to the editor pages of national newspapers. Why this was the case can largely be explained by a combination of media coverage and traditional Western attitudes to Africa.

As in any foreign crisis, the public's knowledge of Rwanda was based essentially on what they read in the newspapers and saw on the television; and in April and May 1994 this reporting was 'appallingly misleading'.[12] As the BBC's Mark Doyle, for example, accepts, 'during the first few days, I, like others, got the story terribly wrong'.[13] For the first four weeks of genocide, the British media failed to identify the killings as anything other than anarchic and as the resumption of a savage tribal war; and this demonstrably impacted the British public's response. Royce Ammon suggests that this style of reporting meant there was little empathy for the suffering being experienced by Rwanda civilians; there were, he says, no 'good people to whom bad things were happening ... no innocents in hell'.[14] Alan Kuperman similarly argues these 'early reports indicated that the Tutsi rebels were winning the civil war ... which contradicted any notion of the Tutsi as victims' and therefore argued against intervention.[15] The reporting was 'devoid of social, political and historical context' and consequently the media consumer was left thinking, as is common in reporting of Africa, that 'That's just the way they are'.[16] As Robinson suggests, '[this] distance framing ... implicitly supported a policy of non-intervention'.[17] As long as the media concentrated on the civil war and drew on clichés of tribal savagery, there was in the minds of the British public no humanitarian crisis. Instead the crisis was understood to be an ancient tribal war, of the sort which Western tradition said had ravaged Africa throughout history and quite simply there was nothing, orthodoxy said, the West could do to stop it.

It was not until the media coverage changed to a focus on the refugee crises that people in the UK began to understand Rwanda as the humanitarian crisis that it truly was. At this stage the coverage shifted to the more familiar image of Africa: what VSO had called the 'starving children with flies in their eyes' picture[18] and the sort of view Seaga Shaw argues is likely to trigger calls for aid.[19] The framing of the refugee story was markedly different from the genocide. Whereas Rwandans had until this point been savages, they were now victims. The reports of suffering, particularly that experienced by women and children, were now empathetic, rather than condemning. The increase in the number of journalists in the region, particularly Goma, also meant there were now more images of the crisis; back in the UK the public could see the genuine trauma being suffered by ordinary-looking people. The change in media framing led to an almost immediate change in the public psyche and for the first time there were calls for action.

But the recognition of the crisis alone was not enough to change the actual response; before that would happen the public also had to believe that something *could* be done. Throughout the genocide, the media focus on the tribal war and ready use of cliché reinforced a belief that there was nothing that could be done to help Rwanda. As Philip Gourevitch describes it, the media stoked a view in the West that Africans 'die of miserable things' and there is nothing the West can do to stop that.[20] However, once the crisis shifted from being seen as genocide and moved to being a refugee crisis, this belief changed. First NGOs and then the media told the British public that their money would help. The celebrity endorsements of the DEC's Rwanda campaign moved the general public to donate, and then images of Red Cross nurses and Save the Children volunteers actually working in Rwanda and Goma reinforced the view that British money was making a difference. Suddenly, there was a belief that intervention would be successful.

It was only when these two factors combined that the public responded; they first had to recognise that a humanitarian crisis existed and they then had to believe that there was something that could be done. Only when the factors aligned was there a clear and definite shift in the public's will to respond to the crisis.

Explaining the Government response

The Government similarly had to go through a two-stage process of recognising the crisis and then believing something could be done, before shifting to a position of supporting intervention. What is particularly evident in the Government response, however, is that elite political support was also fundamental to the decision to intervene.

Recognising the crisis

In the years and months leading up to April 1994, if it had looked hard enough, the Government could have seen clear signs of impending genocide. In Kigali Edward Clay, Britain's High Commissioner, for example, saw for himself the build up of soldiers and the arming of militias, and he heard of ethnically motivated murders. In New York, the UN Secretariat circulated reports from UNAMIR that recorded the increasingly volatile atmosphere in Rwanda; in Washington, intelligence agencies predicted massive loss of life should civil war resume. In the UK, NGOs such as Amnesty International wrote to members about the increasingly common murder of civilians in Rwanda. For historians looking back at the period, there is ample evidence of the impending humanitarian crisis, but this was apparently missed by the FCO.

But as John Coles suggests, 'so often exhaustive accounts, written well after the event, fall into the trap of hindsight and fail to take account of the other [contemporary] pressures on policy makers'.[21] Simply cataloguing the numerous but disparate pieces of evidence and then concluding that the British Government *must* have known about the threat to Rwandan civilians ignores a fundamental fact: the FCO simply had no interest in Rwanda before 1994. Given the other demands on the FCO, most of which were considered more urgent and with a greater potential impact on British interests, to seriously suggest civil servants would have spent time and resources analysing Rwanda is misguided. In this respect the FCO bureaucracy did its job: information that was considered less significant was filtered out at lower levels of the organisation and never reached senior diplomats and ministers, who instead were left free to concentrate on the more pressing issues of Bosnia and EU reform.[22] Junior officials may, for instance, have seen intelligence, such as Dallaire's genocide fax, but there is no evidence that it was passed up the bureaucratic chain to decision makers and ministers. Rightly or wrongly, but absolutely understandably, the FCO did not see the genocide coming.

Even in April, when the genocide did begin, this was not immediately obvious in London; instead Foreign Office mandarins saw what their limited intelligence had suggested was likely – a resumption of civil war. The official UN report on Rwanda might criticise members of the Security Council for 'view[ing] the situation in Kigali after the death of the President as one where the cease-fire had broken down ... rather than one of genocide';[23] but for the UK at least it was a logical view. In April 1994 the FCO did not have officials in Rwanda and had no links with the Rwandan Government. It was unable to communicate with the honorary consul in Kigali because phone lines had been destroyed and the nearest

High Commission, in Kampala, was helpless to report on what was happening. London's intelligence instead came from other countries (particularly France and Belgium), the UN Secretariat and the media; all of which described Rwanda as civil war rather than genocide. Why, then, should the FCO have interpreted the violence in any other way? After all, the civil war had reignited on more than one occasion over the previous three years. History and intelligence told the FCO that April 1994 was no different.

Not until May did this change. Not until May did the FCO begin to see reports from the UN Secretariat that correctly interpreted the events as genocide; not until May did senior officials and ministers begin to read about genocide in the British press; not until May did other countries, such as Spain, Nigeria and New Zealand, start to call the violence genocide; and not until May did British NGOs begin to lobby the Government to demand greater action from the UN. Without independent sources of intelligence, one cannot see how the FCO could have interpreted the violence as genocide any sooner than early-May; until that point it was highly unlikely that the Government would support anything more than the limited role approved for the rump element of UNAMIR, namely to assist in ceasefire negotiations.

But as with the public, it was not until late June that the wider political class, outside of the FCO and some interested MPs, began to fully understand the crisis for what it was. It was only in June and July that Rwanda finally overtook Bosnia in terms of number of questions in the House of Commons; not until late July that ministers began making comments to the press about Rwanda; and not until July that there is documented evidence of there being any 'will' within the Government to respond. It seems that, like the public, the Government equally needed to see pictures of refugees suffering and dying before it recognised the true humanitarian crisis.

Political will and chance of success

Even with the crisis in Rwanda recognised for what it truly was, two factors meant robust intervention was not immediately forthcoming. First, there was not yet a belief that intervention could be successful and secondly, there still was no support for intervention amongst the political elite, the Prime Minister in particular.

The initial lack of political will has variously been explained by racism, by the fear of a repeat of the Somalia debacle, or simply by lack of national interest. Boutros Boutros-Ghali, for example, attributes the slow response to race;[24] the West was quick to respond to the crisis in white Yugoslavia, the argument runs, but nothing was done about the crisis in Rwanda because the victims were black. In relation to Somalia, US National Security Adviser Tony Lake has suggested, 'Rwanda was a casualty of chronology',[25] clearly implying that the will to act in

Rwanda was blocked by the American deaths in 1993. And, as we have seen, Britain's national interest in Rwanda was minimal: there was nothing in Rwanda, General Dallaire claims, 'that impinged on narrowly defined national interests ... not geographically, strategically or economically',[26] or as Oxfam's Anne Mackintosh more cynically suggests, 'Unlike Kuwait, [Rwanda] does not produce oil and was [therefore] of no consequence'.[27]

Alone, these factors do not truly explain the position in 1994. British intervention in Sierra Leone, Angola and Mali and support for numerous UN missions across black Africa, for example, suggests that to argue foreign policy is driven by skin colour alone is an erroneous and dangerous oversimplification. Secondly, to suggest that the response to the crisis in Yugoslavia was quick and robust is also misleading: the response to the 'white man's crisis' was as slow and hesitant as the response to the crisis in Rwanda, and the failure to prevent the massacre of 9,000 men and boys in Srebrenica, amongst many other incidents, suggests a far from robust response.[28] The Somalia effect was clearly paramount in American thinking but the event does not seem to have influenced British decision making quite so markedly. For Malcolm Rifkind, Somalia was not a 'major' influence in the Government's hesitancy to intervene in Rwanda[29] and the incident was rarely used as an analogy in the British press. Arguably, years of violence in Northern Ireland had made the British public and Government less sensitive to the deaths of soldiers than their American cousins and the shadow of Somalia therefore did not fall as darkly over the UK as it did the US. And finally, the national interest argument, as we saw in the Introduction, lacks weight; especially when it is noted that Britain did intervene, both financially and by deploying troops, when still no traditionally defined national interest existed.

The main reason there was such limited political will to intervene was that despite the end of the Cold War and the growth of liberal and cosmopolitan thought, Conservative foreign policy in the early 1990s remained, as the historian Michael Clarke suggests, distinctly realist.[30] The default position of the Government and the bureaucracy was to not intervene in overseas crises unless there was a clear and direct threat to narrowly defined national security or economic interests. Despite the collapse of the Soviet Union, and the consequent peace dividend and talk of more liberal foreign policies, senior Conservative ministers and FCO officials were products of the Cold War and in 1994 remained faithful to the ideal of inviolable state sovereignty. Margaret Thatcher's condemnation of the 1983 US invasion of Grenada, for example, still rang true in 1994, '[we in the West do not interfere] in the affairs of a small, independent nation, however unattractive its regime'.[31] A bottom-up response to any humanitarian crisis grounded simply on moral obligation and advised by the civil service was therefore highly unlikely; without distinct and clear direction from the Prime Minister to the contrary, the default position of non-intervention would dominate Government decision making.

Natural ideological suspicion of intervention was further heightened, in the initial stages of the genocide at least, by the belief that intervention in this particular case was unlikely to be successful. The Government promised financial aid to the region from late April, but as long as the violence in Rwanda continued to be perceived as civil war it was widely held, and not just by the FCO, that nothing could be done to stop the actual killing. Only when the massive scale of the genocide became clear, in early May, did the FCO accept that a greater UN response was needed. But despite approving the deployment of UNAMIR II, the FCO retained a belief that Britain's finite resources were best deployed elsewhere and there were other countries better placed to respond to the crisis in Rwanda. The FCO argued that Rwanda was an African problem that could only have an African solution and therefore UNAMIR had to be African led. So whilst in May and June the FCO was willing to support UN intervention, there was no suggestion from anyone within the Government, the Opposition, the media or the international community that Britain should be involved directly.

Clearly at some point in early July that changed. Douglas Hurd, presumably prompted by a direct request from the UN Secretariat, was the first to suggest British troops should be deployed. Initially, his suggestion was small: a company of just one hundred REME mechanics. However, despite the Foreign Secretary's support, the deployment was rejected by the MOD, which feared that the costs and risks outweighed the benefits; the risk to British troops would have been too great and the chances of stopping the 'ancient tribal warfare' minimal. As we saw in the previous chapter, only when the ceasefire was declared did this assessment change; only then did military commanders advise ministers that a military mission could successfully achieve the aims of alleviating suffering; only then did the two factors, recognition of a humanitarian crisis and a belief that intervention could be successful, meet. This would not now be intervention to stop the killing, British military intervention came too late for that; this would be intervention to stop further deaths and to reduce the risk of resumption of violence. Only in those respects was the mission viewed as likely to be successful.

But even then the third factor, elite political support, was still needed. The MOD advised against intervention until it acknowledged that there was 'a growing political imperative [to act]'.[32] We cannot yet fully explain why or when this change in 'political imperative' happened; we can, however, be reasonably certain from where the change emanated. The MOD's willingness to turn down the Foreign Secretary's request for troops suggests very strongly that the new political will was driven by the Prime Minister himself. Regrettably, until more documents are released, or John Major speaks publicly about his involvement, we cannot fully explain why Major suddenly moved to a position of supporting a British deployment. Whatever the explanation, it was only with this support at the highest level of government that bureaucratic inertia and traditional Conservative suspicion of intervention could be overcome. As was the case in the 1991 intervention in northern Iraq to assist the Kurds, it was almost certainly

John Major who called for British involvement in the military response; only with his direct involvement did the three necessary factors come together and British intervention become a reality.

Intervention twenty years on

If the response to the Rwandan crisis can then be explained by recognition of a crisis, elite political will and high perceived chances of success, is there evidence that these three factors hold true more generally? And conversely, does intervention in other crises help explain the response in Rwanda? These two questions can be, at least partially, answered by looking at the response to two crises from the early twenty-first century, firstly in Libya and secondly in Syria. Of course direct comparison is almost impossible, much has changed since 1994 and all crises have unique elements; but, conscious of those caveats, the answer to both questions appears to be 'yes'.

Libya

In February 2011, encouraged by uprisings elsewhere in the Arab world, unarmed protestors took to the streets of Libya to demand the overthrow of the dictatorial government of Colonel Muammar Gaddafi. Unlike the Presidents of Tunisia and Egypt, who earlier in the year had fallen fairly quickly and relatively peacefully in response to protests, Gaddafi responded in a manner consistent with his previous forty years of rule – the army, police and security services were used to violently put down the insurrection.

The international community responded quickly to the crisis. As the situation deteriorated, first the Security Council issued a statement condemning the violence and then on 26 February approved a resolution expressing 'grave concern' over Gaddafi's response and imposing an arms embargo.[33] Drawing directly on the language of R2P, the resolution called on the Libyan Government to exercise its 'responsibility to protect' its citizens but, having never shown much regard towards the West, the censure was inevitably ignored by Gaddafi. For over a fortnight the UN debated what to do next. The UK and France were bullish on the need for some form of intervention and proposed a no-fly zone; the US remained cautious and sceptical of the impact of intervention; China, Russia, India, Germany and Brazil (the latter three filling rotating seats on the Security Council) all opposed action. Only the support of the Arab League finally tipped the Security Council in favour of intervention and on 17 March, just a month after the violence began, the Security Council adopted Resolution 1973. The Resolution 'reiterated the responsibility of the Libyan authorities to protect Libyan civilians' and, following a late amendment tabled by the US, authorised other nations to take 'all necessary measures' to protect Libyan civilians.[34]

Almost immediately an international coalition began to enforce the no-fly zone and, drawing on the 'all necessary means' clause, proactively targeted Libyan military equipment that was threatening areas of civilian population. The intervention, which was eventually led by NATO, at its peak involved more than 8,000 servicemen, 25 ships and submarines and more than 250 aircraft.[35] Although officially a humanitarian mission, the intervention was far from neutral: air strikes were launched solely against government targets; in contravention of the arms embargo, the rebel army received weapons from Arab countries and 'non-lethal' military equipment from the UK, France and US; and various special forces units (including from the UK) were deployed to provide training and expertise to the anti-Gaddafi rebels.[36] The response to the Libyan crisis appeared to be evidence of the efficacy of R2P; the Security Council drawing on the language of R2P demonstrated its willingness to authorise the use of force to protect civilians and through swift and decisive action large-scale massacres and a protracted civil war were avoided. As Jonathan Eyal succinctly concludes, 'NATO saved many lives'.[37]

Why, then, did the UK intervene in the Libyan war so robustly and so quickly when it had not done so in Rwanda? It is easy to argue intervention in Libya was in the traditionally defined national interest; the crisis certainly had the potential to impact on the peace and security of the Mediterranean region, as this extract from a David Cameron speech shows:

> This is a regime that for years supported terrorism around the world ... and if we don't sort out the current problems the risk is again of a failed pariah state festering on Europe's southern border, threatening our security, pushing people across the Mediterranean and creating a more dangerous and uncertain world for Britain and all our allies.[38]

Despite these claims, the crisis in Libya did not fall into any of the fifteen risks to national security identified in 2010 by the UK's new National Security Council.[39] In fact, the Libyan crisis posed very little direct danger to Britain and intervention arguably increased the threat to national security: providing humanitarian support to the rebels risked prolonging the conflict, thereby impacting British companies' access to the country's vital oil reserves; opposing Gaddafi increased the risk of retaliatory terrorist attacks on the UK; and intervention risked embroiling Britain in another protracted war in a Muslim country. As in Rwanda, a national interest argument fails to adequately explain the intervention.

In Libya there was certainly an element of desire for regime change that (despite the claims of Hazel Cameron and Wayne Madsen discussed in Chapter 2) was not present in Rwanda. Gaddafi was a leader hated equally in Libya in the Arab region and in the wider international community.[40] Libya, like Rwanda, was understood as a violent civil war but unlike Rwanda it was a war in which the West easily discerned a 'good' and 'bad' side. The rebels were fighting for democracy against a leader who was 'mad ... murderous and evil'[41] and whose regime repressed its people and supported international terrorism. In Rwanda, in contrast, both sides were initially believed to be as bad as each other.

Secondly, unlike in Rwanda, the international community agreed that as well as being a civil war, the crisis in Libya was also a humanitarian emergency in which innocent people were suffering. The civil war in Rwanda was reported in the media and understood by politicians to be an ancient tribal war, a war in which there were no innocents; the war in Libya, by contrast, was described as a fight for democracy and as a war to overthrow a leader who had inflicted murderous attacks on his own people. Libya was not just ancient and tribal savagery, it was perceived as rational and just. British intervention was therefore 'right because we believe we should not stand aside while this dictator murders his own people'.[42] The rhetoric of FCO ministers speaking about the two crises reflects this fundamental difference: for William Hague the war in Libya was an opportunity that 'gave Libyan people a chance to determine their own future',[43] for Mark Lennox-Boyd the war in Rwanda was nothing more than 'a tragic civil war'.[44]

Thirdly, unlike Rwanda, the Libyan crisis attracted the attention of the political elite at an early stage and there was political will at the highest levels to respond. As we have seen, the normal response to overseas crises is to do nothing and this can only be reversed by the most senior level of government. In the case of Libya this came quickly; in the case of Rwanda only after many months. Michael Clarke highlights that in Libya 'the impetus to get involved – to "do something" in the face of Gaddafi's escalating brutality – came from Downing Street directly', it was not 'a policy choice that went "up through the system" gathering staff work and refinement on its way to the Prime Minister's desk'.[45] He continues that the bureaucracy of the MOD advised Cameron against any involvement, but the Prime Minister pushed on, supporting and indeed championing intervention. One minister who attended National Security Council meetings on Libya told the *Guardian*, 'the Prime Minister was always the biggest hawk ... he was always the person pushing and saying "how can we get things done"'.[46] Both Libya and Rwanda show that in the UK it is not the case that the Prime Minister simply approves military deployment, the evidence is that it is they who personally drive that decision-making process. It seems that only this very high-level involvement is sufficient to overcome the normative opposition to intervention that ordinarily prevents humanitarian intervention.

Finally, Libya demonstrates that intervention only happens when decision makers perceive there to be a high chance of success. Certainly, as the Chief of Defence Staff and undoubtedly many others warned Cameron, there was a risk that an orthodox ground troop-led intervention in Libya would lead to a protracted war and British casualties. Indeed, it was largely the fear that Western intervention would worsen the situation in Libya and prolong the violence that led the German Government to oppose the UN resolution.[47] These risks were minimised by the very deliberate decision to avoid putting troops on the ground; Resolution 1973 authorised 'all necessary means' but then explicitly prohibited 'a foreign occupation force of any form on any part of Libyan territory'. From the outset it was agreed that it would be the rebel army that would pursue the ground war, it would not be Western soldiers. This decision to intervene through the use of airpower alone minimised both the risk of casualties for intervening countries and the risk of a Muslim backlash to Western presence in another Islamic country.[48]

Therefore, political leaders in the UK, US and France believed the nature of the Libyan conflict meant that intervention had significant potential benefits (which included regime change as well as protecting civilians) at acceptable, almost minimal, risk and cost. For the most part NATO could also easily differentiate between government and rebel forces and keep collateral civilian damage to a minimum;[49] Gaddafi's forces were targeted as they sat in the open desert or as they drove down the main coastal highway. As the *Independent* suggested, 'hitting tanks in the open is meat and drink to coalition aircraft'.[50] The geography of Libya meant aircraft could easily target Gaddafi's tanks, artillery and armoured vehicles and therefore, as Cameron put it, 'stop tanks rolling into Benghazi ... [and] prevent a bloodbath'.[51] Intervention in Libya, by air alone, was in the 'can-do' box.

In direct contrast, the genocide in Rwanda was perpetrated in densely populated towns and villages, by individuals going door-to-door killing with machetes. In this scenario air intervention alone would not have been effective; such killing could only have been stopped by actual boots on the ground and, as Alan Kuperman demonstrates, thousands of boots would have been required for intervention to be effective.[52] Of course the West could have supported the RPF as it did the Libyan rebel army. But whereas the Libyan rebels were believed to be fighting for democracy against an internationally unpopular despot, the RPF did not have such universal support; instead many in the West saw both sides in Rwanda as being as bad as each other. In Libya there was a way to intervene that was perceived as effective and low risk; in Rwanda there was no such option.

Syria

For a short while the crisis in Syria looked as it would lead the intervention debate in a new direction. For the first time politicians and commentators genuinely and explicitly used R2P to justify possible intervention in an actual crisis, but the response to the crisis in Syria seems again to confirm the underlying hypothesis that it is not morality, R2P or national interest that is fundamental to intervention, instead the drivers of intervention are recognition of a crisis, elite political will and perceived chance of success. In the case of Syria, however, whilst two of these factors were present (recognition of a crisis and elite political will), there was insufficient belief that intervention would be successful and as such (as at the time of writing in mid-2014) there has been no intervention.

Like the crisis in Libya, the violence in Syria began when the Government used tanks, gunfire and mass arrests to try to crush street protests inspired by the wider Arab Spring. Beginning in March 2011, the protests quickly spread across the country and the protestors came together to form first armed gangs and then a more unified and formal opposition; by autumn protests had degenerated into full-scale civil war and by December 2012 the UN concluded that the country had spiralled into a sectarian war between the majority Sunni population and the Shiite-dominated Government.[53] In the same report the UN highlighted that 'The unrelenting violence in Syria has resulted in thousands of deaths, untold thousands of wounded, detained and disappeared, and physical destruction on a massive scale'.[54] In August 2013 the crisis took another turn when reports suggested that the Government had used chemical weapons against rebels and civilians; the UN Secretary General called the attack 'a war crime'.[55]

From the outset the international community recognised that the violence was causing terrible human suffering and the West, at least, did condemn President Assad's draconian response.[56] But a firmer stance was hindered by Russian support for the Syrian Government and suspicion that the West was using the UN as a cloak for regime change (both Russia and China vetoed draft Security Council resolutions on Syria in October 2011, February 2012 and July 2012). With the UN Security Council left paralysed, Western countries were forced to respond to the crisis on an almost unilateral basis. For the UK, before August 2013, this meant a three-pronged approach. Firstly, the British Government was a significant donor to the relief programme in the region; by October 2013 the Department of International Development (DFID) had allocated some £500 million of aid.[57] Secondly, ministers publicly called for a diplomatic solution to the crisis. The UK, for example, tabled the three vetoed resolutions mentioned above, led the EU debate on imposing sanctions on Syria, led calls for President Assad to step down and frequently condemned the violence. Thirdly, in a move that demonstrates clearly that the Government believed peace was only possible if Assad was overthrown or stood aside, the FCO actively engaged with the Syrian opposition. For example, the FCO adopted a policy it described as 'intensive engagement with a wide range of Syrian oppositionists'[58] and then provided the rebels with £8 million of non-lethal military equipment, including vehicles, body armour, communications equipment and chemical weapon detection equipment.[59]

The use of chemical weapons, perhaps not of major strategic significance in the actual war, was, however, a game changer politically; it was an act that the international community could not ignore, especially as a year earlier US President Obama had described the use of such weapons as 'a red line ... that would change my calculus'.[60] It was also an act that reinvigorated the will to respond at senior levels of government in the UK and across the Western world. Within days of the reports emerging, Downing Street announced that David Cameron had discussed a response on the phone with presidents Obama, Hollande (France) and Putin (Russia); prime ministers Harper (Canada) and Rudd (Australia); and Chancellor Merkel (Germany). Very soon after the attacks, the Prime Minister had taken the view that 'a firm response from the international community' was required.[61] It quickly became evident that this meant some form of military response and Cameron meant to take a lead in calling for such action. Two of the three necessary drivers of intervention were now present: recognition of a crisis and elite political will.

This call to arms, however, was not entirely driven by the humanitarian suffering. The UK had previously responded to the humanitarian crisis, but serious (or at least public) consideration of military intervention came only after the chemical attack. Speaking on the BBC, the Prime Minister said 'the use of chemical weapons is morally indefensible and completely wrong and what we have seen in Syria are appalling scenes of death and suffering because of the use of chemical weapons'.[62] There was very little reference to the death and suffering caused by conventional weapons; instead Cameron argued for a 'proportionate' response which would 'deter' the Syrian state from using toxic weapons again.[63] However, this remains consistent with our hypothesis: it is not morality that drives intervention but an assessment that, taking into account the level of national interest, the rewards of intervention outweigh the risks. Before the use of chemical weapons, as one senior Cabinet Minister told the author, the risk versus reward calculation and the lack of international support argued against intervention;[64] but the use of sarin gas altered that equation. The British Government decided that the risks of intervention outweighed the risks of failing to respond to a blatant use of chemical weapons against civilians. Like Obama, the British Government believed that Assad's use of chemical weapons crossed a line that tipped the scales in favour of intervention – albeit that in this case intervention, as in Libya, was likely to mean targeting Syria's military infrastructure by air and missile strikes rather than actual troops on the ground.

However, two factors were to constrain a British response. First was the acknowledgment that the UK did not have the military or diplomatic muscle to act unilaterally. Any response would have to be multilateral and would have to include the US, hence Cameron's phone conversations with world leaders. Secondly, in a way that had not been seen before, the Government found itself constrained domestically by a hostile Parliament. At the same time as Cameron was phoning world leaders, over sixty MPs signed a parliamentary motion calling for a full debate on Syria. Whereas there had been no role for Parliament in the decision to deploy troops to Rwanda (or indeed Libya), the weight of opposition to intervention meant that this would not be the case over Syria. In late August, before Cameron could agree a course of action with Obama and other leaders, the British media widely reported that public opinion was against intervention[65] and a number of MPs took to television, radio, newspapers and Twitter to express their opposition to intervention. Despite a constitutional right to engage in military action without a vote in Parliament,[66] the Prime Minister accepted that in this case the political reality was that a vote was needed; military action without parliamentary consensus would have been too damaging to the coalition government. Following calls from the media and MPs alike, Parliament was recalled from its summer recess and a vote on intervention in Syria held on 29 August after a full day of debate. The Government motion was rejected 285 votes to 272; leaving Cameron to acknowledge, 'It is very clear tonight that ... the British Parliament, reflecting the views of the British people, does not want to see British military action. I get that, and the Government will act accordingly.'[67] Military intervention was no longer an option.

There were a number of possible reasons why there was such popular opposition to intervention. First it was widely claimed in the press that the British public were war weary after ten years of involvement in Afghanistan and Iraq.[68] Secondly, there were suggestions that, given the economic environment, the public believed in a need for a focus on the domestic rather than the international agenda.[69] Thirdly, the evidence to support intervention was called into question. MPs and media recalled how Tony Blair had justified the invasion of Iraq on the grounds that Saddam Hussein had chemical weapons and other weapons of mass destruction; like the story of the boy who cried wolf, many MPs were not willing to approve military intervention based on a claim they had heard before. These factors were certainly important, but it seems the main grounds for opposition were the perennial fear that intervention would do more harm than good; that military intervention of any kind would be unsuccessful.

MPs generally agreed with the Government that Syria represented a humanitarian crisis, but most did not share the Prime Minister's opinion that intervention would be beneficial; and this scepticism was largely a result of intervention in Iraq. During the Commons debate, MP after MP reminded the House of the lessons of Iraq; in that one debate there were over one hundred references to Iraq. John McDonnell (Labour, Hayes) said, 'No matter how surgical the strike that is planned by the Americans or by us, [as in Iraq] lives will be lost and lives will be put at risk';[70] Hugh Bayley (Labour, York Central): '[air strikes] failed to bring Saddam to heel and eventually escalated into the second, controversial Iraq war. Once a small military step is taken, conflicts are likely to escalate';[71] Nadhim Zahawi (Conservative, Stratford): 'In Iraq, we have seen what happens when a ruling minority is violently deposed ... My fear is that the envisioned post-Assad Syria would be equally unsustainable.'[72] It was this fear that intervention would lead to greater loss of life, would escalate the war further or would result in unnecessary British casualties that ultimately led Parliament to vote against the Government.

The response to the Syria crisis is therefore entirely consistent with this book's hypotheses: the journey towards intervention was very much led by the political elite (Cameron and Hague in particular), was in response to a recognised humanitarian crisis and was only pursued when the reward of intervention outweighed the risk (an equation which in this case was heavily influenced by the use of chemical weapons). However, Syria introduced new dimensions. First, it demonstrated that the shadow of Iraq still hangs over the UK. The continued popular belief that the overthrow of Saddam Hussein was illegal, was based on inaccurate intelligence and caused untold suffering will undoubtedly influence foreign policy for a number of years. Historians of the future may indeed speak of an 'Iraq Syndrome' as we now speak of America's 'Vietnam Syndrome'. Secondly, the response to the crisis has potentially demonstrated a shift in the constitutional position of Parliament vis-á-vis the prime minister. This is yet to be seen, but Syria may prove to be a turning point in Parliament's role in approving military action; it may now be a political reality that without parliamentary support governments are impotent to approve discretionary military intervention. But what Syria does categorically prove is that even in the age of R2P unless there is a firm belief that intervention can be undertaken successfully, at acceptable levels of risk and at an acceptable cost, it will not go ahead.

Was Britain responsible?

We return finally to Tony Blair's statement of Britain and Rwanda: 'We knew. We failed to act. We were responsible.'[73] Linda Melvern and Paul Williams, in one of the few articles specifically on the British response to the genocide, similarly describe John Major's policy as 'official indifference'.[74] They continue:

> The best that can be said for Britain's policy is that it rested on a tragically flawed interpretation of events on the ground and a desire not to jeopardise the future of UN peacekeeping ... A more accurate interpretation is that Britain's policy of indifference and non-intervention was justified with reference to a deliberately misconceived version of events in Rwanda and a wilful neglect of its obligations under the Genocide Convention.[75]

Ingvar Carlsson likewise condemns Britain and the other members of the Security Council for failing in their 'responsibility to prevent and punish the crime of genocide'[76] and Romeo Dallaire accuses the UK, US and France of 'shirking their legal and moral responsibilities'[77] in Rwanda. But despite these accusations and Blair's *mea culpa* it is hard to see how Britain can in fact be held responsible for the genocide.

Taking a slight step backwards, before a judgement of responsibility can be made we perhaps need to define what it means to be responsible; after all, as Fritz Heider argues, a bystander surely cannot be held responsible for mere association with an emergency, simply being in the wrong place at the wrong time does not make one responsible.[78] Daniela Kroslak provides a useful method for assessing a bystander's degree of responsibility in the case of genocide, 'How much did the bystander *know* about the preparation of the genocide or, during the genocide about its implementation? To what extent was the bystander *involved* with the genocidal regime prior to and throughout the atrocities? And what *capabilities* did the bystander have to intervene in some way, shape or form to prevent or suppress the genocide?' (original emphasis).[79]

Taking these in turn, as we have seen, Britain knew nothing of the preparation of the genocide and for various reasons already discussed failed to truly understand what was happening in the country until at least mid-May. Lack of historical links, the FCO's failure to visit the country more frequently, poor media coverage and the simultaneous occurrence of other world crises meant warning signs from Rwanda were missed. In terms of involvement with the genocidal regime, there simply was none: Britain had no relationship with the interim Government or FAR; at the other extreme, it is in fact accused of engaging in a proxy war against the regime through collusion with the RPF.[80] We are left, then, with the final question of what capability the British Government had to stop the genocide, and the answer is very little. British troops could have been sent to Rwanda, but there were strong and sensible arguments against such a deployment, including significantly the fact that the MOD was almost completely reliant on the US for airlift capacity and this was simply not on offer before the July ceasefire. Alternatively, the UK could have pursued diplomatic efforts to end the genocide more robustly. In reality such efforts were constrained first by Britain's lack of meaningful relationship with, or power over, either side in the war and secondly by the US's intransigence at the Security Council.

Where the British did have the capability to save lives, during the refugee crises both in Tanzania and Zaire, the Government and public did respond and very robustly. In Benaco and Goma, British aid unquestionably saved many lives and in Rwanda itself British troops provided much-needed medical, logistical and engineering support. In this respect the British public, British NGOs and the British Government made a contribution to Rwanda that far exceeded that of most other Western nations; in that one year Britain donated more aid to Rwanda than it had done cumulatively throughout history, making the UK one of the largest donor states to the crisis. Britain may have arrived in Rwanda too late to stop the genocidal killing, but it arrived in time to help stop much of the dying.

Britain could have done more in Rwanda; to argue otherwise is to ignore Britain's place in the world as a member of the Security Council with a large and effective military, but for so many reasons a response would not have been easy or effective. But to argue that anyone in the UK wilfully sat back and knowingly let genocide happen is a misinterpretation of the facts specific to Rwanda and of foreign policy making more generally. Britain did not let the genocide happen because the victims were black, or because of some conspiracy theory that the Government supported the RPF, or even because it did not care. Britain failed to stop the killing in Rwanda because the Government, public and media genuinely did not recognise the genocide for what it was and did not have the capability to stop it. In the case of Rwanda, Britain was not the indifferent bystander or the bystander who did too little; throughout the crisis Britain was simply the ignorant bystander. We must conclude that the UK bears little responsibility for what happened in Rwanda in 1994.

Notes

1 For a fuller account of the UK's relationship with Rwanda since 1994 see: R. Hayman, 'Abandoned Orphan, Wayward Child: The United Kingdom and Belgium in Post-1994 Rwanda', *Journal of East African Studies* 4:2 (2010), pp. 341–60; or D. Beswick, 'Aiding State Building and Sacrificing Peace Building: The Rwanda-UK Relationship 1994 to 2011', *Third World Quarterly* 32:10 (2011), pp. 1911–30.
2 National Archives, London: FCO 371/187917, 'Political Relations between UK and Rwanda 1966', 28 February 1966.
3 DFID, 'Rwanda: Country Assistance Plan 2003–2006', London: DFID, February 2004, p. 17.
4 T. Blair, 'Full Text: Tony Blair's Speech', *Guardian* (2 October 2001).
5 www.toryspeeches.files.wordpress.com/2013/11/william-hague-the-future-of-british-foreign-policy.pdf (accessed on 22 June 2014).
6 Hansard, HC Deb, 9 June 2004, vol. 422, col. 284.
7 Hansard, HC Deb, 19 April 1999, vol. 329, col. 656.
8 Hansard, HC Deb, 17 May 2004, vol. 421, col. 699.
9 R. Thakur, 'No More Rwandas: Intervention, Sovereignty and the Responsibility to Protect', *Humanitarian Exchange* 26 (2004), p. 7.
10 Anonymous interview with author.
11 D. Smith, 'Tribal Feuds', *Scotsman* (7 July 1994).
12 JEEAR, *The International Response to Conflict and Genocide, Lessons from the Rwanda Experience, Volume II: Early Warning and Conflict Management* (Copenhagen: Joint Evaluation of Emergency Assistance to Rwanda, 1996), p. 47.
13 Doyle, 'Reporting the Genocide', p. 145.
14 R. Ammon, *Global Television and the Shaping of World Politics: CNN, Telediplomacy and Foreign Policy*, (Jefferson: McFarland & Co, 2001), p. 127.
15 Kuperman, 'How the Media Missed the Rwanda Genocide', in Thompson (ed.), *Media and the Rwanda Genocide* p. 256.
16 Dahlgren, 'The Third World of TV News', p. 53.
17 P. Robinson, *The CNN Effect: The Myth of News, Foreign Policy and Intervention* (London: Routledge, 2002), p. 115.
18 VSO, *The Live Aid Legacy*, p. 3.
19 Shaw, 'Historical Frames and the Politics of Humanitarian Intervention', p. 359.

20 Quoted in Dawes, *That the World May Know*, p. 23.
21 Coles, *Making Foreign Policy*, p. 124.
22 Hurd, *Memoirs*, p. 541.
23 Carlsson *et al.*, *Report of the Independent Inquiry into the Actions of the United Nations During the 1994 Genocide in Rwanda*, p. 41.
24 L. Murray, *Clinton, Peacekeeping and Humanitarianism: Rise and Fall of a Policy* (London: Routledge, 2008), p. 138; Shaw, 'Historical Frames and the Politics of Humanitarian Intervention', p. 365.
25 Cohen, *One Hundred Days of Silence*, p. 60.
26 R. Dallaire *et al.*, 'The Major Powers on Trial', *Journal of International Criminal Justice* 3 (2005), p. 875.
27 Mackintosh, 'Rwanda: Beyond Ethnic Conflict', p. 465.
28 Rieff, *Slaughterhouse*, p. 177; M Stuart, *Douglas Hurd: The Public Servant* (Edinburgh: Mainstream Publishing, 1998), p. 324; S. Cohen, *States of Denial: Knowing about Atrocities and Suffering* (Cambridge: Polity, 2001), p. 18.
29 Interview with Malcolm Rifkind.
30 M. Clarke, *British External Policy Making in the 1990s* (London: Macmillan, 1992), p. 4.
31 Thatcher, *The Downing Street Years*, p. 331.
32 MOD, letter from Malcolm Rifkind's private secretary to FCO, 25 July 1994.
33 United Nations, New York, UN S/Res (2011) 1970, 26 February 2011.
34 United Nations, New York, UN S/Res (2011) 1973, 17 March 2011.
35 NATO, www.nato.int/cps/en/natolive/topics_71652.htm, accessed 11 June 2014.
36 M. Mohlin, 'Cloak and Dagger in Libya: The Libyan Thuwar and the Role of Allied Special Forces', in K. Engelbrekt, M. Mohlin and C. Wagnsson (eds), *The NATO Intervention in Libya* (Abingdon: Routledge, 2014), pp. 205–7.
37 J. Eyal, 'The Responsibility to Protect: A Chance Missed', in A. Johnson and S. Mueen (eds), *Short War, Long Shadow: The Political and Military Legacies of the 2011 Libya Campaign* (London: Royal United Services Institute, 2012), p. 59.
38 David Cameron press conference, Brussels, 11 March 2011, at www.gov.uk/government/speeches/press-conference-in-brussels, accessed 11 June 2014.
39 HM Government, *A Strong Britain in an Age of Uncertainty: The National Security Strategy* (London: The Stationery Office, 2010).
40 R. Egnell, 'Lessons and Consequences of Operation Unified Protector', in Engelbrekt *et al.* (eds), *NATO Intervention in Libya*, p. 231.
41 Hugo Rifkind, 'There is no Case – Yet – for Any Form of Liberal Intervention', *The Times* (4 March 2011).
42 David Cameron's statement on Libya, 19 March 2011, at www.number10.gov.uk, accessed 5 June 2012.
43 William Hague press conference, London, 31 March 2011, at www.fco.gov.uk/en/news/latest-news/?view=Speech&id=576187382, accessed 11 June 2014.
44 Hansard. HC Deb, 9 May 1994, vol. 243, col. 28w.

45 M. Clarke, 'The Making of Britain's Libya Strategy', in A. Johnson and S. Mueen (eds), *Short War, Long Shadow: The Political and Military Legacies of the 2011 Libya Campaign* (London: Royal United Services Institute, 2012), p. 8.
46 P. Wintour, 'David Cameron's Libyan War: Why the PM Felt Gaddafi had to be Stopped', *Guardian* (2 October 2011).
47 United Nations Department of Public Information, press release SC10200, 'Security Council Approves No-Fly Zone over Libya', 17 March 2011.
48 K. Engelbrekt, 'Why Libya?', in Engelbrekt *et al.* (eds), *NATO Intervention in Libya*, p. 54.
49 A. Nygren, 'Executing Strategy from the Air', in Engelbrekt *et al.* (eds), *NATO Intervention in Libya*, p. 119.
50 B. Brady, 'How Effective Have the Coalition Air Strikes Been?', *Independent* (3 April 2011), p. 12.
51 Hansard, HC Deb, 21 March 2011, vol. 525, col. 703.
52 Kuperman, *The Limits of Humanitarian Intervention*,, p. 87.
53 UNHCR, 'Independent International Commission of Inquiry on the Syrian Arab Republic', 20 December 2012, pp. 3–4.
54 *Ibid.*, p. 1.
55 UN, 'Report on Alleged Use of Chemical Weapons in the Ghouta Area of Damascus', 16 September 2013.
56 FCO press release, 'Foreign Secretary Condemns the Killing of Demonstrators by the Syrian Security Forces', 8 April 2011.
57 DFID press release, 'UK Aid Syria Response', 8 October 2013.
58 FCO press release, 'Foreign Office Minister Meets Syrian Kurdish Opposition Leader', 18 January 2012.
59 K. Sengupta, 'Revealed: What the West Has Given Syria's Rebels', *Independent* (11 August 2013).
60 S. Thomas, 'Obama Draws Red Line for Syria', *NBC News*, 20 August 2012.
61 Prime Minister's Office, press release, 'Syria: PM Call with Chancellor Merkel', 25 August 2013.
62 BBC News Online, 'Syria: Cameron Says Use of Chemical Weapons "Cannot Stand"', 27 August 2013, www.bbc.co.uk/news/uk-23851292, accessed 22 June 2014.
63 T. Ross, 'MPs Recalled to Parliament to Vote on Syrian Crisis', *Daily Telegraph* (27 August 2013).
64 Anonymous interview with author.
65 On 28 August, for example, the front-page headline of the *Sun* was 'Brits Say No to War'. A YouGov poll commissioned by the newspaper showed the public opposed missile strikes on Syria by 2 to 1 and that 74% opposed the sending of ground troops to Syria.
66 White, *Democracy goes to War*, p. 20.
67 Hansard, HC Deb, 29 August 2013, vol. 566, col. 1556.
68 M. West, 'Britain is War Weary and Suffering from "Vietnam Syndrome" after Decade of Fighting in Middle East', *Daily Mail* (18 June 2013).

69 M. Hastings, 'We've Got Enough Problems at Home without Charging into Another Foreign Bloodbath', *Daily Mail* (28 May 2013).
70 Hansard, HC Deb, 29 August 2013, vol. 566, col. 1462.
71 Hansard, HC Deb, 29 August, vol. 566, col. 1531.
72 Hansard, HC Deb, 29 August, vol. 566, col. 1533.
73 Blair, *A Journey*, p. 61.
74 Melvern and Williams, 'Britannia Waived the Rules', p. 2.
75 *Ibid.*, p. 22.
76 Carlsson, 'The UN Inadequacies', p. 844.
77 Dallaire *et al.*, 'The Major Powers on Trial', p. 887.
78 H. Bierhoff, *Prosocial Behaviour* (New York: Psychology Press, 2002), p. 162.
79 Kroslak, *The Responsibility of External Bystanders*, p. 4.
80 Cameron, *The Cat's Paw*, p. 113.

Select bibliography

Adelman, H. and A. Suhrke (eds), *The Path of a Genocide: The Rwanda Crisis from Uganda to Zaire* (New Brunswick: Transaction, 2001)

—— 'Early Warning and Response: Why the International Community Failed to Prevent the Genocide', *Disasters* 20:4 (2007)

Albright, M., *Madam Secretary: A Memoir* (London: Macmillan, 2003)

Allen, T. and J. Seaton (eds), *The Media of Conflict: War Reporting and Representations of Ethic Violence* (London: Zed Books, 1999)

Allison, G., *Essence of Decision: Explaining the Cuban Missile Crisis* (Boston: Little, Brown and Co., 1971)

Barnett, M., 'The UN Security Council: Indifference and the Genocide in Rwanda', *Cultural Anthropology* 12:4 (1997)

—— *Eyewitness to a Genocide: The United Nations and Rwanda* (Ithaca: Cornell University Press, 2003)

BBC, *Mission Angola: Defence of the Realm* (TV programme first aired BBC One, 29 August 1996).

—— *Values: Getting our Way* (TV Programme, first aired BBC One, 22 February 2010).

Beattie, L., 'The Media and Africa: Images of Disaster and Rebellion', in G. Philo (ed.), *Message Received* (Harlow: Longman, 1999)

Bell, M., 'TV News: How Far Should we Go?' *British Journalism Review* 8:1 (1997)

Bellamy, A., 'Whither the Responsibility to Protect? Humanitarian Intervention and the 2005 World Summit', *Ethics & International Affairs* 20:2 (2006)

—— and P. Williams, *Understanding Peacekeeping* (Cambridge: Polity Press, 2010)

Bennett, G., *Six Moments of Crisis: Inside British Foreign Policy* (Oxford: Oxford University Press, 2013)

Berdal, M., 'Peacekeeping in Africa, 1990–1996: The Role of the United States, France and Britain', in O. Furley and R. May (eds), *Peacekeeping in Africa* (Aldershot: Ashgate, 1998)

Beswick, D., 'Aiding State Building and Sacrificing Peace Building: The Rwanda–UK Relationship 1994 to 2011', *Third World Quarterly* 32:10 (2011)

Blair, T., *A Journey* (London: Hutchinson, 2010)

Brown, B. and D. Shukman, *All Necessary Means: Inside the Gulf War* (London: BBC Books, 1991)

Brunk, D., 'Curing the Somalia Syndrome: Analogy, Foreign Policy Decision Making, and the Rwandan Genocide', *Foreign Policy Analysis* 4 (2008)

Budge, I., *The Changing Political System: Into the 1990s*, 2nd edn (London and New York: Longman, 1988)
—— *The New British Politics*, 4th edn (Harlow: Pearson Longman, 2007)
Burkhalter, H., 'The Question of Genocide: The Clinton Administration and Rwanda', *World Policy Journal* 11:4 (1994)
Bush, G., *Decision Points* (London: Virgin Books, 2010)
Callamand, A., 'French Policy in Rwanda', in H. Adelman and A. Suhrke (eds), *The Path of a Genocide: The Rwanda Crisis from Uganda to Zaire* (New Brunswick: Transaction, 1999)
Cameron, H., 'Britain's Hidden Role in Rwandan State Violence', *Criminal Justice Matters* 82:1 (2010)
—— 'British State Complicity in Genocide: Rwanda 1994', *State Crime* 1:1 (2012)
—— *Britain's Hidden Role in the Rwandan Genocide: The Cat's Paw* (Abingdon: Routledge, 2013)
Caplan, G., 'Rwanda: Walking the Road to Genocide', in A. Thompson (ed.), *The Media and the Rwanda Genocide* (London: Pluto Press, 2007)
Carlsson, I., 'The UN Inadequacies', *Journal of International Criminal Justice* 3 (2005)
—— *et al.*, *Report of the Independent Inquiry into the Actions of the United Nations During the 1994 Genocide in Rwanda* (New York: United Nations, 1999)
Carruthers, S., *The Media at War: Communication and Conflict in the Twentieth Century* (Basignstoke: Macmillan Press, 2000)
Chandler, D., *From Kosovo to Kabul and Beyond: Human Rights and International Intervention*, 2nd edn (London: Pluto Press, 2006)
Clapham, C., 'Rwanda: The Perils of Peacemaking', *Journal of Peace Research* 35:2 (1998)
Clarke, M., *British External Policy Making in the 1990s* (London: Macmillan, 1992)
——'Foreign Policy', in A. Seldon (ed.), *Blair's Britain* (Cambridge: Cambridge University Press, 2007)
—— 'The Making of Britain's Libya Strategy', in A. Johnson and S. Mueen (eds), *Short War, Long Shadow: The Political and Military Legacies of the 2011 Libya Campaign* (London: Royal United Services Institute, 2012)
Clements, B., 'Examining Public Attitudes towards Recent Foreign Policy Issues: Britain's Involvement in the Iraq and Afghanistan Conflicts', *Politics* 31:2 (2011)
Clinton, B., *My Life* (London: Arrow Books, 2005)
Cooke, A., *The Campaign Guide 1994: A Comprehensive Survey of Conservative Policy* (London: Conservative & Unionist Central Office, 1994)
Cohen, H., *Intervening in Africa: Superpower Peacemaking in a Troubled Continent* (Basingstoke: Macmillan Press, 2000)
Cohen, J., *One Hundred Days of Silence: America and the Rwanda Genocide* (Lanham: Rowman & Littlefield, 2007)
Coles, J., *Making Foreign Policy: A Certain Idea of Britain* (London: John Murray, 2000)
Coonaughton, R., 'The Military, Peacekeeping and Africa', in O. Furley and R. May (eds), *Peacekeeping in Africa* (Aldershot: Ashgate, 1998)
—— *Military Intervention and Peacekeeping: The Reality* (Aldershot: Ashgate, 2001)

Courtemanche, G., *A Sunday at the Pool in Kigali* (Edinburgh: Canongate, 2003)
Coyne, C., 'The Politics of Bureaucracy and the Failure of Post-War Reconstruction', *Public Choice* 135 (2008)
Cradock, P., *In Pursuit of British Interests: Reflections on Foreign Policy under Margaret Thatcher and John Major* (London: John Murray, 1997)
Curtis, M., *The Ambiguities of Power: British Foreign Policy since 1945* (London: Zed Books, 1995)
—— 'Britain's Real Foreign Policy and the Failure of British Academia', *International Relations* 18:13 (2004)
Dahlgren, P., 'The Third World on TV News: Western Ways of Seeing the "Other"', in W. Adams (ed.), *Television Coverage of International Affairs* (Norwood: Ablex, 1982)
Dallaire, R., *Shake Hands with the Devil: The Failure of Humanity in Rwanda* (London: Arrow Books, 2004)
——, K. Manocha and N. Degnarain, 'The Major Powers on Trial', *Journal of International Criminal Justice* 3 (2005)
Dannreuther, R., *International Security: The Contemporary Agenda* (Cambridge: Polity Press, 2007)
Dawes, J., *That the World May Know: Bearing Witness to Atrocities* (Cambridge: Harvard University Press, 2007)
De Heusch, L., 'Rwanda: Responsibilities for a Genocide', *Anthropology Today* 11:4 (1995)
Des Forges, A., *Leave None to Tell the Story: Genocide in Rwanda* (New York: Human Rights Watch, 1999)
—— 'Shame: Rationalising Western Apathy on Rwanda', *Foreign Affairs* (June 2000)
Destexhe, A., 'The Third Genocide', *Foreign Policy* Winter (1994)
—— *Rwanda and Genocide in the Twentieth Century* (London: Pluto Press, 1995)
De Waal, A. and R. Omaar, 'The Genocide in Rwanda and the International Response', *Current History* 94:591 (1995)
Dickie, J., *Inside the Foreign Office* (London: Chapmans, 1992)
—— *The New Mandarins: How British Foreign Policy Works* (London: I.B. Tauris, 2004)
Diehl, P., *Peace Operations* (Cambridge: Polity Press, 2008)
DiPrizio, R., *Armed Humanitarians: US Interventions from Northern Iraq to Kosovo* (Baltimore: Johns Hopkins University Press, 2002)
Dixon, P., 'Britain's "Vietnam Syndrome"? Public Opinion and British Military Intervention from Palestine to Yugoslavia', *Review of International Studies* 26 (2000)
Dowden, R., 'The Rwandan Genocide: How the Press Missed the Story. A Memoir', *African Affairs* 103 (2004)
—— *Africa: Altered States, Ordinary Miracles* (London: Portobello Books, 2009)
Doyle, M., 'Reporting the Genocide', in A. Thompson (ed.), *The Media and the Rwanda Genocide* (London: Pluto Press, 2007)
Drury, C. *et al.*, 'The Politics of Humanitarian Aid: U.S. Foreign Disaster Assistance, 1964–1995', *Journal of Politics* 67:2 (2005)

Dumbrell, J., *Clinton's Foreign Policy: Between the Bushes, 1992–2000* (London: Routledge, 2009)

Durch, W., 'Building on Sand: UN Peacekeeping in the Western Sahara', *International Security* 17:4 (1993)

Evans, G., 'Crimes against Humanity: Overcoming Indifference', *Journal of Genocide Research* 8:3 (2006)

Foley, C. and K. Starmer, 'Foreign Policy, Human Rights and the United Kingdom', *Social Policy and Administration* 32:5 (1998)

Frizzell, C., 'Public Opinion and Foreign Policy: The Effects of Celebrity Endorsements', *Social Science Journal* 48 (2011)

Garnett, M., *Principles and Politics in Contemporary Britain*, 2nd edn (Exeter: Imprint Academic, 2006)

Geeta, S., 'Role of the United Nations in Namibian Independence', *International Studies* 30:1 (1993)

Goose, S. and F. Smyth, 'Arming Genocide in Rwanda', *Foreign Affairs* 73:5 (1994)

Gourevitch, P., *We Wish to Inform you that Tomorrow we Will be Killed with our Families* (London: Picador, 2000)

Gribbin, R., *In the Aftermath of Genocide: The US Role in Rwanda* (New York: iUniverse, 2005)

Hannay, D., *New World Disorder: The UN after the Cold War: An Insider's View* (London: I.B. Tauris, 2008)

Hatzfeld, J., *Machete Season: The Killers in Rwanda Speak*, trans. L. Coverdale (New York: Farrar, Strauss and Giroux, 2005)

Hawley, A., 'Rwanda 1994: A Study of Medical Support in Military Humanitarian Operations', *Journal of Royal Army Medical Corps* 143 (1997)

Hayman, R., 'Abandoned Orphan, Wayward Child: The United Kingdom and Belgium in Post-1994 Rwanda', *Journal of East African Studies*, 4:2 (2010)

Hehir, A., *Humanitarian Intervention: An Introduction* (Basingstoke: Palgrave Macmillan, 2010)

Heppell, T., 'Weak and Ineffective: Reassessing the Party Political Leadership of John Major', *Political Quarterly* 78:3 (2007)

Hilsum, L., 'Reporting Rwanda: The Media and the Aid Agencies', in A. Thompson (ed.), *The Media and the Rwanda Genocide* (London: Pluto Press, 2007)

—— *Sandstorm: Libya from Gaddafi to Revolution* (London: Faber & Faber, 2012)

Hintjens, H., 'Explaining the 1994 Genocide in Rwanda', *Journal of Modern African Studies* 37:2 (1999)

Holbrooke, R., *To End a War* (New York: Modern Library, 1999)

Holmes, G., 'Did *Newsnight* Miss the Story? A Survey of How the BBC's "Flagship Political Current Affairs Programme" Reported Genocide and War in Rwanda between April and July 1994', *Genocide Studies and Prevention* 6:2 (2011)

Huliaras, A., 'The "Anglo-Saxon Conspiracy": French Perceptions of the Great Lakes Crisis', *Journal of Modern African Studies* 36:4 (1998)

Human Rights Watch, *The Rwandan Genocide: How it Was Prepared* (London: Human Rights Watch, 2006)

Hurd, D., *Memoirs* (London: Abacus, 2004)

International Panel of Eminent Experts *Rwanda: The Preventable Genocide* (Addis Ababa: Organisation of African Unity, 2000)

Jakobsen, P., 'National Interest, Humanitarianism or CNN: What Triggers UN Peace Enforcement after the Cold War?', *Journal of Peace Research* 33:2 (1996)

Janssen, D., 'Humanitarian Intervention and the Prevention of Genocide', *Journal of Genocide Research* 10:2 (2008)

Jentleson, B. and R. Britton, 'Still Pretty Prudent: Post Cold-War American Public Opinion on the Use of Military Force', *Journal of Conflict Resolution* 42:4 (1998)

Joint Evaluation of Emergency Assistance to Rwanda, *The International Response to Conflict and Genocide: Lessons from the Rwanda Experience, Volume I: Historical Perspectives* (Copenhagen: Joint Evaluation of Emergency Assistance to Rwanda, 1996)

—— *The International Response to Conflict and Genocide: Lessons from the Rwanda Experience, Volume II: Early Warning and Conflict Management* (Copenhagen: Joint Evaluation of Emergency Assistance to Rwanda, 1996)

—— *The International Response to Conflict and Genocide: Lessons from the Rwanda Experience, Volume III: Humanitarian Aid and Effects* (Copenhagen: Joint Evaluation of Emergency Assistance to Rwanda, 1996)

—— *The International Response to Conflict and Genocide: Lessons from the Rwanda Experience, Volume IV: Rebuilding Post War Rwanda* (Copenhagen: Joint Evaluation of Emergency Assistance to Rwanda, 1996)

Jones, A., *Genocide, War Crimes and the West* (London: Zed Books, 2004)

—— *Genocide: A Comprehensive Introduction* (London: Routledge, 2006)

Junor, P., *The Major Enigma* (London: Michael Joseph, 1993)

Kaarbo, J. and M. Hermann, 'Leadership Styles of Prime Ministers: How Individual Differences Affect the Foreign Policymaking Process', *Leadership Quarterly* 9:3 (1998)

Kaldor, M., *New and Old Wars: Organised Violence in a Global Era*, 2nd edn (Cambridge: Polity Press, 2006)

Kavanagh, D. and A. Seldon, *The Powers behind the Prime Minister* (London: HarperCollins, 1999)

Kay, A., 'When Americans Favor the Use of Force', *International Journal of Public Opinion Research* 12:2 (2000)

Keane, F., *Season of Blood: A Rwandan Journey* (London: Penguin Books, 1996)

Kennedy-Pipe, C. and R. Vickers, 'Britain in the International Arena', in P. Dunleavy *et al.* (eds), *Developments in British Politics*, 8th edn (London: Palgrave Macmillan, 2003)

Kent, R., 'The UN and the Rwanda Genocide: Could it Ever Happen Again?', *Humanitarian Exchange* 26 (2004)

Khan, S., *The Shallow Graves of Rwanda* (London: I.B. Tauris, 2000)

Kitfield, J., 'Can the National Security Bureaucracy Carry out an Ambitious Afghanistan Strategy?', *National Journal* (May 2009)

Knecht, T. and S. Weatherford, 'Public Opinion and Foreign Policy: The Stages of Presidential Decision Making', *International Studies Quarterly* 50 (2006)

Kovanda, K., 'The Czech Republic on the UN Security Council: The Rwandan Genocide', *Genocide Studies and Prevention* 5:2 (2010)
Krenn, M., *The Color of Empire: Race and American Foreign Policy* (Washington DC: Potomac Books, 2006)
Kroslak, D., 'The Responsibility of External Bystanders in Cases of Genocide: The French in Rwanda, 1990–1994' (PhD thesis, University of Wales, 2002)
—— *The Role of France in the Rwandan Genocide* (London: Hurst & Co., 2007)
Kuperman, A., 'Rwanda in Retrospect', *Foreign Affairs* 79:1 (2000)
—— *The Limits of Humanitarian Intervention: Genocide in Rwanda* (Washington DC: Brookings Institution Press, 2001)
Lebor, A., *Complicity with Evil: The United Nations in the Age of Modern Genocide* (New Haven: Yale University Press, 2006)
Lemarchand, R., 'The Crisis in the Great Lakes', in J. Harbeson and D. Rothchild (eds), *Africa in World Politics* (Boulder: Westview Press, 2000)
—— 'The 1994 Rwanda Genocide', in S. Totten and W. Parsons (eds), *Century of Genocide: Critical Essays and Eyewitness Accounts*, 3rd edn (New York: Routledge, 2009)
Livingstone, S. and T. Eachus, 'Rwanda: US Policy and TV Coverage', in H. Adelman and A. Suhrke (eds), *The Path of a Genocide: The Rwanda Crisis from Uganda to Zaire* (New Brunswick: Transaction, 1999)
Mackintosh, A., 'Rwanda: Beyond Ethnic Conflict', *Development in Practice* 7:4 (1997)
McNulty, M., 'Media Ethnicization and the International Response to War and Genocide in Rwanda', in T. Allen and J. Seaton (eds), *The Media and Conflict: War Reporting and Representations of Ethnic Violence* (London: Zed Books, 1999)
——'French Arms, War and Genocide in Rwanda', *Crime, Law & Social Change* 33 (2000)
MacQueen, N., *The United Nations since 1945: Peacekeeping and the Cold War* (Harlow: Pearson Education, 1999)
Madsen, W., *Genocide and Covert Operations in Africa 1993–1999* (Lewiston: The Edwin Mellen Press, 1999)
Major, J., *The Autobiography* (London: HarperCollins, 1999)
Mayall, J., 'Humanitarian Intervention and International Society: Lessons from Africa', in J. Welsh (ed.), *Humanitarian Intervention and International Relations* (Oxford: Oxford University Press, 2006)
Magnarella, P., 'The Background and Causes of the Genocide in Rwanda', *Journal of International Criminal Justice* 3 (2005)
Mahadeo, M. and J. McKinney, 'Media Representations of Africa: Still the Same Old Story', *Policy & Practice: A Development Education Review* 4 (2007)
Meisler, S., *A Man of Peace in a World of War: Kofi Annan* (Hoboken: Wiley, 2007)
Melvern, L., 'Missing the Story: The Media and the Rwandan Genocide', *Contemporary Security Policy* 22:3 (2001)
—— 'The Security Council: Behind the Scenes', *International Affairs* 77 (2001)
—— 'The Security Council in the Face of Genocide', *Journal of International Criminal Justice* 3 (2005)

—— *Conspiracy to Murder: The Rwandan Genocide*, revised edn (London: Verso, 2006)
—— 'Rwanda and Darfur: The Media and the Security Council', *International Relations* 20:1 (2006)
—— *A People Betrayed: The Role of the West in Rwanda's Genocide* (London: Zed Books, 2009)
—— and P. Williams, 'Britannia Waived the Rules: The Major Government and the 1994 Rwandan Genocide', *African Affairs* 103 (2004)
Meredith, M., *The State of Africa* (London: Free Press, 2006)
Mermin, J., 'Televison News and American Intervention in Somalia: The Myth of a Media Driven Foreign Policy', *Political Science Quarterly* 112:3 (1997)
Moeller, S., *Compassion Fatigue: How the Media Sell Disease, Famine, War and Death* (London: Routledge, 1999)
Murray, L., 'Somalia and the "Body Bag Myth" in American Politics', *International Politics* 44 (2007)
—— *Clinton, Peacekeeping and Humanitarianism: Rise and Fall of a Policy* (London: Routledge, 2008)
Myers, G., T. Klak and T. Koehl, 'The Inscription of Difference: News Coverage of the Conflicts in Rwanda and Bosnia', *Political Geography* 15:1 (1996)
Neack, L., 'UN Peace-Keeping: In the Interest of Community of Self?', *Journal of Peace Research* 32:2 (1995)
Olsen, G., 'Western Europe's Relations with Africa since the End of the Cold War', *Journal of Modern African Studies* 35:2 (1997)
Page, B., R. Shapiro and G. Dempsey, 'What Moves Public Opinion', *American Public Science Review* 81:1 (1987)
Pape, R., 'When Duty Calls: A Pragmatic Standard of Humanitarian Intervention', *International Security* 37 (2012)
Patel, P., 'The Challenge of Peacekeeping in Africa', *Contemporary Review* 279:1628 (2001)
Patman, R., 'US Foreign Policy in Africa', in M. Cox and D. Stokes (eds), *US Foreign Policy* (Oxford: Oxford University Press, 2008)
Pattison, J., 'The Ethics of Humanitarian Intervention in Libya', *Ethics and International Affairs* 25:3 (2011)
Philo, G. *et al.*, 'The Media and the Rwanda Crisis: Effects on Audiences and Public Policy', in G. Philo (ed.), *Message Received* (Harlow: Longman, 1999)
Porteous, T., *Britain in Africa* (London: Zed Books, 2008)
Power, S., 'Why the United States Let the Rwandan Tragedy Happen', *Atlantic Monthly* (September 2001)
—— *A Problem from Hell: America and the Age of Genocide* (London: Flamingo, 2003)
Prunier, G., *The Rwandan Crisis: History of a Genocide* (London: Hurst & Co., 2005)
Ramsbotham, O. and T. Woodhouse, *Humanitarian Intervention in Contemporary Conflict* (Cambridge: Polity Press, 1996)
Reynolds, D., *Britannia Overruled: British Policy and World Power in the 20th Century* (Harlow: Longman, 2000)
Rieff, D., 'The Illusions of Peacekeeping', *World Policy Journal* 11:3 (1994)

—— *Slaughterhouse: Bosnia and the Failure of the West* (New York: Simon & Schuster, 1996)

Roberts, A., 'The So Called "Right" of Humanitarian Intervention', in *Yearbook of International Humanitarian Law 2000* (The Hague: TMC Asser, 2001)

—— 'The United Nations and Humanitarian Intervention', in J. Welsh (ed.), *Humanitarian Intervention and International Relations* (Oxford: Oxford University Press, 2006)

Robertson, G., *Crimes against Humanity* (London: Penguin, 1999)

Robinson, P., 'The News Media and Intervention: Triggering the Use of Air Power during Humanitarian Crises', *European Journal of Communication* 15 (2000)

—— *The CNN Effect: The Myth of News, Foreign Policy and Intervention* (London: Routledge, 2002)

Ross, R., 'Some Early Lessons from Operation Haven', *RUSI Journal* 136 (1991)

Royal United Services Institute, *Accidental Heroes: Britain, France and the Libya Operation* (London: Royal United Services Institute, 2012)

Rurangwa, R., *Genocide: My Stolen Rwanda* (London: Reportage Press, 2009)

Seldon, A., *Major: A Political Life* (London: Phoenix, 1997)

Shaw, I.S., 'Historical Frames and the Politics of Humanitarian Intervention: From Ethiopia, Somalia to Rwanda', *Globalisation, Societies and Education* 5:3 (2007)

Smith, K., *Genocide and the Europeans* (Cambridge: Cambridge University Press, 2010)

Smith, M., 'Britain and the United States: Beyond the Special Relationship', in P. Byrd (ed.), *British Foreign Policy under Thatcher* (Oxford: Philip Allan Publishers, 1988)

Soroka, S., 'Media, Public Opinion and Foreign Policy', *Harvard International Journal of Press Politics* 8:1 (2003)

Stanton, G., 'Could the Rwandan Genocide Have Been Prevented?', *Journal of Genocide Research* 6:2 (2004)

Staub, E., *The Roots of Evil: The Origins of Genocide and Other Group Violence* (Cambridge: Cambridge University Press, 1992)

Stockton, N., 'In Defence of Humanitarianism', *Disasters* 22:4 (1998)

Storey, A., 'Non-Neutral Humanitarianism: NGOs and the Rwanda Crisis', *Development in Practice* 7:4 (1997)

Strauss, S., *The Order of Genocide: Race, Power and War in Rwanda* (Ithaca: Cornell University Press, 2006)

Strobel, W., *Late Breaking Foreign Policy: The News Media's Influence on Peace Operations* (Washington DC: US Institute of Peace Press, 1997)

Stuart, M., *Douglas Hurd, the Public Servant: An Authorised Biography* (Edinburgh: Mainstream Publishing, 1998)

Thakur, R., 'No More Rwandas: Intervention, Sovereignty and the Responsibility to Protect', *Humanitarian Exchange* 26 (2004)

Thatcher, M., *The Downing Street Years* (London: HarperCollins, 1993)

Totten, S., 'The Intervention and Prevention of Genocide: Sisyphean or Doable?', *Journal of Genocide Research* 6:2 (2004)

Towle, P., *Going to War: British Debates from Wilberforce to Blair* (Basingstoke: Palgrave Macmillan, 2009)
Uvin, P., 'Reading the Rwandan Genocide', *International Studies Review* 3:3 (2001)
Valentino, B., *Final Solutions: Mass Killings and Genocide in the 20th Century* (Ithaca: Cornell University Press, 2005)
Vassall-Adams, G., *Rwanda: An Agenda for International Action* (Oxford: Oxfam Publications, 1994)
Vaux, T., *The Selfish Altruist: Relief Work in Famine and War* (London: Earthscan, 2001)
Verdeja, E., 'On Genocide: Five Contributory Factors', *Contemporary Politics* 8:1 (2002)
VSO, *The Live Aid Legacy: The Developing World through British Eyes* (London: VSO, 2001)
Wallace, W., 'Foreign Policy', in D. Kavanagh and A. Seldon (eds), *The Major Effect* (London: Macmillan, 1994)
Wallis, A., *Silent Accomplice: The Untold Story of France's Role in the Rwandan Genocide* (London: I.B. Tauris, 2007)
Wanta, W. and Y. Hu, 'The Agenda Setting Effects of International News Coverage: An Examination of Differing News Frames', *International Journal of Public Opinion Research* 5:3 (1993)
Waugh, C., *Paul Kagame and Rwanda: Power, Genocide and the Rwandan Patriotic Front* (London: McFarland, 2004)
Weiss, T., *Humanitarian Intervention* (Cambridge: Polity Press, 2007)
—— 'RtoP Alive and Well after Libya', *Ethics and International Affairs* 25:3 (2011)
—— and C. Collins, 'Politics of Militarised Humanitarian Intervention', in S. Totten and P. Bartrop (eds), *The Genocide Studies Reader* (New York: Routledge, 2009)
Weissman, F., *In the Shadow of 'Just Wars': Violence, Politics and Humanitarian Action* (London: Hurst & Co., 2004)
Wertheim, S., 'A Solution from Hell: The United States and the Rise of Humanitarian Intervention, 1991–2003', *Journal of Genocide Research* 12:3 (2010)
Wheeler, N., 'Legitimating Humanitarian Intervention', *Melbourne Journal of International Law* (2001)
White, N., *Democracy Goes to War: British Military Deployments under International Law* (Oxford: Oxford University Press, 2009)
Whittle, M., '10 Airborne Workshop Deploys to Rwanda', *Craftsman* (September 1994)
Williams, P., 'Who's Making UK Foreign Policy?', *International Affairs* 80:5 (2004)
Willum, B., 'Legitimizing Inaction Towards Genocide in Rwanda: A Matter of Misperception', *International Peacekeeping* 6:3 (1999)
Woolridge, M., 'Reporting Africa', *Irish Quarterly Review* 84:336 (1995)
Zanetti, V., 'Global Justice: Is Intervention Desirable?', in T. Pogge (ed.), *Global Justice* (Oxford: Blackwell, 2001)

Index